Advance Praise for
Parents *Do* Make a Difference

"Michele Borba's book is bursting with wise and practical ideas for helping kids develop the strengths of character—qualities like caring, self-discipline, and perseverance—that make us fully human."
—**Thomas Lickona,** author of *Educating for Character*

"*Parents* Do *Make a Difference* is a godsend for parents. Dr. Borba speaks clearly and authoritatively about the things that matter most to a child's success—not grades or test scores, but the ability to set goals, cooperate, and empathize with others, to be self-reliant and self-motivated, and above all, have high self-esteem."
—**Thomas Armstrong,** author of *Awakening Your Child's Natural Genius* and *In Their Own Way*

"Michele Borba's new book is invaluable. Drawing on a lifetime of rich experience, the author understands parents' concerns and speaks to them wisely and compassionately. Best of all, she spells out what parents need to know in easily accessible language and easily learnable stages."
—**Nathaniel Branden,** author of *The Six Pillars of Self-Esteem* and *A Woman's Self-Esteem*

"Packed with helpful suggestions and insights. This book is a wonderful guide to help kids become winners."
—**Louise Hart,** author of *The Winning Family: Increasing Self-Esteem in Your Children and Yourself* and *On the Wings of Self-Esteem*

"*Parents* Do *Make a Difference* makes a huge contribution to the well-being of children. It's positive, practical, and instantly usable. Kids across America will surely become more confident and self-reliant as a result of this wonderful book."
—**Naomi Drew,** author of *Learning the Skills of Peacemaking*

"Dr. Michele Borba's years of research and experience make her uniquely qualified as an expert in this field. The many practical and creative suggestions offered here are sound, effective ways of developing successful human beings. I'm certain that this outstanding book will become an extremely valuable guide and resource for both parents and teachers."

—**Robert W. Reasoner,** president, International Council for Self-Esteem and retired school superintendent

"*Parents* Do *Make a Difference* is able to address the core issues of parenting. Cross-culturally, Dr. Michele Borba has brought valuable insights to teaching professionals. Her parenting ideas have also been widely adopted by parent educators in Hong Kong."

—**Ivan Yiu,** assistant community services secretary for children & youth, Tung Wah Group of Hospitals, Hong Kong

"Every child arrives in life with a birthright to healthy self-esteem and to be welcomed, nurtured, and inspired by parents who abide by the practices Michele Borba recommends in this book. Applying these principles would quickly help the world become a much healthier and happier place."

—**Senator John Vasconcellos,** 13th District, California State Senate

"Finally, a 'cookbook' for parents and educators on how to raise successful kids. My seminar attendees have asked me for years, 'Wouldn't it be terrific if children could be exposed to these principles of self-esteem?' Michele, you've done it. The world needs your recipes for success—what a difference they'll make in our kids' futures!"

—**Bob Moawad,** chairman/CEO, Edge Learning Institute, and past president, National Association for Self-Esteem

"Michele Borba has done it again—she's written another must-have, must-read book! Parents of grown children will ask, 'Why didn't they have this when my kids were younger?' and then buy it for their grown kids so the grandkids will be raised sensibly. I highly recommend this book to anyone who cares about kids."

—**Hanoch McCarty,** coeditor of *A 4th Course of Chicken Soup for the Soul*® and coauthor of *Acts of Kindness*

"This book is loaded with practical, proven ideas for teachers and parents to use in their efforts to be the best influence they can be. Children of all ages will be helped to develop skills they need to be their personal best in the new millennium."
—**Dorothy Rouse,** board member and former teacher, Los Gatos Union School District, Los Gatos, California

"By applying the strategies from *Parents* Do *Make A Difference* I experienced such stunning success with a severely disturbed foster child that it caused an astonished juvenile court judge to label her transformation "miraculous." He even led his courtroom in a round of applause for her success and credited her rehabilitation to Dr. Borba's techniques. One could only imagine how using these techniques could profoundly impact the lives of all children."
—**Dawn Hamill,** foster child advocate

"As one who works with foster children, I consistently look to Michele Borba for her expertise, insightful guidance, and sound advice. I personally have seen miracles occur in the lives of foster children who have been touched by the skills detailed in *Parents* Do *Make A Difference.* Because of this book, foster children's lives are being changed—more importantly, their lives are being saved."
—**Madelene Hunter,** recipient of the California Foster Parent's Association's President's Award; founder, Madelene Hunter Foundation Serving Foster Children, San Diego

"I strongly endorse Michele Borba's new book, *Parents* Do *Make a Difference.* Grounded in solid research, her message has the potential to truly help parents help their children be more successful in school and in life."
—**Richard Herzberg,** executive director, Bureau of Education & Research

Parents
Do Make
a Difference

Parents *Do* Make a Difference

How to Raise Kids with *Solid Character, Strong Minds, and Caring Hearts*

Michele Borba, Ed.D.

Jossey-Bass
San Francisco

Jossey-Bass books and products are available through most bookstores. To contact Jossey-Bass directly, call (888) 378-2537, fax to (800) 605-2665, or visit our website at www.josseybass.com.

Substantial discounts on bulk quantities of Jossey-Bass books are available to corporations, professional associations, and other organizations. For details and discount information, contact the special sales department at Jossey-Bass.

Manufactured in the United States of America.

Library of Congress Cataloging-in-Publication Data
Borba, Michele.
    Parents do make a difference: how to raise kids with solid character, strong minds, and caring hearts / by Michele Borba. — 1st ed.
      p. cm. — (The Jossey-Bass psychology series)
    Includes bibliographical references and index.
    ISBN 0-7879-4605-2 (acid-free paper)
    1. Success in children. 2. Self-actualization (Psychology) in children. 3. Self-confidence in children. 4. Child rearing. I. Title. II. Series.
    BF723.S77 B67 1999

                                       98-58112

FIRST EDITION
PB Printing 10 9 8 7 6 5 4 3 2 1

Contents

Foreword by Jack Canfield   xiii

Preface: You Do Make a Difference!   xv

Acknowledgments   xix

Introduction   1

Success Skill 1   Positive Self-Esteem   7

Success Skill 2   Cultivating Strengths   32

Success Skill 3   Communicating   56

Success Skill 4   Problem Solving   84

Success Skill 5   Getting Along   115

Success Skill 6   Goal Setting   143

Success Skill 7   Not Giving Up   166

Success Skill 8   Caring   193

Final Thoughts   226

References   231

Index   239

About the Author   245

To the ones who make the difference in my life:
My parents, Dan and Treva Ungaro
My husband, Craig
and
My children, Jason, Adam, and Zachary

Foreword

Jack Canfield, coauthor of *Chicken Soup for the Soul*®

Some psychologists have been asserting that parenting doesn't matter all that much—that the child's genetic makeup, which is determined at birth, is the most important factor in how a child turns out. As an educator and a parent of three who has taught thousands of students, I can just as confidently assert that the nature-not-nurture position is patently silly. Anyone with a lick of common sense knows, and any parent who has lived day by day with a child growing up knows, that of course parents make a difference. Sure, there are the influences of genes and peer group and the culture around us. But for heaven's sake, parents know for sure that they have a big impact, for better or worse, on their children's lives and that they had definitely better keep on doing the very best job they can!

Because you love your kids and want only the best for them, I am sure you have wondered what really matters most in parents. How do you raise kids with solid characters, strong minds, and caring hearts? As a parent and a parent educator, I'm always looking for new information and insights myself.

Well, you can stop wondering, because your question has finally been answered. What you have in your hands is the instruction manual on how to raise a decent, successful human being. It is a veritable treasure chest of ways to make your love for your children come alive so that you can help them learn to love themselves, realize their potential, get along and empathize with others, communicate effectively, solve problems, go for their most cherished dreams, and lead more successful and fulfilled lives. The fact is, this may well be the only book you will ever need on raising great children.

Michele Borba has gathered together some of the finest ideas and activities ever collected in one volume for parents. You will find evaluation lists that help you identify your child's skill strengths and weaknesses, dozens of quick parenting tips, simple steps that show you how to develop each success skill, and scores of practical activities you can use to teach your child the eight skills that matter most in success.

But that's not all! Michele has also included engaging stories about real kids falling short of their potential and the simple solutions their parents used to turn their lives around. She has listed wonderful children's literature selections and videos for family viewing that embody the eight success skill themes, as well as websites and valuable parenting resources. And she pulls it all together with a solid structure based on research. You'll have enough ideas to keep you busy for years!

My only recommendation: use this book! Keep it by your bedside and refer to it constantly. Consistently using the ideas Michele suggests will help your kids lead more successful lives not only now but also for the rest of their lives. Raising your kids in a loving, secure home and teaching them these success skills is the way you will make the most enduring difference in their lives. And what a difference you will make!

Jack Canfield
Santa Barbara, California
March 1999

Foreword

Preface

You Do Make a Difference!

Last week I was in Lansing, Illinois, presenting a workshop for parents. I finished my talk and was sorting my materials when I noticed a parent standing a few feet away. She appeared to want to ask me something but was obviously reluctant. I introduced myself and asked if she needed anything. Her response troubled me deeply. "I just don't know what to believe anymore," she began. "I always hoped I could make a difference in my child's life, but raising kids today, you just never know. I'm competing against their friends, the media, the movie industry, even their music. And now I'm hearing these reports saying parents don't matter at all in how our kids turn out. So I was just wondering, do parents really make a difference?"

I thought of how many other parents must be sharing the same concern. I can't count the times teachers have asked me if they make a difference in their students' lives. How sad to doubt our significance even for a second! After all, *we not only make a difference but also can have an enduring impact on their lives, now and forever.*

Now I'm sure most of us would agree there are some "givens" we can't change about our children, such as their genetic makeup and their innate temperament. But even those *are not* etched in stone: we can still modify or enhance those characteristics. Sure, we can't change an impulsive child into one who is passive, but we can teach him how to temper his aggressiveness so that he can react more calmly. Of course we can't turn a timid child into one with an outgoing personality, but we can help her learn how to be more comfortable around others. And the latest brain research on how young minds form shows just how powerful we are in helping develop our children's brain circuits for the acquisition of music, math, logic, motor development, social attachment, language, and emotional control.

And how can anyone ever negate the power of a caregiver's love? A dad spending hours each night helping his child learn to catch because the boy so much wants to make the team; a stepmom gently showing her youngster how to cope with defeat; a teacher instilling in her student a "never give up" spirit; a foster parent helping a child recognize her artistic capabilities. Such moments can never be minimized, because they help children form images of who they are and teach them lessons of life that guide them the rest of their lives. Parents and teachers create the framework for children's success by helping them learn to believe in themselves, and doing so lays the foundation for their emotional well-being.

When I think back on my own childhood, images of love, encouragement, and warm family memories flood my mind. I recall evenings on my dad's lap listening to him read to me for hours. I have no doubt that those experiences instilled in me a lifelong love of books. Four decades later I can still hear my mom's words, "Treat everyone with kindness, Michele," in the same tone she used when I was young. The values that my parents modeled—perseverance, compassion, acceptance, and believing in myself—are the same ones that guide my life today. And they are the same values I try to model to my own children. You don't need research to prove your influence: just one moment of catching your child imitating your behavior or repeating your words or emulating your values should confirm that you *do* make a difference.

Some of the most powerful research in psychology addresses the issue of resilient children: kids who have been dealt numerous risk factors— poverty, sexual, physical or emotional abuse, dysfunctional family lives, severe handicaps—but go on to lead successful, fulfilled lives. How did they overcome such trauma? Dozens of studies point to one variable: each child had in his life a caring adult who stuck by him and offered him hope. No one can deny that those adults made a significant difference on those children's lives. So whatever role you play in a child's life—mom, dad, stepparent, teacher, foster parent, counselor, scout leader—you can be critical in her life. Although this book is written primarily for parents, my hope is that it will be used by all caregivers. Besides, working together always increases our potential to help children become their best.

Common sense tells us we can significantly influence the direction of children's lives. And there's a simple reason: *the skills for living successfully are learned—not inherited; we can make an enormous difference because we can teach these skills to our children and to our students.* Handling life's ups and downs, getting along with others, setting a goal and not giving up until it is reached, knowing how to find solutions and resolve conflicts, communicating assertively, and doing it all with compassion and empathy are the skills that build solid characters, strong minds, and caring hearts, and they are all skills that can be taught. Although our love and affection may not necessarily make our children more self-confident and friendly, we can nurture the skills that do enhance the traits of successful living. And regardless of your children's innate temperament and genetic makeup, you can expand their potential by teaching them how to live more successful and fulfilled lives.

There's much we can do to enrich our children's lives to help them become their best. And that's really what raising kids is all about. Good parenting and great teaching are not about how to turn out little prodigies but rather how to help our children live their lives to the best of their abilities. And that in itself is an immensely powerful role. This book will show you the way.

Michele Borba
Palm Springs, California
March 1999

Acknowledgments

Countless special people guided and supported me and made a difference in helping me write this book over these past five years. I would like to express heartfelt appreciation:

To the extraordinary teachers and administrators who allowed me the privilege of conducting research at their school sites to analyze the effectiveness of these eight skills of success and my *Esteem Builder* program. In particular I thank Gary Le Count and the staff of Jefferson Elementary School in Hays, Kansas; Dan Wilson and the staff of Crest View Elementary School in Brooklyn Park, Minnesota; principal Ron Sveinson and the staff of William F. Davidson Elementary School in Surrey, British Columbia; and Karen Whittle and the staff of Washington Elementary School in Great Bend, Kansas. One of the greatest honors of my life was working with such extraordinarily dedicated teachers. This book would not have come to fruition without their practical wisdom on how best to teach children these skills.

To the hundreds of teachers and parents from whom I have been privileged to learn during these past two decades—those attending my seminars who so openly shared their ideas; teachers whose classrooms I've observed and from which I always walked away more appreciative than ever of our education profession; and those whom I've known on a personal level—their practical wisdom has significantly shaped my writing. I am especially grateful to Judy Joslyn, Karen Wasinger, Bob Tamblyn, Diane Archer, Nate and Pat Swift, Kelly Welsh, Janice True, Cindy Morse, Jim Meyers, Susanna Tsoi, Ken Kostka and his staff at Lakeview Elementary in Robbinsdale, Minnesota; Ivan Yiu and the Tung Wah Community Hospital staff in Hong Kong; and all the primary teachers with whom I worked for two summers from the New Zealand Principals' Federation. Special thanks go to Debbie de Ganna and the staff at Stockton Unified School District, where many of these parenting ideas were first introduced at parent workshops.

To all the individuals who were involved in conducting and analyzing the pilot site research, including Stacie Taylor, Terri Fitzharris, Dr. Diane Frey, Joel Chaney, Dr. David Kingsley, and Dr. Jack Dugan. To the folks at Jalmar Press and publishers of *Esteem Builders:* Bradley Winch Sr., Brad Winch, and Jeanne Iler for being there at the beginning and offering undying support in the first phase of my research.

I especially thank Robert Reasoner, whose work has been an inspiration not only to my own work but also to all of us in the field of self-esteem. I thank him for his invaluable suggestions, his heartfelt support in helping me with this research project, and for his steadfast dedication to helping all children become their best.

To Dr. Nathaniel Branden, for having a more significant impact on my work than he probably recognizes: his own work in the field of self-esteem was what started me on a twenty-year quest to discover how to help children succeed. Two decades later, he graciously introduced me to his agent as well as to Jossey-Bass. I thank him profoundly for his extraordinary generosity in helping me get this book published and for his encouragement, which helped me complete this project.

To my colleagues: Dr. Richard Herzberg, for first persuading me to do a seminar on success and then convincing me that the seminar would make a great book—as usual he was right; Dr. Merrill Harmon, for being there at the beginning to help me formulate the model of the eight skills of success; Dr. Thomas Lickona, for reading through the first draft and offering such insightful suggestions; and Jack Canfield, for his twenty years of support for my work and constant willingness always to share such wise advice.

To two special friends: Jane Bluestein, for taking time to patiently talk me through the discouraging times; and Barbara Keane, for helping me hang in there by being just so fun and so loyal and by doing hundreds of hours of my carpooling so I could type and type and type. And to Judy Baggott, Cat Ayala, Jane Brewer, Andrea Funk, Madeline Hunter, Bonnie Gus, and Joan Weinger for their encouragement and friendship.

To my agent, Nat Sobel, for believing in this project and in me as a writer, and for knowing that Alan Rinzler would be the absolute perfect editor. To all the staff at Jossey-Bass—especially Wendy Bass, Kim Corbin, Katie Crouch, Bruce Emmer, Michele Jones, Danielle Neary, Margaret Sebold, Jennifer Whitney, and Lasell Whipple—their professionalism and dedication to producing only the best is a marvel. Most important, I thank my editor, Alan Rinzler, for so many things: his belief and commitment to this project; his uncanny ability always to pinpoint where a change was needed; his superb suggestions and insights; his formatting of this book into the exact vision I dreamed; and for taking care at every step, from the conception of this book to the finished product, to make it be the best it could be. I am blessed to have had an editor rich in skill *and* compassion.

And to my family: to my husband, best friend, and partner, Craig, for continually filling my days with love and fun and for being there to encourage me through every phase of this book and my life; to my parents, Dan and Treva Ungaro, for reading every line of every draft, always finding time to mail off critically needed research, and mostly for their never-ending love and steadfast support. What a different place the world would be if every child could have such parents! To my mother-in-law, Lorayne Borba, for her continual encouragement and upbeat phone calls that always ended with "I know you can do it"; and finally to my sons, Jason, Adam, and Zach, for all the love and laughter they bring to my life. And for all the times they asked, "Aren't you done yet?"—well, it's done!

Parents
Do Make
a Difference

NOTE TO THE READER

All of the stories in this book are based on cases of children and their families and teachers whom I have known and worked with over the last twenty years. A few stories are composite cases of children I have treated, and their actual names as well as their parents' names have been changed to protect their privacy. All examples from schools are gathered from my actual observations. The exceptions are children interviewed for newspapers or written about in books as examples of children displaying these eight success traits.

Introduction

Raising children is always serious and sometimes scary. You and I both know it, because one of the bonds we share as parents is that we worry about our kids. "Am I doing enough?" "Did I do too much?" "Was I too hard?" "Should I be stricter?" We lie awake agonizing over our parenting skills and questioning our choices. Of course, the reason we worry is because we love our kids so much and want them to become decent, responsible, fulfilled adults. But how do we go about helping our children become successful, worthwhile human beings? What should really concern us? This is what this book is all about. It answers our question: In raising successful children, what really matters most?

It has taken me more than two decades to understand what helps children succeed. I started my quest as a teacher. Through the years, I've worked with students of all ages, abilities, and settings. I began as a special education teacher and taught learning disabled, autistic, physically handicapped, and emotionally disturbed students. After school, my husband and I worked at our private practice with troubled youths. My first students had one thing in common: their disabilities greatly handicapped them in their effort to achieve personal, social, or intellectual successes.

One year, I was assigned to teach a class of "regular" elementary students. The range of their abilities ran from gifted to below-average intelligence.

I quickly recognized that the children's IQ scores had little to do with how successful they were in my classroom. Race, gender, and economic background didn't make a real difference either. So what did?

One day, I remembered something about my first group of special education students, who had such severe handicaps. A few of the students weren't letting their limitations hold them back. Remarkably, they were succeeding in spite of their disadvantages. Then it dawned on me: *these kids were successful because they had learned a few skills that helped them thrive.* But what were the skills that mattered most in helping them succeed?

Over the next several years I pursued my search in various roles. As a doctoral student, I read thousands of pages on the best studies about success. As an educational consultant presenting workshops to teachers across the United States, I always asked, "What skills do you think are most important in helping students succeed?" As a researcher, I interviewed dozens of experts and observed hundreds of students both in the United States and abroad. Then I spent hundreds of hours tallying the findings.

Finally, something happened that greatly expanded my understanding of what children need. In the next five years I gave birth to three sons. And—here is another bond we share—I became passionate about being the world's best parent. For the first time, I realized that it was critical not only to find out what matters most in helping my kids become their best but also to make sure that what I did find could be easily taught.

What I eventually began to see in all my roles was a trend: eight skills were consistently named as critical to success by researchers, parents, experts, and educators. These appeared so often, I knew they could not be dismissed: *positive self-esteem, cultivating strengths, communicating, problem solving, getting along, goal setting, not giving up,* and *caring.* Conveying these skills makes a difference in our children's lives. But how do we teach them?

I spent the next few years developing simple ways to teach children these eight skills of success. I then presented them in workshops for hundreds of teachers and parents across the United States. After each session, I was flooded with phone calls and letters from participants telling me of the positive changes in their children after using the strategies for only a short while. My next step was to prove that teaching them made a difference in children's lives.

TRIED, TRUE, AND PROVEN: THESE SKILLS MAKE A DIFFERENCE!

Three elementary schools volunteered to become pilot sites and test the effectiveness of teaching students these skills of success: William F. Davidson School in Surrey, British Columbia; Crest View Elementary in Brooklyn Park, Minnesota; and Jefferson Elementary in Hays, Kansas. For the next two years, every teacher at those three schools agreed to emphasize a different success skill each month and to teach students strategies to enhance the skill. The students' behaviors were closely monitored and evaluated.

The results, analyzed by researchers at Wright State University, bore out the positive gains the teachers had been noticing. Suspensions and detentions were significantly lower, and students' self-esteem was higher. Students' verbal and physical aggressive behaviors were cut in half. Perhaps most revealing was that 90 percent of the teachers at all sites said their students were better behaved and more positive, respectful, cooperative, and productive.

I've since shared these activities with over half a million parents and teachers in North America, Europe, Asia, and the South Pacific and continuously receive positive reactions. The activities have been used with children in foster homes, learning disability labs, gang prevention units, preschools, Boys and Girls Clubs, scout troops, church groups, and regular classrooms, as well as with gifted students. Every experience has convinced me that by teaching the skills we can boost every child's potential in life.

The best proof that the skills were valuable came from students. One child's comment said it all: "I can use the skills not just in school, but also at home. I bet I can use these for the rest of my life." The student recognized that the skills were also *life skills.* They matter for our kids, not just now but forever.

HOW THESE SKILLS HELP YOUR CHILD

What you have in your hands can help your child become her personal best. These eight skills benefit *every* child, of *any* gender, economic background, culture, temperament, or learning ability. Although the activities work best for children ages three to twelve, they can be adapted for any age. Here's how teaching these eight skills will help your child live a more successful life:

- *Positive Self-Esteem* helps your child develop an optimistic, "I can do it" attitude, because she has developed strong self-beliefs and believes she can succeed.

- *Cultivating Strengths* helps your child recognize his strengths, compensate for his limitations, and enhance his self-confidence, thus allowing him to fulfill more of his personal potential.

- *Communicating* helps your child acquire knowledge and enhance interpersonal skills, because she has learned to focus on and comprehend a speaker's message.

- *Problem Solving* helps your child learn to rely on himself, because he has developed a repertoire of skills to solve problems and make responsible choices.

- *Getting Along* helps your child be more cooperative by helping her acquire critical interpersonal skills that allow her to nurture and maintain friendships and deal with stormy relationships.

- *Goal Setting* helps your child be more self-motivated, because he has the skills to choose a goal, develop a plan to achieve it, and then stay on course toward success.

- *Not Giving Up* helps your child persevere, because she knows that personal effort is critical to success and understands that mistakes are not fatal.

SUCCESS TIP
The Eight Skills of Success

Skill	Description	Goal
The Skills of Personal Success		
Positive Self-Esteem	Helping your child develop solid, positive self-beliefs and an "I can do it" attitude so that she feels capable of succeeding.	Self-confidence
Cultivating Strengths	Enhancing your child's awareness of his special talents and strengths so that he develops pride in his individuality and increases his personal potential.	Self-awareness
The Skills of Emotional Success		
Communicating	Helping your child listen attentively, speak up, and get her message across to increase knowledge and reduce misunderstandings.	Understanding
Problem Solving	Teaching your child how to calmly find the best solutions and make responsible decisions.	Self-reliance
The Skill of Social Success		
Getting Along	Enhancing your child's friendship-making skills and helping her deal with stormy relationships.	Cooperation
The Skills of Motivational Success		
Goal Setting	Helping your child learn to target what he wants to achieve and to set the steps to succeed.	Self-motivation
Not Giving Up	Guiding your child to completing what she starts even though it may be difficult.	Perseverance
The Skill of Moral Success		
Caring	Enhancing your child's compassion and sensitivity toward others' feelings and needs.	Empathy

- *Caring* helps your child be more compassionate and empathic and think about the needs and feelings of others. It's our best hope for helping our kids live in a world of tolerance and peace.

HOW TO USE THIS BOOK

There is no right or wrong way to use this book, so use it any way that works best for you. You don't need to work through the book in order; feel free to jump around. Choose the skills you feel will be more useful for your child and then commit yourself to teaching them to enhance his successes in life. Although the content in this book is quite serious, the activities are designed to be fun, relaxing, and enjoyable. I hope this is the tone in which you and your child will work together.

Do remember that exposing your child to a strategy only one time is never enough for her to learn a new skill. Many researchers say new behaviors take a minimum of twenty-one days to learn. My strongest recommendation is to *choose any skill you think is important for your child and reinforce the same skill for twenty-one days.* Consistent, repeated messages about these skills are exactly what your child needs to learn them.

Raising happy, productive, thriving, and well-adjusted children, whatever their abilities, is our greatest challenge as parents. Our kids certainly need our love, encouragement, patience, respect, energy, ingenuity, resourcefulness, nurturance, and understanding. But in addition, these eight skills for success are the tools and abilities that research says are most important in boosting our children's potential to become their best. It is the combination of our love and our teaching these skills that gives our kids the best chance of leading happy and fulfilling lives.

Positive Self-Esteem

Developing an "I Can" Attitude and a Solid Belief in Self

Four-year-old Jessica sat and sulked as she waited to be picked up from the birthday party. She had begged to stay home, but her mom made her go. "Parties are always stupid," she whined. "Nobody ever plays with me, and the games they make you play are dumb." By the time Jessica's mom drove up, her daughter was close to tears. "I'm never going to another party again," she cried. Her mom tried to console her, then went to tell the hostess she was taking her daughter home. "I'm so sorry Jessica had such a bad time," explained the other mother. "The other girls tried to get her to play the games, but she wouldn't participate. The games really were easy, but Jessica told me they were all too hard. It's almost as though she'd made up her mind she couldn't do them." Jessica's mom sadly shook her head. She'd heard the same comments about her daughter from other parents. "Why can't Jessica have fun like the other kids?" she asked herself. "If only I could help her believe in herself more. But how?"

Six-year-old Yuri came barreling into the classroom on the first day of school full of energy and optimism. He was adorable, and he had a smile that made you melt. Motivated? Nothing could stop him! He excitedly explained to his teacher, "My mom says I'm going to learn to read this year. When do we start?" And with that he darted off to recess before the teacher could say a thing. "What an incredible kid!" the teacher thought, and then it dawned on her how equally incredible his mom was. Yuri, you see, was in this teacher's special education class because he had severe learning disabilities and an attention deficit. His mom knew learning was not going to be easy for him. She also wisely recognized that she could help soften some of the inevitable rough spots he would face in life by helping her son develop a firm belief in himself. The teacher could see that Yuri's mom's faith in her son along with the faith he had developed in himself would help him cope with his learning problems. He was a lucky little boy.

Regardless of what state or country I'm in, the question parents at my workshops ask me most frequently is, "What's the most important thing I can do to help my child succeed?" I have been asked the question so often, I decided to pose the same question to teachers attending my seminars. After all, they deal with hundreds of children and certainly know what helps students succeed. For the next five years I surveyed more than ten thousand teachers from coast to coast, and their number one response *everywhere* was, "Help children learn to believe in themselves." Scores of child development experts have reached the same conclusion. Simply stated: *for our children to succeed, they must first believe they can succeed.*

Without feeling "I can do it," a child is gravely handicapped from succeeding in every arena: at school, at home, with others, at work, on athletic fields, and in life. With little faith in himself, the child will approach experiences with a "Why bother, I can't do it anyway" attitude, greatly minimizing his chances for happiness and personal fulfillment. The cumulative impact that an "I can't" attitude has on his self-esteem is tragically predictable: How can he possibly feel good about himself with so few positive experiences to affirm that he is worthwhile and competent?

"I can" attitudes don't develop automatically; our children learn them, and the first place they learn them is from us. Clear-cut evidence shows that parents who expect their children to succeed and communicate the belief, "I know you can," produce children who do. Nurturing this first success skill is one of the greatest gifts you can give your child, because it is the foundation for healthy self-esteem and success.

WHAT YOU WILL LEARN IN THIS CHAPTER

This first chapter describes ways you can lay the foundation for your child's success in school and in life by helping her learn to believe in herself. You'll learn how to:

- Set expectations that stretch your child's capabilities and expand her potential, without snapping her confidence.

- Make your encouragement more enhancing to your child's self-esteem.

- Give evidence to your child that she is succeeding so that she can develop an "I can" attitude.

- Help your child develop a positive inner dialogue and reduce negative self-talk habits.

- Use positive practices of discipline that effectively change misbehavior while still protecting self-esteem.

- Turn negative, destructive labels into more positive, affirming ones that nurture positive images.

HOW IS YOUR CHILD DOING NOW?

The statements below describe behaviors usually displayed by children who have developed a strong "I can" attitude. To evaluate your child's strengths in this first success skill, write the number you think best represents your child's current level on the line following each statement and then add all the scores to get his total score. If your child scores 40 to 50, he's in great shape with the skill. If he scores 30 to 40, he can benefit from skill enhancement. A score of 20 to 30 shows signs of potential problems. If your child scores 10 to 20, consider getting help to increase this skill.

5 = Always 4 = Frequently 3 = Sometimes 2 = Rarely 1 = Never

A child with a strong "I can" attitude: My child

Sets high expectations for himself; says "I know I can do it." _____

Acts confident and self-assured.   _____

Regards self as worthwhile and special.   _____

Generally has a positive, optimistic attitude about himself.   _____

Seldom says "I can't" or "I don't know."   _____

Takes pride in his accomplishments.   _____

Seldom is overly dependent on others for help;
    is never clingy or dependent.   _____

Has confidence in himself and his abilities.   _____

Is willing to try new tasks.   _____

Says "I can" as a first response to any request.   _____

                                                     Total Score _____

FOUR STEPS TO DEVELOPING POSITIVE SELF-BELIEFS

A child's firm belief in herself does not develop automatically. It must be nurtured and learned. There are four steps you can take to help your child develop positive self-beliefs. The first and most important step is instilling in your child that you believe in her and love her for who she is, not for what she does. The second step is learning to set the kind of expectations that stretch your child to try new possibilities without pushing her further than what she's capable of achieving. Because a large part of your child's beliefs are developed internally, the third step nurtures a positive inner dialogue that fosters strong self-beliefs. The final step is helping your child recognize that her success possibilities are unlimited once she develops an "I can" attitude. Following are the four steps to nurturing positive self-beliefs in your child:

Step 1: Convey to Your Child, "I Believe in You"

Step 2: Set Expectations That Enhance Success

Step 3: Nurture Strong Internal Self-Beliefs

Step 4: Help Your Child Develop an "I Can" Attitude

STEP 1: CONVEY TO YOUR CHILD, "I BELIEVE IN YOU"

When our children feel we believe in them, they grow to believe in themselves. When kids doubt our confidence in their capabilities, they tend to lower their expectations of themselves and fall short of their potential. This first step shows how to set the kinds of expectations that convey to your child, "I believe in you!" and help him form a positive portrait of himself.

Our children do try to live up to our expectations. We know that the first place children learn to believe in themselves is from their parents. Intentionally, as well as unintentionally, we continually send messages to our kids—through our words, our looks, and even our body language—that help form their self-beliefs. On the one hand, if your child interprets your messages positively—"Mom thinks I'm responsible," "Dad feels he can trust me," "My teacher thinks I can do it"—he will try to fit himself into that view. On the other hand, if your child thinks you feel that he won't be able to accomplish much on his own, he almost surely will begin to share your opinion and lower his expectations to accommodate your view. This step describes the kinds of proven routines that enhance children's positive self-beliefs.

SUCCESS TIP
Family Conditions That Nurture Self-Esteem

Dr. Stanley Coopersmith, author of *The Antecedents of Self-Esteem*, conducted a famous study to determine the kinds of conditions that enhance self-esteem; he discovered three critical factors. First, he found that children with high self-esteem clearly felt they were loved unconditionally, with no strings attached. Second, contrary to conventional wisdom, the children with high self-esteem were raised with clear, fair rules that their parents consistently enforced, so they knew what was expected. Finally, because their parents took time to listen and paid attention to their ideas, they grew up believing that their opinions were respected and meaningful. Coopersmith found that parents who give their children the kind of love that conveys acceptance, who have fair and clear expectations, and who treat them respectfully produce children who believe in themselves. How would you describe the three esteem conditions in your family? Are your words and actions conveying to your child, "I believe in you," or are they in need of repair?

Using Labels That Foster Strong Self-Beliefs

I waited anxiously to pick my young son up from his first day of preschool, hoping his day went well. As usual, he was first out the door and ran full speed to me, almost knocking me over with his hug. "It was fun!" he exclaimed, and I sighed with relief. He was always a bundle of joy and energy, and he could light the world with his smile. Unfortunately, not everyone described him using my positive term, sometimes substituting the word hyper *instead.*

I noticed his teacher's eyes following my child. Her look told me she'd already chosen the second label to define my son—the last way I wanted his school year to start. Before she could say a word I quickly introduced myself and blurted, "My son just loves it here. Don't you just love his spirit?" She appeared temporarily stunned, so I quickly added, "I just hope nobody ever tries to tame his spirit. We need more people in this world with such spunk." I can honestly say I left her standing there speechless. I secretly smiled when we met again at our parent conference a few weeks later. Her first words that day were, "Your child is such a joy. I just love his spirit and energy!" I agreed with her, of course, and breathed a sigh of relief. She was seeing my child in the positive way I had hoped for.

Sometimes parents and teachers unintentionally send messages that diminish children's sense of worth. One of the deadliest habits that chips away at children's self-confidence is any form of stereotyping. Nicknames like Shorty, Clumsy, Crybaby, Slowpoke, Klutz, or Nerd can become daily reminders of incompetence. They can also become self-fulfilling prophecies. Regardless whether the labels are true or not, when children hear them they begin to believe them. And the label very often sticks and becomes difficult to erase. Here are four things you can do to help prevent your child from forming negative self-images:

1. **Avoid using negative labels about your child, whether you are in front of him or with others.** Labeling children with such terms as *shy, stubborn, hyper,* or *clumsy* can diminish self-esteem.

2. *Never* **let anyone else label your child.** Labeling is deadly, but you can immediately turn any negative label into a positive one. Negative label: "Your son is so shy!" Positive new label: "Not at all; he just is a great observer."

3. **Avoid making comparisons.** Never compare your child to anyone—especially siblings! "Why can't you be more like your sister? She's always so neat, and you're such a slob!" Making comparisons can strain a child's individuality and undermine her sense of self-worth.

4. **Refrain from using genetic labels.** Labels can limit your child's view of himself. "You're as lazy as your uncle." "You're going to be poor in math like I was." "You take after your Aunt Sue; you're shy just like her."

The box that follows shows how you can turn negative, demeaning labels into more affirming terms that help children develop more positive self-images. One good rule to remember about labeling is, *If the nickname does not boost your child's feelings of adequacy, it's best not to use it.*

SUCCESS TIP
Creating a Positive New Label

Think of your own child and identify any current label that could be destructive to his self-esteem: *lazy, selfish, dumb, slow, irresponsible, sloppy, unreliable, uncoordinated, inconsiderate, stubborn, rebellious.* Now develop a new, more positive term you could use to replace the negative label, and write it down. Use the new term with your child as well as around others to help him see himself more positively. Here are a few to get you started:

Old Negative Label	New Positive Label
Hyperactive	Energetic
Shy	Cautious
Unpredictable	Flexible
Daydreamer	Creative
Aggressive	Assertive

Using Constructive Discipline

"I don't know how to get my daughter to stop whining. It's driving me crazy!" the father told me. "It seems like the only way Jenny knows how to talk."

"What do you say to her to try to stop her whining?" I asked.

"Well," said the father, "I tell her over and over, 'Stop whining. None of your sisters act that way.' I try to tell her how bad a habit it is. I tell her, 'You sound just like a crybaby, and nobody will like you if you keep it up,' but now she's whining more than ever! I swear she does it because she knows it makes me mad. Is there a better way to get her to stop?"

All kids misbehave at one time or another. How we react to our child's misbehavior can be destructive or productive to their beliefs about themselves, and the responsibility of responding appropriately makes a parent's job especially tricky. Here are three simple discipline practices I suggested to Jenny's father to help stop her whining behavior. You can use these same practices to curtail almost *any* misbehavior and still protect your child's self-portrait.

I Messages vs. You Messages.   When you are not pleased with your child's behavior, it's helpful to declare your disapproval starting your message with the word *I* instead of *You.* Notice how just changing *You* to *I* turns the father's critical, judgmental message into one focusing on Jenny's misbehavior and not on her self-worth.

"You" message: *You sound just like a crybaby. Nobody will like you if you keep it up.*

"I" message: *I don't like to hear you whine, because people don't like to be around whiners.*

Separate the Child from Her Behavior.   Jenny's father told her to stop whining, but never told her how to express herself differently. He also belittled her by making the comparison "None of your sisters act that way." The right kind of discipline should help children learn right from wrong, recognize consequences, and discover how to improve the misbehavior, *while still protecting their self-worth.* The corrective message tells Jenny both what's wrong with her behavior and what new behavior her father expects. The message also focuses only on her behavior, not on the child.

Critical: *Stop whining. None of your sisters act that way.*

Corrective: *I want to hear your thoughts, but say them without a whiny tone.*

Encourage Your Child's Attempts.   Jenny's father was right to be concerned about his daughter's whining: her habit was certain to hinder relationships. By focusing only on Jenny's whining, he was not only failing to stop her misbehavior but also actually increasing it. Here's why. By being so critical, he was overlooking the times Jenny was trying *not* to whine.

Although there were not many, there were still a few. Expecting her to change her habit all at once was unrealistic, and Jenny gave up trying.

After we talked, the father recognized that he should acknowledge any effort—successful or not—his daughter made to improve. Doing so would help her believe success was really possible. He continued to encourage Jenny's efforts until her newer behavior of speaking without whining was locked in.

 SUCCESS TIP
Effective Encouragement

To make your encouragement more enhancing to your child's self-esteem, be sure that it is

- *Deserved.* Children know when they have really earned the praise they receive, so be sure the praise you give is deserved: "You took special care making your bed today—I can tell. You smoothed the covers, and that made it look so much better!"
- *Immediate.* The best time to give praise is on the spot, as soon as you observe the effort: "Give yourself a pat on the back, Sam. You stayed calm when your blocks fell apart."
- *Specific.* When you observe good behavior, word your message so that your child knows exactly what was done well: "Kelly, you were so kind to Kara today when you helped her tape her torn drawing. You made her tears go away."
- *Individual.* Effective praise is directed to the deserving child. Do not make comparisons.
- *Repeated.* To help your child make the new behavior a habit, you must repeat the praise.

STEP 2: SET EXPECTATIONS THAT ENHANCE SUCCESS

Research reveals that one of the most powerful determinants of children's success is the kind of expectations their parents set for them. This step helps you learn to set expectations that encourage kids to try new possibilities, expand their potential, *and* nurture their self-confidence.

Several summers ago, our family vacationed in a quaint community called Lake Arrowhead. My plan was to spend each morning peacefully reading the paper on the dock, while my three sons fished. The very first day my plan failed because my youngest son lost his fishing pole in the lake. His excuse: "A gigantic fish bit the bait and swam off with it." Because he was young, we forgave him, chipped in our change, and bought him an inexpensive new pole. The following day my older sons decided to fish right next to their brother and watch his every move so that they wouldn't have to hear his "gigantic fish" excuse if he lost another pole. The day began like I'd planned it: I sat drinking my coffee and reading the paper, while my kids fished. This time they were on full alert. By my third sip, I knew my day would once again be anything but relaxing. I looked up to find all three kids—and everyone else on the dock—yelling and wildly pointing into the lake. I ran just in time to see a gigantic orange fish swimming away with my son's pole as he screamed, "I told you! I told you! Now do you guys believe me?"

We stood there in disbelief. Then a local fisherman told us about one of the residents several years ago, who, tired of his pet fish, dumped them into the lake. The fish, Japanese carp, were no more than three inches in length at the time, but the fishermen explained a fascinating principle about the breed: the carp's length is affected by the size of its container. He told us, "Carp contained in a small aquarium grow to about two to six inches in length. If you put the same fish in a larger tank, they'll grow to be six to ten inches long. If they're in a small pond, they can become almost a foot in length. Because the fish were thrown into the lake, they grew to be over two feet in length and were certainly strong enough to steal a small pole from a young child." All of us stood on that dock shaking our heads in amazement. Probably no one was more pleased with the story than my youngest son, overjoyed that we finally believed him. I spent the rest of the week thinking about the fisherman's words when it dawned on me how similar the principle of the carp's length is to the old psychological premise of expectations: your success is often determined by how much others believe in you.

The kind of messages we send our children is critical. Expecting too little from our kids limits their success, because they lose the incentive to try new possibilities. Unrealistic expectations can also damage our kids: "Why didn't you get all A's?" "How did you not make the team?" "You got a 98 percent—which two did you miss?" Pushing our kids because we want the best for them may be misinterpreted by them as "You're not good enough." Successful expectations gently stretch our children's potential to become their best without pushing them to be more than they can be. And these expectations *never* destroy children's feelings of adequacy.

Four Questions to Help Gauge Your Expectations

Here are four questions to ask yourself to make sure the expectations you set for your children are ones that stretch their potential without unintentionally diminishing their self-worth. The questions correspond to four important criteria; the expectations must be all of the following:

1. **Developmentally appropriate.** "Is my child developmentally ready for the tasks I'm requiring, or am I pushing him beyond his internal timetable?" Learn what's appropriate for your child's age, but still keep in mind that developmental guidelines are not etched in stone. It's always best to start from where your child is.

2. **Realistic.** "Is my expectation fair and reasonable, or am I expecting too much?" Realistic expectations stretch kids to aim higher, without pushing them beyond their capabilities. Be careful of setting standards too high. Putting your child in situations that are far too difficult increases her risk of failing and of lowering her feelings of adequacy.

3. **Child-oriented.** "Is what I'm expecting something my child wants, or is it more something I want for myself?" We all want our children to be successful, but we have to be constantly wary of setting goals for our kids that are based on our dreams instead of theirs.

4. Success-oriented. "Am I setting the kind of expectations that tell my child I believe he's responsible, reliable, and worthy?" Effective expectations encourage kids to be their best so that they can develop a solid belief in themselves.

SUCCESS TIP
The Power of Expectations

One of the most famous classroom studies on the power of expectations was conducted by Robert Rosenthal, a Harvard psychologist, and Lenore Jacobson, a San Francisco principal. The study began by testing a group of kindergarten through fifth-grade students and then giving their teachers the names of students found to have "exceptional learning abilities." What the teachers did not know was that the names of these "exceptional" students had been chosen entirely at random by the researchers. When students were retested at the end of the school year, the students who the teachers thought had "exceptional learning abilities" not only made significant academic progress but also gained as many as fifteen to twenty-seven IQ points! Their teachers described these children as happier, more curious, better adjusted, more affectionate than average, and likely to be very successful in their future lives. *The only change that year was that the teachers' expectations of the students had changed.* Because the teachers had been led to expect more of these children, the children came to expect more of themselves. The researchers demonstrated the power expectations have on enhancing human potential.

STEP 3: NURTURE STRONG
INTERNAL SELF-BELIEFS

Children with poor self-beliefs often have long bombarded themselves with a steady stream of derogatory messages. Their potential for success is greatly limited, because they don't believe in their capabilities. This step helps children become their best by helping them developing positive inner dialogues.

I'd spent the day at the inner-city school gathering data for my research and had only a fourth-grade class left to observe. I was standing in the back when I heard a noise like that of a crying kitten somewhere in the room. Surprisingly, it didn't seem to distract the students, but it sure got to me. What was making the noise? It didn't take long to trace it to the teacher's storage room, and what I found still haunts me. The source of the noise was not a kitten but a clearly upset little boy. I figured he must have misbehaved and was sent to the storage room as a consequence. He sat at a small table facing a poster that read, "Think about why you're here." Then I realized that as he was staring at the poster, the child was saying, over and over, "Because I'm dumb. Because I'm dumb. Because I'm dumb." I wondered how many hundreds of times he must have been replaying the same message in his mind each day. I left, almost as upset as the child, knowing that in those brief minutes he had developed some devastating beliefs about himself that would take a number of positive experiences to erase.

Research indicates that 85 percent of the time we talk, we aren't speaking to someone—we're speaking to ourselves! Self-talk is a critical part of how children acquire beliefs about themselves. One of the most powerful ways to help your youngster develop a firm belief in herself is to teach her to practice positive self-talk. If she learns the skill now, she'll use it forever.

Six Ways to Turn "Can't" into "Can"

Six months after Jose appeared to adjust to his new school, the eight-year-old suddenly began protesting that he didn't want to go to school and complaining that he had no friends. His stepmom noticed how often he reacted to situations by saying, "I can't" or "Why bother?" as though he assumed he would fail. Jose's teacher confirmed he was using the same negative self-talk at school. His teacher and parents agreed that Jose's new pessimistic attitude would be disastrous to his self-beliefs, but what could they do? Then Jose's teacher mentioned an article on teaching kids positive self-talk and its potential to enhance self-confidence. His parents decided to try the ideas, even though they knew it would take time and hard work. A few weeks later, when Jose's teacher called to say that he seemed much happier, was trying harder, and was even making friends, the parents knew their efforts had actually paid off. Jose's new behavior meant one thing: he was developing a more positive picture of himself.

Helping a child break the habit of using negative self-talk is not easy. As when you try to break any habit, you'll need to be consistent in your efforts to help change your child's behavior, usually for a minimum of three weeks. Here are the six ideas Jose's parents used to help their son develop a more positive self-picture and reduce his negative self-talk.

1. **Model positive self-talk.** Recognizing that kids learn much of their self-talk from listening to others, Jose's parents deliberately began saying more positive messages out loud so that Jose would overhear them. One day his stepmom said, "I love the recipe I used today. I really liked how it turned out." The same day, his dad said, "I like how I really stuck to my 'To Do' list today and finished everything I'd planned." At first they felt strange affirming themselves, but when they noticed their son praising himself more, they overcame their hesitancies.

2. **Develop a family "I can" slogan.** Whenever someone in Jose's family said, "I can't," other family members learned to say to the person, "Success comes in cans, not in cannots." The simple little slogan became an effective way of encouraging family members to think more positively.

3. **Point out "stinkin' thinkin'."** To remind Jose that negative talk was not allowed, his parents created a private signal—pulling on their ear—whenever he said a negative comment in public.

4. **Confront negative voices.** The parents gently encouraged Jose to talk back to his negative voice. They began by explaining how they confront their inner negative talk. His dad said, "I remember when I was in school. Sometimes right before I'd take a test I'd hear a voice inside me say, 'This stuff is hard. You're not going to do well on this test.' I used to hate that voice, because it would take my confidence away. I learned to talk

back to it; I'd just say, 'I'm a good learner. I'm going to try my best. If I try my best, I'll do OK.'"

5. **Turn negatives into positives.** The family developed a rule to combat negativity they called "one negative equals one positive." Whenever a family member made a negative comment, the sender was required to turn it into something positive. If Jose said, "I'm so stupid," his parents encouraged him to say something positive: "I'm pretty good at spelling." Consistently enforcing the rule gradually diminished Jose's use of negative statements.

6. **Send positive self-statement reminders.** The parents' final step was to remind him to praise himself inside his head when he deserved it. The day he brought home a good spelling test, his stepmom said, "Jose, you did a great job on your spelling test today. Did you remember to tell yourself inside your head what a super job you did?" After his soccer game, his dad said, "Jose, that was a great side kick you used today. I hope you praised yourself, because you sure deserved it." It took a while before Jose felt comfortable using the technique, but gradually his comfort level increased as he slowly erased his negative thinking patterns.

 SUCCESS TIP
Using Positive Self-Statements

Teach your child to reduce her self-defeating talk by helping her learn to say positive phrases instead. It's best to help your child choose only one phase and help her practice saying the same phrase five or six times a day until she learns it. Here are a few.

I know I can do it.   I can handle this.   I have confidence in me.   I'll just do my best.

STEP 4: HELP YOUR CHILD
DEVELOP AN "I CAN" ATTITUDE

As adults, we need to think we're improving, getting better at something, and making progress. Knowing that we're doing well helps us believe in our abilities and causes us to forge ahead and make continued efforts. An awareness that we're improving is like a pat on the back that encourages us to keep trying.

Children, like adults, need to see improvements, especially in school subjects, where their growth is constantly being measured. This final step shows you ways to give your child evidence that she is succeeding, allowing her to develop an "I can" attitude.

 SUCCESS TIP
Avoid Making Comparisons!

Children should only compare their current work to their own previous work—never to the work of their classmates or siblings. Competition may be stimulating for children who already have firm beliefs in themselves, but it can be paralyzing to children who are low in self-confidence.

Five Ways to Help Your Child See Success

One of the most powerful skills parents and teachers can teach a child is to record her own progress so that she can see her successes. As she sees her improvements, her self-beliefs can do nothing but grow! The following activities build "I can" attitudes by helping children record and measure their progress and accomplishments.

1. **Recording progress.** Each week, have your child record her academic progress on an audiotape so that she can "hear about" her abilities. The recording need not be more than a minute per session and can be about any number of subjects: poetry, a passage from a book or her report, math facts, spelling words, or even an interview with a friend.

2. **Making a favorite work folder.** Purchase a large manila folder from a stationery store—the sturdier the better—or even a strong box. Each week, ask your child to choose the school paper he is most proud of and put it inside

the work folder. Then help your child look at his earlier work in the folder and compare it to his present progress so that he can see his improvements.

3. **Putting up a bulletin board.** Put up a bulletin board for your child to display her best work papers. Date each paper as it is completed and place it on the board in chronological order. Your child can instantly compare her previous work to the work she is doing now. This idea is particularly effective if you help your child choose work from the same academic area each time, such as all multiplication papers or all handwriting papers.

4. **Starting an accomplishment journal.** Give your child a blank journal or composition notebook. Encourage her to record her accomplishments and successes in the journal on a regular basis. For younger children, consider photographing or drawing their accomplishments and gluing them into a scrapbook.

5. **Doing paper chains.** Keep on hand an ample supply of light-colored construction paper cut into 1" × 5" lengths. Each time your child has a special accomplishment, write it on a paper strip, pass the strip through the next strip in the ring, and glue the ends together to form a chain. Continue adding new links and hang the chain around your child's room as proof of success.

A Word About External Rewards

We all want our kids to succeed, and when they do, our approval means a great deal to them. But always rewarding kids for their successes—such as giving them money for good grades or treats for nice behaviors—can send negative messages we may not recognize: "I'm going to work hard to get good grades because Mom and Dad will give me something" or "Why should I change my behavior? There's nothing in it for me." The deadliest scenario is the one in which a child grows up believing that his parents love him only when he achieves. One of the best ways to nurture your child's self-confidence is to acknowledge his efforts and attempts whether they are successful or not. The cornerstone of a child's belief in himself is knowing he is loved unconditionally—*no matter what the outcome.*

SUCCESS TIP
Making an "I Can"

Here's a fun way to increase your child's awareness of her capabilities. Carefully remove and discard the top of a soup-size can; clean the can and cover it with colored paper. Decorate the outside with the words *I CAN* and perhaps even glue on a picture of your child. Each time your child accomplishes something special, help her write or draw the accomplishment on a slip of paper, and put it in the can. Accomplishments can include any new skill your child has learned: setting the table, tying her shoes, riding her bike, counting to one hundred, buttoning her jacket, finishing a book. The "I can" messages become visual reminders of her growing list of capabilities.

WHAT ONE PARENT DID

Robin was eleven years old when her dad noticed how often she was saying negative statements about herself: "I'm so stupid," "I can't do anything right," and "I'll never get any better" were becoming everyday comments. He couldn't understand why she'd say such things: she was a sweet girl with so many wonderful qualities, and they loved her dearly. Unfortunately, Robin didn't believe in the good parts about herself; she was developing her self-concept based on only her negative messages. Her self-confidence was plummeting. Worried, her parents met with the school counselor, who offered ways to free Robin from her negative-thinking trap.

Over the next few weeks, her parents did four things that helped rebuild their daughter's confidence. First, her parents admitted that they had been ignoring their daughter's feelings and took time to really listen, so Robin would know they understood she felt unhappy. It affirmed how much they cared and that her feelings were important. Although they acknowledged her feelings, they did not necessarily accept her conclusions. When Robin said, "I'm so stupid and can never do anything right," her father responded, "I know you think you're not smart, and that must make you feel bad. But I also know you're a great kid, and good at a lot of things. We'll work on making school easier for you, Robin." That evening her parents did the second thing: they arranged for a tutor to work on rebuilding Robin's confidence in math.

Next, Robin's parents began countering her negative thinking by offering her a more balanced perspective. If Robin said, "I can't do anything right," they would say, "I know you feel disappointed about your math grade, but remember how good you are in soccer and art? Nobody can be good at everything. We think you're good in a lot of areas, even though it may not seem like it right now." Finally, they enrolled her in an art class. She not only enjoyed art but was also really good at it. They hoped it would boost her confidence. By concentrating on giving their daughter the support she needed, Robin's parents helped Robin form more positive self-beliefs. Gradually, her self-confidence blossomed.

SUCCESS TIP
Ways to Say "I Believe in You!"

The following is a list of empowering statements you can use to convey to your child that you believe in him. Keep them handy.

I knew you could do it!	That's better than ever.	That's a great idea.
You almost have it.	You're on the right track now.	You're doing a great job.
You're doing much better.	Every day you improve!	You must have practiced!

Excellent! Super! Great! The best! Magnificent! Awesome! Hooray! Superior! Spectacular performance! You have it! You're really thinking! Keep it up! Good going! That's it! Tremendous! Fantastic! You've got it! Nice job! Wow! Congratulations! Impressive! I'm proud of you!

FINAL THOUGHTS ON ENHANCING
POSITIVE SELF-ESTEEM

If you could give your child one quality that would most enhance her chances for leading a successful, meaningful, and fulfilling life, what would it be? Scores of child development experts say the greatest gift would be positive self-esteem. Perhaps nothing will play a more significant role than the strength of her self-beliefs in determining the caliber of your child's productivity, inner strength, contentment, competencies, goal attainments, interpersonal relationships, and achievements.

As parents, we have the opportunity every day to reinforce our children's self-beliefs. Our expectations for our children, our reactions and words to them, can give them votes of confidence or chip away at their self-worth. Perhaps one of the most important questions we should ask ourselves each evening is, If my child's self-beliefs were based only on my words and actions today, what would he believe about himself as a human being? Our answer should guide how we interact with our children each following day.

POINTS TO REMEMBER

- Look for the positives and focus on what is good about your child. If we're not careful, we can overlook the good things our child does and focus on the negatives.

- Have faith in your child, so she can have faith in herself.

- Children with flimsy self-beliefs must be shown their progress in highly concrete terms to help them believe they are improving. Just saying, "You're getting better!" isn't enough. Samples of actual work, tape recordings, or videotapes of the skill over a period of time are powerful evidence that helps kids see they really are progressing.

- Reinforce your child for trying. Our kids need to believe we love them whether they succeed or fail. Every effort your child makes increases the possibilities that he will succeed.

- Compare your child's current work only to her previous work—never to the work of her siblings or classmates.

- Remember, success breeds success, so create opportunities for your child to succeed.

RESOURCES FOR FURTHER ACTION

For Parents

Esteem Builders, by Michele Borba (Torrance, Calif.: Jalmar Press, 1989). Dozens of esteem-enhancing activities to help students be the best they can be.

"Help Me, I'm Sad," by David G. Fassler and Lynne S. Dumas (New York: Viking Penguin, 1997). Solid advice for parents on recognizing, treating, and preventing childhood and adolescent depression.

Home Esteem Builders, by Michele Borba (Torrance, Calif.: Jalmar Press, 1993). Dozens of simple esteem-building activities for parents to implement with their children; accompanies *Esteem Builders.*

"I Think I Can, I Know I Can!" by Susan Isaacs and Wendy Ritchey (New York: St. Martin's Press, 1989). Offers a simple five-step program on how to change children's negative self-talk voices into positive ones.

The Magic of Encouragement: Nurturing Your Child's Self-Esteem, by Stephanie Marston (New York: Morrow, 1990). Indispensable guide to the enhancement of children's self-esteem featuring simple-to-use activities as well as solid rationales for using them.

Twenty-First-Century Discipline, by Jane Bluestein (Albuquerque, N.Mex.: Instructional Support Services, 1998). Solid, practical advice for teaching children responsibility and self-control.

What Do You Really Want for Your Children? by Wayne Dyer (New York: Avon, 1985). Straightforward advice about raising children and increasing their self-esteem.

The Winning Family: Increasing Self-Esteem in Your Children and Yourself, by Louise Hart (Oakland, Calif.: Celestial Arts, 1993). Simple ideas for creating an esteem-building family.

Your Child's Self-Esteem: The Key to His Life, by Dorothy Briggs (New York: Doubleday, 1970). A self-esteem classic describing how self-esteem is the key to a child's life.

For Children Ages Three to Seven

Amazing Grace, by Mary Hoffman and Caroline Binch (New York: Dial, 1991). Although classmates say she cannot play Peter Pan in the school play because she is black and a girl, Grace discovers that she can do anything she sets her mind to.

The Carrot Seed, by Ruth Krauss (New York: Scholastic, 1971). A child has faith in the carrot seed she plants, despite the fact that no one believes it will grow. It does!

I'm Terrific, by Marjorie Weinman Sharmat (New York: Scholastic, 1977). An affirmation of "self-terrificness."

Leo the Late Bloomer, by Robert Kraus (New York: Windmill, 1971). A young lion finally learns to read, draw, and talk, much to his parents' delight.

The Little Engine That Could, by Watty Piper (New York: Scholastic, 1979). The classic of positive thinking: "I think I can."

For Children Ages Eight to Twelve

Castle in the Attic, by Elizabeth Winthrop (New York: Bantam, 1986). William learns a mighty lesson from the Silver Knight: the power you need to fight any obstacle is within you.

The Night of the Twisters, by Ivy Ruckman (New York: Crowell, 1984). The terrors of a tornado help young Dan recognize his inner strengths and develop a firm belief in self.

Success Is a Fly in the Eye of a Frog, by Gene Bedley (Irvine, Calif.: People-Wise, 1995). A delightful tale about animals discovering the real meaning of success.

Videos for Family Viewing

City Boy (Public Media Video, 1993). Drama based on a year in the life of Nick O'Brien, a motherless child raised in tough foster homes, who rides the rails in search of his father. A birth defect on his right hand has not hindered his self-esteem. For older children.

Flight of the Navigator (Walt Disney Home Video, 1986). A twelve-year-old boy is whisked away by an alien spaceship and must rely on his belief in himself and his skills in order to find his way back home. (PG)

The Sword in the Stone (Walt Disney Home Video, 1963). The animated Disney version of the story of a young boy who is destined to become King Arthur but first must prove himself. (G)

Where the Lilies Bloom (MGM/UA, 1974). Four Appalachian children must fend for themselves when their father dies. They also must keep his death a secret so that they won't be taken away by the State and separated from one another. (G)

Where the Red Fern Grows (Vestron Video, 1974). The story of a boy's love of his two hunting dogs and how his heart-wrenching experiences teach him to believe in himself and develop responsibility. Based on Wilson Rawls's novel. (G)

The Wizard of Oz (MGM/UA, 1939). The extraordinary classic based on L. Frank Baum's story of a young Kansas girl who goes over the rainbow and searches for the wizard to help her. In the end she finally learns she had the power to solve her problems all along—she just had to believe in herself. Watch with your kids: the flying monkeys still give me nightmares.

Websites for Parents

"Attention Deficit Disorder Home Page" [http://www.attn-deficit-disorder.com/]. For parents interested in learning more about attention deficit disorder (ADD).

"Family World Home Page" [http://family.go.com/]. A collaborative effort of more than forty parenting magazines offering parenting articles and links to Internet resources.

"Foster Parents" [http://fostercare.org/fphp]. A discussion network especially for foster parents offering special hints as well as available resources.

"KidSource" [http://www.kidsource.com]. An on-line parenting resource about health care, education, and product information.

"Our-kids" [listserv@maelstrom.stjohns.edu]. A support group for parents of children with special needs.

"Parenthood Web" [http://www.parenthoodweb.com]. Resource topics include family health, problems at school, behavioral issues, family-related matters, homework help, and more.

"Parent Soup" [http://www.parentsoup.com]. Parent chat rooms and a wealth of parenting resources.

"Parents' Place" [http://www.parentsplace.com]. An on-line parenting resource offering articles, books, as well as a place to chat with other parents.

Cultivating Strengths

Developing Personal Potential and Enhancing Individuality

It's an another frustrating morning for Jessica's parents. Their nine-year-old daughter is complaining of another headache and says she's too sick to go to school. His parents know the real reason is that reading is so difficult for her. This year it's torture, because she has to read out loud everyday. She's sure the rest of the kids think she's stupid, because she reads so slowly. Jessica's parents look helplessly at each other as their child begs to stay home. They've spent hours trying to find a way to build her self-confidence. "If only she'd recognize some of her positive qualities," they sigh. "She's a good athlete and a nice kid, but all she thinks about is what she can't do." Their biggest concern at the moment is how to get her on the bus.

Lucas has had intensive speech therapy for six years, and, despite his progress, he still stutters. The ten-year-old's jitters are understandable: his turn to give his class speech is next. Lucas knows he will probably stutter; he just hopes he can finish his talk this time. He takes a deep breath and silently says inside his head the positive comments he has learned at home. "I'm good at soccer and drawing," he tells himself. "I'm good at math. I have a lot of friends." Lucas feels less tense already. His parents taught him how to focus on his positive qualities long ago. "Some things, like your speech, will be hard for you," they told him. "God also gave you special positive qualities, Lucas. You're athletic, artistic, and a great friend, and you have a smart mind. The secret is to concentrate on the things you do well and make them even stronger. Those are the qualities that will help you succeed in life." Lucas softly repeated his strengths one more time and then confidently stood up, ready to speak.

All children are born with the potential to succeed in life. Brain researchers tell us that the kinds of positive experiences children have determine whether their full potential will be achieved. The tragedy is that so many children never have the chance to be all they can be because their innate strengths are never nurtured. Their potential for leadership, art, music, creativity, teamwork—or dozens of other possible talents—remains buried. The purpose of cultivating strengths is not to produce little prodigies but instead to enrich our children's lives by helping them recognize and then develop what makes them unique.

By focusing on your child's strengths rather than on his weaknesses, you can only help increase his self-esteem. There's another reason why we need to nurture our children's strengths: doing so will buffer their stresses, cushion their difficult times, and help them compensate for their limitations. When children value their uniqueness, they protect themselves from many of those dragons out there: drugs, alcohol, self-destruction, making poor choices, and choosing the wrong friends. No matter what happens, they know they can believe in themselves, because they are aware that they are unique and worthy individuals.

WHAT YOU WILL LEARN IN THIS CHAPTER

Every child deserves to wake up each morning knowing she is special. This chapter teaches you how to identify and cultivate the unique strengths and qualities that enhance your child's potential. You'll learn how to:

- Pinpoint your child's already existing positive qualities and areas of excellence.

- Increase your child's self-confidence by helping him recognize his special strengths.

- Expand your child's potential by using proven talent-building parenting practices to develop her strengths.

- Give effective praise that not only enhances your child's strength awareness but also increases his self-knowledge and self-esteem.

HOW IS YOUR CHILD DOING NOW?

The statements below describe behaviors usually displayed by children who have developed a strong knowledge of their strengths and personal potential. To evaluate your child's strengths in this second success skill, write the number you think best represents your child's current level on the line following each statement and then add all the scores to get her total score. If your child scores 40 to 50, she's in great shape with the skill. If she scores 30 to 40, she could benefit from skill enhancement. A score of 20 to 30 shows signs of potential problems. If your child scores 10 to 20, consider getting help to increase this skill.

5 = Always 4 = Frequently 3 = Sometimes 2 = Rarely 1 = Never

A child with strong knowledge of her strengths and personal potential:	**My child**
Can easily describe her special strengths and positive qualities.	_____
Is proud of her special qualities, assets, and talents.	_____

Feels adequate and special; enjoys being herself.   _____

Focuses mostly on her strengths instead of her weaknesses
    or past failures.   _____

Is comfortable accepting praise; rarely shrugs off compliments.   _____

Speaks mostly positively about herself, rarely negatively.   _____

Has a few developed hobbies or special interests.   _____

Is not oversensitive to criticism.   _____

Has confidence in herself and her abilities.   _____

Enjoys expressing her uniqueness and individuality.   _____

Total Score   _____

THREE STEPS TO DEVELOPING
YOUR CHILD'S POTENTIAL

There are three steps to developing your child's personal potential and self-esteem. The first step is one of our most important parental tasks: identifying all the possible areas of excellence that exist in our children. Once you discover your child's strengths, the second step is to point them out to your child so that he's aware of them. This step helps your child develop new positive images of himself as well as confirm existing attributes of which he is already aware. The final step expands your child's potential by helping him develop his strengths to their fullest. These steps enhance the second skill critical to success—cultivating strengths.

> **Step 1:** Identify Your Child's Unique Strengths and Qualities
> **Step 2:** Point Out Strengths So That Your Child Sees Them
> **Step 3:** Provide Opportunities to Develop Strengths

STEP 1: IDENTIFY YOUR CHILD'S UNIQUE
STRENGTHS AND QUALITIES

Discovering our children's unique qualities and strengths is one of our most important parenting tasks. This first critical step helps you identify what makes your child unique. The more you understand who this child is, the more effective you will be in helping her recognize her strengths and in enhancing her potential for success.

My favorite finger play I used when my children were little was so simple. I'd hold up their thumbs and have them repeat after me: "Of all the people in the world, I'm special you see. I'm a thumb body!" I'd take a few seconds to remind them of their special qualities, then we would end by giving quick "thumb hugs" or by having our thumbs touch. I don't know who loved that rhyme more—my sons or I.

You begin helping your child recognize she's a "thumb body" when you identify her special qualities and strengths. She might have a talent for music, athletic ability on the soccer field, or artistic capability. Her strength could be a mental attribute: she might have a keen memory for details. Or perhaps it's a social skill: she has a kind and generous heart. Maybe she has strong knowledge in a particular area: dinosaurs, computers, rocks, or constellations. The list of your child's potential gifts is endless. Your task is to identify those gifts.

Finding your child's special qualities could become an avenue to enhance his self-esteem and competence. He could develop a special interest or hobby into a specialized area of enjoyment that will last a lifetime or even become a career. A talent could also be one that relates to a personal learning style that, once nurtured, will help your child become a more successful lifelong learner. It is important to remember that your child's special strengths may not be your own strengths or preferences. Put aside your biases—they can keep a talent locked up forever. Instead, try to be open to all the wondrous possibilities.

Seven Ways to Discover Your Child's Strengths and Abilities

Set aside some time to really think about your child and write down your thoughts. My girlfriend decided to keep an ongoing profile of each of her children's strengths. The leather journal is now a fabulous family keepsake. These seven ideas help you identify your child's positive qualities and strengths.

1. Think in terms of categories. Think honestly about your child in every way: socially, emotionally, physically, morally, and intellectually. Make a list of your descriptions. Now look for any possible talents and positive strengths already present in your child. Underline any area that could be a potential area to nurture for strengths.

2. Ask others. Talk with others who know and care about your child, such as scout leaders, teachers, ministers, friends' parents, baby-sitters, grandparents, siblings, and friends. Add their opinions about your child's special traits to your list. Their ideas might surprise you.

3. Observe quietly. Over the next several days, silently watch your child in different situations: at school, with friends, playing by himself, with his family. Tune into what he seems to enjoy and chooses to do. Write down his choices.

4. Pull from your memories. Look through scrapbooks, old photo albums, and videos. What were her past birthday and holiday gift wishes? Our talents often lie in our interests.

5. Listen, really listen. Put up a "Do Not Disturb" sign and invite your child to join you for some uninterrupted listening. Ask him what he considers to be his special assets. What subjects does he love or hate? Is there a special camp he wants to go to this summer? Any new hobbies or interests? Jot them down. They will help you develop a thorough understanding of your child.

6. Poll your family. Brainstorm as a family the special talents of every member. Post the strengths and keep adding to the list as new discoveries are made.

7. Check off talents. Your goal is to answer the question, What makes my child special and unique? The checklist in the next Success Tip provides one hundred strengths and qualities to get you started. Check off areas you feel best describe your child's innate skills or talents. *Make sure these strengths are already present in your child and not ones you wish were there.* When you have identified your child's positive qualities, write them down. Keep the list handy; you will use it throughout this chapter. As you discover new attributes, add them to your list.

SUCCESS TIP
One Hundred Strengths and Positive Qualities

Visual Talents

O Drawing
O Photography
O Recall for details
O Painting
O Active imagination
O Visualizes
O Map skills
O Good sense of direction
O Artistic

Logical/Thinking

O Computer
O Organized
O Problem solver
O Abstract thinking
O Math/numbers
O Thinking games
O Deciphers codes
O Common sense
O Science
O Quick thinker
O Learns quickly
O Keen memory
O Knowledgeable
O Intelligent

Bodily Kinesthetic/Physical Strengths

O Role playing
O Acting
O Creative movement
O Dancing

O Dramatics
O Specific sports
O Running
O Athletic
O Physical strength
O Grace
O Endurance
O Balance
O Dexterity
O Coordination

Musical Talents

O Instrument
O Singing
O Rhythm
O Remembers tunes
O Composes music
O Reads music
O Responds to music

Personality Traits

O Creative
O Initiative
O Follows through
O Trustworthy
O Patient
O Reliable
O Sensitive
O Courageous
O Caring
O Hardworking
O Adaptable

- O Easygoing
- O Responsible
- O Generous
- O Confident
- O Independent
- O Neat
- O Determined
- O Truthful
- O Insightful
- O Gentle
- O Mature
- O Happy
- O Open
- O Prompt
- O Optimistic
- O Loyal
- O Serious
- O Honest
- O Disciplined
- O Affectionate
- O Strong character
- O Faithful

Social Skills

- O Friendly
- O Leader
- O Helpful
- O Good-natured
- O Sportsmanship
- O Courteous
- O Fair
- O Takes turns
- O Team player
- O Cooperates

- O Shares
- O Empathic
- O Understanding
- O Peacemaker
- O Fun
- O Charming
- O Encouraging
- O Humorous
- O Good listener
- O Likable

Linguistic Talents

- O Reading
- O Vocabulary
- O Speaking
- O Remembers facts
- O Creative writing
- O Poetry
- O Debate
- O Humor, joke telling
- O Storytelling

Physical Appearance

- O Neat
- O Attractive
- O Good posture
- O Special feature

Nature and Outdoor Abilities

- O Observer
- O Loves animals
- O Curious
- O Hiking
- O Science collections

STEP 2: POINT OUT STRENGTHS
SO THAT YOUR CHILD SEES THEM

Just knowing our children's strengths isn't good enough: we must pass our findings on to our children. The more you can expand your child's awareness of her qualities, the greater the likelihood her self-confidence will increase, because she'll focus on her positive attributes. This next step shows you how to point out your child's present strengths, of which she may not even be aware, enabling her to recognize her special areas of excellence.

SUCCESS TIP
The Law of Compensation

Victor and Mildred Goertzel studied the childhoods of four hundred of some of the most creatively gifted and talented individuals in our century, including Einstein, Schweitzer, Gandhi, Roosevelt, Churchill, and Edison. The researchers were startled to discover that three-fourths of these prominently gifted individuals had tremendous handicaps in their lives, including troubled childhoods, emotionally fragile or alcoholic parents, and serious learning problems. What helped them compensate for their handicaps and become so successful? From an early age, each individual had a "significant someone" who helped him recognize a hidden talent he possessed, and encouraged its development.

Stresses and handicaps are facts of life. Although we cannot eliminate childhood pressures, we can minimize their impact by nurturing our children's talents and strengths.

When my two youngest children were preschoolers, we had a family trauma: our youngest son was the same height as our middle son. Comments from strangers—"Oh, what cute twins!"—were certainly not boosting our middle son's confidence. To help him recognize his special qualities, my husband and I began focusing on a physical attribute that was uniquely his. It wasn't hard; his gorgeous blue eyes are quite unusual in our brown-eyed family. My husband and I began complimenting his asset: "Your eyes are so

Parents Do Make a Difference

*beautiful" or "We're so lucky to have a little boy with such pretty blue eyes."
His grandparents were brought into the plan. "How's my grandson with the
gorgeous blue eyes?" Even his brothers began introducing him as "the brother
with the great eyes."*

*It wasn't until the first day of kindergarten that I knew he really believed
the praise. He came home that day literally bouncing. "How was school?"
I asked.*

*"Oh, it was so great, Mom!" he said. Without missing a beat he added,
"Somebody must have told the teacher about my beautiful blue eyes." I
paused, a bit startled (his father and I hadn't said anything to his teacher),
and asked, "Why do you think so?"*

*"She knows, all right," he explained. "She made sure I sit at the blue table
every day—probably to match my eyes!" And he barreled out the door with
a smile that could light the world. I knew then he had recognized another of
his strengths and didn't need reminding. He had added another new positive
image inside himself forever.*

 SUCCESS TIP
Birthday Celebration Letter

A special way to recognize your child's positive qualities and strengths is by writing a
Celebration Letter to her on each birthday. Highlight the year's special moments and,
most important, validate her strengths. Acknowledge any efforts she took to improve
her talents. Enjoy the letter together, then save all of them to present to her on her
twenty-first birthday. They will be a treasured memento of her uniqueness, and they
took only minutes once a year.

Four Keys to Unlocking Children's Strengths

Reinforcing your child's positive strengths and qualities is an important
strategy in enhancing self-esteem and success. Here are four keys to unlocking your child's awareness of his personal talents and areas of excellence.

1. Choose one to three positive qualities to strengthen. Look at your checklist of your child's strengths and positive traits. Choose one or two attributes you want your child to recognize about himself right away. Make sure the strengths are already present in your child and are not ones you wish were true about him. Jot down the terms you will use to point out the strengths to your child. Use the same term every time you praise the quality.

2. Find opportunities to praise the strength frequently. You can start out giving one strength message a day and gradually work your way up to two to four strength reminders. Flooding your child with too many compliments per day is probably not valuable. They begin to lose their effectiveness and become too predictable. Usually it takes at least three weeks for a new image to develop, so keep praising your child's strengths for at least twenty-one days.

3. Praise the strength only when deserved. Compliment the child only when her actions deserve recognition and you mean it. Children are great at distinguishing the genuine from the insincere.

4. Describe specific examples of the strength. Point out examples when your child displays the strength. He may not be able to see these strengths on his own. Be specific in your praise so that your child knows exactly what he did to deserve recognition.

 SUCCESS TIP
How to Describe Strengths

Grace	"You are so graceful when you dance. Your hands and body move so smoothly to the music."
Artistic ability	"You're very artistic; your drawings always have such great details and color combinations."
Caring	"You are so caring. I noticed how you stopped to ask that older woman if she needed help crossing the street."
Positive attitude	"You always seem to have something upbeat and positive to say about people. It brightens everyone's day."

Seven Ways to Help Children Recognize Their Strengths

Nine-year-old Maureen complained of headaches every morning before she left for school. The real problem was that she felt stupid. School was getting harder and harder. She always compared herself to other kids, and in her mind she always came out inferior. Maureen's parents hired outside tutors, but the truth was that learning would always be difficult. Her parents and I recognized that this child desperately needed to see herself more positively. When we brainstormed her strengths, we all agreed she clearly was artistic. The trick was now to help Maureen believe she was. I suggested seven ways they could help her recognize her artistic capabilities. Their consistent efforts in pointing out her talent gradually increased Maureen's self-confidence. She began to focus on a personal strength instead of always on her weaknesses.

Here are the seven techniques Maureen's parents used that month to help their daughter recognize her artistic strength. To use the techniques with your child, choose the qualities you would like to reinforce right now in your child. Think how you could change Maureen's parents' comments about her artistic capabilities to nurture your own child's talents. Finally, decide when you will begin to use them to help your child recognize his strengths.

1. **Describe the strength.** "Maureen, your drawing today has so many great details. You certainly are artistic."

2. **Recount past successes.** "Your teacher is still talking about that drawing you did of our family last month. She certainly thinks you're artistic."

3. **Describe the effect of the strength on others.** "Did you notice Grandma's face when she saw your drawing? Wow, did she ever think you're artistic!"

4. **Express your feelings about the strength.** "Ever since I was a little girl I have always wanted to be able to draw like you. I admire people who are artistic."

5. **Photograph the strength.** "Maureen, I found this photograph of you drawing at your desk. I framed it and am going to leave it right here on

the counter. Every time I see it I smile because it reminds me of how artistic you are."

6. **Let your child overhear your praise.** "Wait until you see Maureen's drawings today! She's so artistic. You'll love looking at her new pictures."

7. **Give opportunities to show the strength.** "Mr. Jones called to ask if you could please help the younger scouts with their drawings at the next meeting."

 SUCCESS TIP
Putting Praise in Writing

- *Lunch bag memo.* Write a little note on a paper napkin and put it in your child's lunch bag: "Chandra, remember to use that beautiful smile of yours today! See you at dinner. Dad."
- *Magnet communication.* Keep a set of magnets on your refrigerator to attach short notes: "Alex, Grandma said she loved your letter. You're so thoughtful. Love, Mom."
- *Post-It message.* Keep a set of self-adhesive notes handy to stick brief messages for your child everywhere. "You're so organized, Carrie. Your desk looks great!"
- *Pillowgram.* Slip a message under your child's pillow: "Kevin, I loved looking at your drawings today. You're so artistic! Sleep tight! Love, Dad."

Five Ways to Cultivate Children's Talent

All children deserve to hear from parents what makes them unique. It not only develops a loving relationship but also nurtures their self-esteem. Your child's self-esteem is acquired from all the images he has developed about himself. If his pictures are mostly positive, his self-esteem is high. If he has developed images that are negative or ones he is not comfortable with, his self-esteem is low. These five activities are fun ways to help your child recognize his uniquenesses and special qualities. These strategies enhance his potential for success because they help create in your child a deep-seated belief: "I have the abilities, I know what I'm good at, and I believe in myself."

1. **Strength talk.** Explain the meaning of *strength* to your child. You might say, "Usually when we think of the word *strength* we think of muscles and weight lifting. The kind of strengths I'm talking about are things that make you powerful on the inside. These are your unique strengths that make you special. Everyone has different kinds of strengths and talents. It's important to discover what your special strengths are so that you can build on them to make yourself even stronger and to benefit others."

2. **Strength mobiles.** Construct a mobile from an old clothes hanger and yarn. Your child can draw pictures of his strengths on paper and hang them from the hanger using lengths of yarn. Hang the finished mobile over your child's bed.

3. **Strength photographs.** Take several photographs of your child's special strengths in action. If your child is athletic, a good friend, and reliable, the photos might be of your child hitting a baseball, playing with friends, and taking care of her pets. Frame the snapshots and put them around your child's room.

4. **Business cards.** Help your child print up his own personalized business cards on your computer. The cards can include not only your child's name and address but also a few of his talents: "Kevin Morgan: outstanding baseball player, kind friend, and great kid." He will love giving them out to his friends and relatives.

5. **Special-me poster.** One mother, Sara, told me that her daughter, Sheila, had such low self-esteem that every time Sara praised her strengths, Sheila discounted them. Sara decided that if her daughter wouldn't "hear" the strengths, she would "show" them to her. Using photographs, magazine cutouts, and marking pens, she helped her daughter make a poster of her unique strengths. The only place Sheila felt comfortable hanging it was in her closet, so that's where the poster went. Sara says the poster is still there a year later, and Sheila refers to it whenever her confidence is running low.

SUCCESS TIP

Learning to Accept Compliments

Hearing about her strengths can make your child feel better about herself—*but only if she learns to accept the compliment.* To help your child learn to accept praise, post a list of sample comments, and take turns saying them to each other. When it's your child's turn to receive the compliment, tell her to hold her head high, look you straight in the eye, and warmly say "Thank you!" or one of the other phrases below.

"Thanks for noticing!"	"Thank you!"	"I'm glad you like it."
"I appreciate that!"	"Thanks for telling me."	"I'm pleased you think so!"

STEP 3: PROVIDE OPPORTUNITIES TO DEVELOP STRENGTHS

You have identified your child's strengths and qualities and helped your child recognize them. The last step is to provide opportunities for the strengths to grow so that your child's confidence blossoms.

The little girl was almost three when she saw her first Olympic figure skating competition on television. Each day, she sat glued to the set watching the women skaters. The night the women's gold medal in figure skating was awarded, the youngster stood on a cardboard box, pretending it was an Olympic podium. She announced to her family that one day, she too was going to win a medal. Everyone laughed, but the girl's mother saw the determination in her eyes and that moment vowed to help her daughter achieve her dream. She bought the little girl her first pair of ice skates and signed her up for skating lessons. Every day, the little girl rigorously practiced her skating skills and prayed that she would have the strength to achieve her dreams. Over the following years, the family made tremendous financial and personal sacrifices to ensure that the child's potential developed to its fullest and they prayed for strength to persevere.

After twelve years of long, hard work, the young girl stood on a podium, this time not cardboard, with an Olympic gold medal hanging from her neck. Her mother, watching from the stands, knew that her child's dream had finally come true. Tara Lipinski made Olympic history that day as the youngest woman to receive the figure skating medal.

What makes a Tara Lipinski? A Tiger Woods, a Michael Jordan, a Chris Evert Lloyd? Why do some children develop their talent to such heights that they become superstars? A noted educator, Benjamin Bloom, and a team of researchers at the University of Chicago conducted a five-year study of 120 immensely talented young people. Among them were Olympic swimmers, accomplished sculptors, tennis champions, concert pianists, and exceptional mathematicians and scientists. All were recognized as outstanding in their ability. Bloom explained in his book *Developing Talent in Young People* that, surprisingly, these world-class talents weren't simply born talented—they were brought up to become talented. Although each child's road to achievement was slightly different, all the parents used remarkably similar practices to nurture talent. The most heartening news from Bloom's study was this: *given the right conditions, almost any child can rise higher, shine brighter, and succeed.*

Six Parenting Practices That Nurture Talent

As most of us know, the odds that our children will become superstars are remote. Still, we can use these parents' practices with our children to help them live richer lives. Following are six of the most significant talent principles the parents of superstars used to cultivate their children's talents. We can borrow these practices to nurture our own children's strengths, helping them become their best.

1. **Emphasize encouragement.** Parents made sure their children's early talent development was positive, fun, and *not pushed.*

2. **Make practice times enjoyable.** The parents made their children's practice times fun and usually sat with their kids as they practiced.

3. Provide resources to cultivate the talent. The children's talents improved because parents constantly provided the necessary resources to nurture their skills.

4. Show your interest. The superstars' parents attended every major activity to show support, and they often learned the skill just so they could spend more time with their children.

5. Stand by—win or lose. Each superstar had an encouraging parent standing by his side, celebrating his wins and cushioning his losses.

6. Focus on the talent. All parents placed great emphasis on their children's evident talents and spent a tremendous amount of time cultivating it.

SUCCESS TIP
Ways to Develop Your Child's Talent

Experts tell us that children's talents rarely develop by chance, but instead are cultivated and nurtured. Here are eight ways to develop your child's talent.

1. Find classes, camps, or lessons related to the talent. Teachers, park and recreation programs, camp directories, and the yellow pages are possible resources. Offer this opportunity to your child.
2. Take your child on field trips or outings to view the talent in action.
3. Seek out experts for advice on ways to nurture the strength.
4. Set aside space for your child to practice the skill.
5. Subscribe to a magazine that features the talent.
6. Use your library to check out videos and books about the talent. Ask the children's reference librarian for ideas and resources.
7. Use the Internet to find websites describing any available resources related to the field. Query experts by e-mail.
8. Find someone in your community with the talent to mentor your child.

Four Ways to Applaud Your Child's Efforts

Publicly acknowledging your child for his efforts to develop his talent increases the effectiveness of your praise. Your child hears the compliment not only from you but also from other family members. Besides, it makes your child feel good to be recognized before an audience. A characteristic of strong families is that they take time to celebrate each other's achievements. Here are four ways your family can honor one another's special qualities. Have fun and use every success—as well as every effort—as an excuse for celebrating!

1. **Celebration banners.** I was in an industrious mood one year and decided to make celebration banners for each of my children. They were nothing more than strips of bright-colored felt. Using felt letters, I glued each child's name across the top and hung the banners on wooden dowels. I bought a few tiny trinkets to show their special talents—a paintbrush, soccer ball, and a drum—and glued them on along with all the ribbons, buttons, and little pins they had earned from scouting, sports, and school over the years. The banners were simple to make, but I let my family believe this was a very creative endeavor. We have a tradition now that whenever a child deserves recognition for a success or effort related to his talents, I hang his banner on the front door. Curiosity makes everyone eventually ask the child what he did to deserve having his banner on display. It's our way of celebrating our children's successes and efforts.

2. **Celebration placemats.** A father shared with me how his family celebrates their strengths. Each person has her own special placemat that she personalizes using permanent marking pens. The child's placemat is put out at dinner only for honoring improvement in a talent, so everyone immediately knows there's something to celebrate.

3. **Displayed treasures.** At Christmastime when I was little, I couldn't wait to go to my girlfriend's house and see her family's Christmas stockings. Each sister's stocking was covered with different little trinkets her mother sewed on, representing the girl's interests and talents. Everyone always stopped to ask each sister what the trinkets stood for. Consider displaying your child's special mementos of his special talents in a special box, on a piece of colored felt, or even glued inside a picture frame.

Make sure the display is prominent so that your child receives public recognition.

4. Talent brag board. Set aside a bulletin board or wall space where family members can share their talents and skills. You can pin up articles, photographs, or news clippings describing their talents, along with inspirational quotes encouraging family members to keep developing their talents and positive qualities.

WHAT ONE PARENT DID

Kevin was an energetic seven-year-old who loved to be outdoors on a baseball diamond. Settling down and doing his schoolwork was not as fun. Like many boys his age, Kevin's attention span was short, and he needed constant reminders to "Get to work!" Lately he was focusing so much on his weaknesses that his self-esteem was plummeting. His parents and teacher met to develop a plan both to improve his concentration and to rebuild his self-confidence.

Kevin's parents decided that their first step was to help their son focus on his positive qualities. They helped him list his strengths and hung copies of the list on the refrigerator and on his bathroom mirror, bedroom ceiling, and closet door. They asked him which strengths he felt he was best at, and from his choices they created this affirmation: "I'm good at a lot of things. I'm good at baseball, I'm a kind friend, and I'm fun to be around." Kevin said the affirmation to himself several times a day. After a few weeks, his parents and teacher noticed the positive change in Kevin's attitude: he was not only more confident but also more willing to work on schoolwork for longer periods of time.

FINAL WORDS ON CULTIVATING YOUR CHILD'S STRENGTHS

Many researchers agree on one thing: there is a talent hiding in every child. Parents are often the greatest determinants of whether their children's talents will lie dormant or be nurtured into full bloom. How skilled your child becomes in his talent depends on many factors: his motivation, temperament, and maturation level; his teacher's being the right match; and the availability of resources. Sometimes it's all just a matter of having the right timing.

Keep in mind that you just never know where your efforts may lead. Your child may use his talent to develop a lifelong hobby or expand his knowledge. His new interest may help him find new friends or discover a possible life career. It might build his confidence or help him compensate for a handicap; someday he might even become a superstar. Who knows? Whatever the outcome, your labors are worth every effort. Maybe the greatest reason it is all worthwhile is that you are giving your child the gift that withstands time: his knowing what makes him special.

POINTS TO REMEMBER

• Encourage each of your children's originality and creativity. Stress that everyone has special uniqueness.

- Accept what makes your child unique and special. A person's feeling of self-worth starts with his knowing he is fully accepted for all that he is. Recognize that your child's strengths may lie in areas that don't reflect your own personal preferences.

- You can help your child discover her special strengths and positive qualities by pointing them out each time she demonstrates them.

- Affirm your own positive qualities with your child. You may feel uncomfortable at first, but you can't expect your children to make positive self-statements unless they hear you making them, too.

- Remember the most crucial parental admonition: *never* compare your child's strengths to anyone else's: Grandma's, Dad's, a friend's, yours, or, especially, a sibling's.

RESOURCES FOR FURTHER ACTION

For Parents

Awakening Your Child's Natural Genius, by Thomas Armstrong (New York: Tarcher, 1991). More than three hundred practical suggestions showing parents how they can play a pivotal role in helping their children realize their true gifts.

Developing Talent in Young People, by Benjamin Bloom (New York: Ballantine, 1985). The fascinating results of a study on 120 immensely talented Americans and the practices used by their parents and teachers that helped them realize their full potential.

In Their Own Way: Discovering and Encouraging Your Child's Personal Learning Style, by Thomas Armstrong (New York: Tarcher, 1987). An excellent resource for helping pinpoint and enhance children's unique learning styles.

Understanding Your Child's Temperament, by William B. Carey (Old Tappan, N.J.: Macmillan, 1997). This reference helps parents understand the nine temperament traits inborn in every child and how to work with them from infancy through adolescence.

For Children Ages Three to Seven

The Bedspread, by Sylvia Fair (New York: Morrow, 1982). A gloriously written account of two elderly sisters with two very different views of life. The message they convey is wonderful: "There is no one way that is better. Our uniqueness make us special."

I Wish I Were a Butterfly, by James Howe (Orlando, Calif.: Harcourt Brace, 1987). A wise dragonfly helps a despondent cricket recognize his uniqueness and gain self-acceptance.

The Magic Fan, by Keith Baker (Orlando, Fla.: Harcourt Brace, 1989). Beautiful fan-shaped cutout pictures enhance this tale of a young boy who gradually recognizes his inner powers.

Quick as a Cricket, by Audrey Wood (Child's Play, 1982). Rhymes and vibrant pictures portray a child's affirmations of his strengths and attributes.

The Story of Ferdinand, by Munro Leaf (New York: Viking Penguin, 1936). A classic tale celebrating uniqueness.

Tacky the Penguin, by Helen Lester (Boston: Houghton Mifflin, 1988). A perfect, comical read-aloud about a wonderful, unique penguin named Tacky.

For Children Ages Eight to Twelve

Do Bananas Chew Gum? by Jamie Gilson (New York: Lothrop, Lee & Shepard, 1980). A boy with learning disabilities receives the special help he needs, and finds success.

Mostly Michael, by Robert Kimmel Smith (New York: Dell, 1987). A boy receives a diary for his birthday and fills it with revelations about his life and search for identity.

There's a Boy in the Girls' Bathroom, by Louis Sachar (New York: Knopf, 1987). A humorous and touching story of a young boy in search of his identity.

Trial by Wilderness, by David Mathieson (Boston: Houghton Mifflin, 1985). As the sole survivor of a plane crash, Elena survives in the wilderness by calling upon her courage.

Videos for Family Viewing

A Dog of Flanders (Paramount Home Video, 1960). The story of a young boy who hopes to become a great classical painter. He draws with homemade charcoal by day and dreams of famous painters by night until he finally finds an artist patron.

My Side of the Mountain (Paramount Home Video, 1969). A thirteen-year-old Canadian boy runs away from home to get closer to nature and reveals his pronounced strengths in dealing with the wilderness. Based on the book. (G)

Pollyanna (Walt Disney Home Video, 1960). This child's clear strength is an incredible positive attitude and her ability to spread it throughout the town. A wonderful Disney film to enjoy as a family. (G)

The Red Shoes (Family Home Entertainment, 1990). The animated version of Hans Christian Andersen's tale is the story of two little girls who fall in love with ballet and of their dream of futures on the stage. A poignant story of caring, goal setting, identifying personal strengths, and not giving up. (G)

Rookie of the Year (20th Century-Fox, 1993). After breaking his arm, a young boy discovers that he has an amazing fastball pitch, which earns him a spot as the new star pitcher for the Chicago Cubs.

Websites for Kids

"Animals Tracks Kids Stuff" [http://www.nwf.org/kids/]. Wonderful for nature-loving kids with an interest in science. Games, riddles, facts, and links to sites all about animals.

"Astronomy Picture of the Day" [http://antwrp.gsfc.nasa.gov/apod/astropix. html]. A great way to introduce kids to astronomy: every day a different astronomy picture is displayed with accompanying information.

"Aunt Annie's Craft Page" [http://www.auntannie.com]. This site offers scores of creative art projects for kids to do. Great for your artistic, visual child.

"The Big Busy House" [http://www.harpercollins.com/kids/]. For kids who love books; this site features interviews with authors and explains how a book is made.

Parents Do Make a Difference

"Global Show 'n Tell Museum Wings" [http://www.telenaut.com/gst/]. A site for kids to display their talents, skills, favorite interests, and collections.

"Gordon's Entomological Home Page" [http://www.insect-world.com]. An introduction to insects. A great way for a science-oriented child to start a bug collection or just find out fascinating bug information.

"KidPub" [http://www.kidpub.org/kidpub/]. If your child likes to write stories, this is the site for her. She can submit her work so that kids all over the world can read it.

"Kidstuff" [http://pathfinder.com/kids/]. A way to familiarize your child with a wealth of different interest possibilities. Offers special editions of kid's magazines, such as *Sports Illustrated* and *Time*. Visit the Underwater World site to find out all about the ocean.

"Yahooligans" [www.yahooligan.com]. Offers a directory of kid websites organized by interests.

"Yuckiest Site on the Internet" [www.yucky.com]. Helps develop children's interest in science; educational information about insects, worms, and other "yucky" science creatures.

Communicating

Learning How to Speak Up, Listen Attentively, and Reduce Misunderstandings

Six-year-old Noah spent the morning building a Lego fort. He was almost done when his brother barreled in, grabbed a handful of Legos, and ran off with the pieces Noah needed to finish. Noah jumped up and chased Joshua to the kitchen, bumping straight into his mother. "What's wrong?" asked his mom. Noah was so angry he couldn't speak. Instead he pulled Joshua's arm and wrestled him to the ground. Their mom finally pulled the boys apart and cried, "What's the matter with you two? Why can't you tell each other why you're so upset instead of always fighting?" Noah looked at her, startled. "Why tell someone you're mad?" he thought. "It's easier just to hit him." And then he went to sit in his room, grounded again for fighting.

Five-year-old Toni was upset at her classmate, Leticia, for grabbing the sponge paints from her. She had waited so long for her turn, she felt like exploding. Then she remembered what her stepmom always said: "Use your words, Toni. They're more powerful than your fists." She turned to face Leticia and firmly said, "I am really mad, because you grabbed the paints from me. I want you to give them back." Surprised, Leticia looked up and stopped painting. "She sounds like she really means it," thought Leticia. "Here," she said, giving the sponges to her classmate. "You take them." Toni smiled and thought to herself, "Using your words really does help."

Teaching children how to become effective communicators is one of the greatest gifts you can ever give them. Few skills enhance children's growing-up years or increase their chances of becoming confident and independent adults as much as this third skill of success. The reason: your child uses communication skills every moment he's awake—and he uses them in *every* arena of his life.

Experts agree that children who are poor communicators are tremendously disadvantaged when trying to achieve success: because these kids frequently misconstrue directions or forget key facts or ideas, their grades drop. If they don't remember the information they hear, their knowledge dwindles. In addition, misunderstandings of verbal and nonverbal messages can put their friendships at risk. If they cannot make their views understood, their future success in the workplace can be curtailed. And if communication in your family is weak, even your own relationship with your child can suffer. Understanding both verbal and nonverbal language is the key to solving problems, acquiring knowledge, and accepting others. Without this skill, our children are greatly shortchanged in their chances of success in life.

Effective communication skills and success are just too tightly connected for us to assume that our kids will acquire these skills by chance. Just as our children must learn reading, writing, and arithmetic to be their best, they must also learn to be effective communicators. And you are your child's most important communication instructor.

WHAT YOU WILL LEARN IN THIS CHAPTER

This chapter discusses the many ways you can enhance your child's success in school and in life by teaching her effective communication skills. You'll learn how to:

- Keep the lines of communication open between you and your child to help her always feel comfortable speaking up.

- Enhance your child's social competence by helping her read other people's nonverbal messages.

- Establish family meetings and traditions in your home to help your child practice communication skills, have a voice in your household, resolve family problems, and speak up to get her point across.

- Improve your child's listening skills by helping her recall the most important ideas she's just heard, so as to enhance both her school success and her knowledge base.

- Teach your child beginning note-taking skills by showing her how to write down key facts for review at a later date.

- Help your child learn to use "I messages" as a peaceful way to communicate feelings and concerns.

HOW IS YOUR CHILD DOING NOW?

The statements below describe behaviors usually displayed by children who have developed strong communication skills. To evaluate your child's strengths in this third success skill, write the number you think best represents your child's current level on the line following each statement and then add all the scores to get his total score. If your child scores 40 to 50, he's in great shape with the skill. If he scores 30 to 40, he could benefit from skill enhancement. A score of 20 to 30 shows signs of potential problems. If your child scores 10 to 20, consider getting help to increase this skill.

5 = Always 4 = Frequently 3 = Sometimes 2 = Rarely 1 = Never

A child with strong communication skills:	My child
Rarely has problems speaking up and speaking his mind in school and at home.	_____
Makes frequent and appropriate eye contact with the speaker.	_____
Shows interest in the speaker: nods, smiles, asks relevant questions.	_____
Stays focused in the conversation without changing the topic or interrupting.	_____
Can verbalize his feelings appropriately to get his needs met.	_____
Can remember directions or facts the first time he hears them.	_____
Correctly reads others' nonverbal cues: gestures, body language, facial expressions.	_____
Understands the most important ideas from what he hears.	_____
Shows he understands the speaker's feelings.	_____
Uses appropriate tone of voice, gesture, and posture when communicating.	_____
Total Score	_____

FOUR STEPS TO DEVELOPING STRONG COMMUNICATION SKILLS

There are four steps to improving your child's communication skills. Because watching how you communicate is the best way for your child to acquire the skill, the first step conveys ways to tune up your attentive listening behaviors. These ideas help keep the lines of communication open so that your child feels comfortable speaking up; they lay the foundation to enhancing success at communication.

Because scores of studies show that the greatest percentage of communication is sent through our body language and not our spoken words, the second step enhances your child's nonverbal behaviors. The third steps boosts your child's listening skills to help her remember what she hears and recognize the most important points in verbal messages. And, because research shows that the way to ensure your child learns communication skills is for her to use them, the final step shows you how to set family meetings and establish home traditions to provide opportunities for your child to practice getting her point across in real life. Following are the four steps to nurturing children's verbal and nonverbal communication skills:

Step 1: Encourage Your Child to Speak Out
Step 2: Help Your Child Send and Receive Nonverbal Messages
Step 3: Enhance Your Child's Listening Skills
Step 4: Provide Opportunities to Use Communication Skills

STEP 1: ENCOURAGE YOUR CHILD TO SPEAK OUT

Communication skills are best taught not by telling our kids about them but by showing them with our own behavior. Using the skills in this step establishes the foundation for your child's communication capabilities, because you'll be modeling the same effective listening behaviors you want your child to copy. So the first step we must all learn is how to listen more attentively—especially to our kids. Using the technique is also one of the easiest and most powerful ways of keeping the lines of communication open so that your child always feels comfortable sharing his thoughts with you.

Eleven-year-old Summer hung up the phone and shouted, "Mom! Where are you?"

"Now what?" Summer's mom thought. She had had another exhausting day at work and was trying to get dinner ready, and being a single parent

made it especially hard. She didn't need any interruptions now. "I'm in the kitchen, Summer. Don't yell!"

Summer burst in. "Maria just invited me to her sleepover Saturday." She grabbed a cookie and pleaded, "Can I go?"

"Don't eat that, Summer," her mom scolded. "You know you're supposed to lose five pounds."

"But can I go, Mom?" she pleaded. "If I don't tell Maria tonight, she'll invite someone else." The phone rang, cutting off her words.

"Can't you see I'm busy, Summer?" and her mom turned to answer the call. "Let's talk about this after dinner."

"OK," her daughter answered in a barely audible voice. She slowly walked to her room thinking to herself, "Why bother? She doesn't care. She's always too busy to listen."

I've yet to meet parents who want their children to think they aren't interested in their ideas or don't care about their kids' feelings or who hope their children won't openly share their experiences with them. Yet those are the messages children pick up, all because of how parents react when their children talk. There are countless ways we can discourage our kids from expressing themselves: by cutting our kids off ("Let's not talk about this now" or "We've been through this before"), by denying their feelings ("Just forget about it" or "You don't mean that"), by lecturing ("You should do this . . ." or "You know you shouldn't . . ."), by ordering them ("Stop complaining!"), by putting them down ("That's pretty immature" or "I never did that"). Often the biggest communication discouragers have nothing to do with what we say but rather with what we do when our kids talk to us: roll our eyes, shrug our shoulders, raise our eyebrows, frown, turn away, or shake our head.

We may not mean to discourage our children from speaking up, but that's exactly how they interpret our actions: "Mom isn't interested in what I say," "Dad doesn't care how I feel," "She doesn't want to hear my side," "He doesn't think my ideas are important." And our poor listening habits can take a major toil on the growth of our children's communication skills. If children are made to feel their ideas and feelings aren't important, their self-esteem is diminished. If children aren't given opportunities to practice expressing themselves, the development of their communication skills is hindered. And then there is the most painful outcome: if the poor habits continue and our kids don't feel we'll listen, they just may turn to someone else to talk to. Our relationships with our children may suffer, often taking years to rebuild.

If we really want our children to open up and share their ideas, feelings, and concerns as well as become effective communicators, we need to tune up our own listening behaviors.

The Power of Listening Attentively

Eight-year-old Jonathan was placed in my special education classroom because of severe attention deficits and learning disabilities. As I grew to know him I discovered a sharp mind, a memory filled with historical facts, and a heart of pure gold. One morning I found him at the art center busily creating a beautiful paper heart.

"That's lovely, Jonathan," I commented.

"Thanks. It's for my Mom," he explained. "She always makes my feelings feel good." I couldn't wait to meet this mother to see just what she did to make her child's "feelings feel good."

I had the opportunity the following week at our parent-child reading party. It was obvious that Jonathan's mom was a master at listening to her son. Each time Jonathan talked, she'd stop everything, look into her son's eyes, and listen with genuine interest. Her words usually were nothing more than repeating back small tidbits of what Jonathan just said, to let him know she was hearing him. Occasionally she'd add, "Uh huh," or "Really?" She acknowledged him simply by saying how she thought he was feeling: "You seem so happy" or "Jonathan, you look proud." The effect on her son was dramatic: his whole demeanor brightened when he realized his mom really was interested in what he had to say. Using the simple technique of active listening encouraged Jonathan to talk and obviously "made his feelings feel good."

A Four-Part Formula That Invites Kids to Talk

Using the technique of active listening is one of the easiest and most powerful ways to encourage your child to speak up and share his feelings, ideas, and experiences. The best lessons in active listening were those I learned not from a textbook or class but from my son Adam, when he was just two. Whenever we would talk, he had a habit of taking my chin in his hand and pulling my face toward him so that my eyes were directly in front of his face. His actions were crystal clear: Adam wanted my complete attention. The way he knew I was listening was by seeing my eyes focused exclusively on his eyes. That's what our kids want most—knowing we're really listening and interested in what they have to say. Using active listening with our kids conveys that message to them.

What follows is a four-part formula for using active listening, adapted from the work of Drs. Thomas Gordon and Haim Ginott, outstanding communication experts. As with any technique, learning the formula takes practice and effort, but the benefits are enormous for enhancing your family's communication. This is also a wonderful way to develop a warmer and more intimate relationship with your child. And, best yet, watching you use active listening is the best way for your child to recognize what good listening behaviors look and sound like. He'll be more likely to use the skill in his own life.

Part 1: Listen with Full Attentiveness

Eleven-year-old Yuki came back from gymnastics quite upset and sank into the couch. Seeing her daughter's distress, her mom quickly put down her book, sat facing her, and gently took her hand. She wanted her daughter to know she was completely there for her.

Yuki's mom is demonstrating the first part of active listening: stop everything and focus completely on your child so that he feels you are hearing him. Your full attentiveness makes it easier for your child to talk and keeps your lines of communication open.

Part 2: Offer a Word to Encourage the Dialogue

"I'm never going back there again," cried Yuki. "Oh?" her mom said, and waited to see if her daughter would say anything more. When she didn't, she simply restated the last thing Yuki said: "You're never going back."

"That's for sure, never!" exclaimed her daughter. "All my teacher does is yell at me, because I can't do anything right."

The second part of active listening is usually the hardest: don't interrupt your child or offer any opinion. Your silence at this stage can be golden. Your being there to listen is usually all your child really needs. Besides, the last thing kids want to hear is our advice. To let him know you're interested, just offer a nonjudgmental word or two to encourage his talking, such as, "Oh?" "I see," "Really?" or even "Mmmm." Dr. Gordon also suggests simply repeating back your child's last phrase:

Child: "I can't stand being around Kevin this year."

Adult: "You can't stand being around Kevin."

Child: "You bet I can't. He's so bossy and mean all the time."

Part 3: Reflect the Feeling Content of the Message to Your Child
Yuki's mom had wondered if the class would be too hard. Now she knew. The distraught look on her daughter's face crushed her, so she said, "You look so upset, Yuki." Then she waited for her daughter's reaction to see if she was right. It didn't take long: "Sure I'm upset. How would you feel if your teacher picked on you in front of all the other kids?"

When you recognize how your child is feeling, describe the feeling to your child: "Looks like you're angry," "You seem really frustrated," "Sounds like you're irritated," or "You seem unhappy." This simple act helps keep your dialogue open, because your child knows you are really trying to understand him.

The biggest communication mistake parents make at this point is trying to solve the problem for their kids. So don't say anything for a few seconds; wait for your child to answer. Usually your child will tell you whether your reflection is wrong or right, and you can respond to his reaction. Either way, the communication between you continues, which is exactly what you want to have happen.

Part 4: Reassure Your Child with Empathy
Yuki's mom gently put her arm around her daughter and said, "I'm so sorry you had such a bad day."

"The class is just too hard, Mom," Yuki sighed. "Do you think I can maybe enroll in another class instead?"

Her mom smiled. That was just what she was thinking, and she said, "That's a great idea, Yuki. Let's look into it first thing after school tomorrow. Thanks for telling me your problem." Yuki gave her mom a quick hug and ran off to call her friend.

End your conversation with a response that conveys your support: "I hope things work out," "I'm so sorry," or "I'm here if you need me." Wait to see if your child needs anything else: advice, a hug, reassurance, or even a quick game of hoops, and thank your child for sharing.

I find that the hardest part of active listening is not giving my advice unless my kids ask for it. Sometime the urge is so strong, I have to say inside my head, "Don't say anything. Be quiet." And I'm always glad I do stay quiet: my kids are more talkative, and they generally solve their own problems just because they talked it through aloud. I'm sure my goal is the same as yours: always to keep the communication doors open so that my kids will feel comfortable coming back and telling me anything!

 SUCCESS TIP
Rebuilding Communication Through Writing

A Baltimore father, whose wife recently moved out, found his communication temporarily strained with his twelve-year-old son. He came up with a unique way of keeping their relationship alive: each night he left a short note on his son's pillow, reaffirming his love and assuring him he was always there for him. For several days the son never said a thing, but the father swore he'd keep writing. His efforts paid off: one morning the son walked into the kitchen, gave his dad a hug, and said, "Thanks for the notes, Dad. I've been so afraid that I did something to make Mom want to go away, and didn't want to talk about it. Can we talk now?" Sometimes writing to your child can be a way to rebuild your communication.

STEP 2: HELP YOUR CHILD SEND AND RECEIVE NONVERBAL MESSAGES

Experts say that the greatest percentage of communication is sent through our body language and not our spoken words. This step helps you enhance

SUCCESS TIP
Improving Conversation with Your Kids

Edward Ford and Steven Englund, authors of *For the Love of Children*, suggest three principles to improve conversation with kids. They're especially helpful with preadolescents!

1. *Talk about common interests.* Discuss topics you mutually share, such as past experiences, the planning of an upcoming event, or a movie, actor, song, or play you both know.

2. *Stay noncritical.* Judging, criticizing, or offering advice are communication stoppers. Try to exercise patience and be open to hearing your child's ideas.

3. *Ask questions that elicit more than one-word responses.* Make skillful use of your questions so that your child must respond with more than a one-word answer: "How would you have ended that book?" "What would you have done differently in the game?" "What are your feelings about . . . ?"

your child's social competence by improving her nonverbal behaviors so that she can send and receive emotional messages correctly.

My son Jason was four years old when I began working on my doctorate in counseling and psychology at the University of San Francisco. I remember going to class and then coming home and eagerly practicing my counseling skills on my family. I thought I was doing so well, until an experience taught me I had a long way to go to master my techniques.

One day, Jason was helping me dry dishes and accidentally broke a favorite family plate. At the sound of the crash, I turned and saw his distraught look as well as my smashed plate. All the counseling skills I'd been working on flashed before me: I took three deep breaths to calm down, got down to eye level and gently said, "I see how upset you are Jason. It's OK; accidents happen." I thought I had done well, but my son's next comment immediately squelched my confidence: "Why are you angry, Mom? It really was an accident." I was surprised: I had tried to sound so calm. I exclaimed,

"But I'm not angry." At which Jason quickly pointed out, "Then you should tell your face that, Mom. It looks angry." And of course he was right! I had worked so hard on trying to sound calm and tell him I wasn't upset, I had overlooked the importance of using a calm facial expression. Jason had heard my words but picked up on my grimace and furrowed brow. That's when I recognized how critical our nonverbal messages are in communication.

Most of the time our kids aren't listening to our words nearly as much as they are watching our posture, gestures, and facial expressions, and hearing the tone of our voice. Albert Mehrabian, author of *Silent Messages,* conducted a series of classic studies and found that the percentage of communication actually sent through spoken words is only 7 percent! The greatest portion of our messages—over 55 percent—is communicated through our body language, and 38 percent is through the tone of our voice.

As I worked on my doctorate, I learned that adults weren't the only ones who needed to work on nonverbal communication skills: they are essential for our children's success. It is important to help children understand that their body posture, facial expressions, and voice tone constantly send messages to speakers and that if they don't interpret or send nonverbal messages correctly, serious misunderstandings can occur.

Five Ways to Help Kids Read Nonverbal Messages

Drs. Stephen Nowicki and Marshall Duke, child psychologists at Emory University in Atlanta, conducted tests with more than one thousand children and found that one out of ten children, despite normal and even superior intelligence, has significant problems in nonverbal communication. This disability may explain why these children have trouble getting along with others and just don't seem to fit in. They also discovered that the most popular and well-adjusted children are highly competent in recognizing particular emotional signals and in expressing their feelings to others. The researchers' recommendation: enhance your child's skills in reading nonverbal messages! The following are five ideas for getting started.

SUCCESS TIP
Teach Two Critical Skills:
Eye Contact and Smiling

Researchers have discovered that well-liked children consistently use the nonverbal skills of eye contact and smiling. Using them increases children's social successes dramatically. These are also two of the easiest success behaviors to enhance in your child. Here's how: as you're talking with your child, gently remind her to use eye contact: "Look at me," "Put your eyes on my eyes," or "I want to see your eyes." And whenever your child displays a great smile, point it out! "What a great smile!" or "That smile of yours will win people over." By consciously reinforcing these two important skills and modeling them regularly, your child will soon be smiling more and using eye contact, and you will be enhancing her success potential.

1. **Make an emotion scrapbook.** Help your child collect pictures of a variety of facial expressions and paste them into a scrapbook. Be sure to include the six basic emotions: happy, sad, angry, surprised, afraid, and disgusted. Now make a game of naming the emotions with your child by asking, "How is this person feeling?" You can also help your child learn to predict the body language and voice tone that would accompany each facial expression: "If you were angry, how would your voice sound?" "How would a sad person stand?" "What about a person who is disgusted?"

2. **Guess people's emotions.** With your child, watch other people's faces and body language at a playground, park, or shopping mall. Try together to guess their emotional states: "How does her face look?" "He's standing with his arms crossed; how do you think he's feeling right now?" "Listen to the sound of that man's voice. How do you think he feels?" "See how that woman is seated next to the man. She's crossing her legs and folding her arms. Do you suppose she wants to be with him or not?"

3. **Watch silent movies.** Turn off the sound on your television and watch the show together. Make a game out of trying to guess how the actors feel just from what you see. There are dozens of nonverbal things

people do to express their feelings. Point out those behaviors to your child to help him recognize how people communicate with their body language. Tension behaviors include blinking eyes rapidly, biting nails, twirling hair, clenching jaws, and grinding teeth. Withdrawal or uninterested behaviors include folded arms, crossed legs, rolling eyes, and not facing the speaker. Expressions of interest include nodding, smiling, leaning into the speaker, and standing or sitting close to the person.

4. Play emotion charades. A fun, quiet car game is to have family members play charades—but only with their face and body. Riders must try to guess the person's emotion.

5. Observe good listening behaviors. Be on the alert for people demonstrating good listening habits; point them out to your child. "Do you see how that lady is facing the man while he's talking? She's showing him that she's interested in what he has to say." "Look how that girl over there is nodding her head while the other girl is talking. That's a great way to show you're listening." "Did you notice how Aunt Ellen always has her eyes on you while you talk? It makes you feel she wants to hear what you're saying." The better your child understands what good nonverbal listening behaviors look like, the greater the chance he will use them on his own.

SUCCESS TIP
"Bridge of Your Nose" Technique

One of my students was so shy that whenever students were paired to share an idea, she'd quietly ask me, "Do I have to look at my partner?" By accident one day, I said to her, "Don't look at your partner's eyes—just look right between them at the bridge of his nose. He'll never know the difference." The technique worked like a charm! With a few practices, she no longer needed the technique and instead looked confidently right into her partner's eyes. Suggest the tip to your child if he feels uncomfortable using eye contact.

Parents Do Make a Difference

STEP 3: ENHANCE YOUR
CHILD'S LISTENING SKILLS

Experts say that, except for breathing, we listen more than any other single activity, yet it is one of our most underdeveloped success traits. Considering how critical listening is to our children's success in classrooms, at home, with friends, and in the workplace, it is essential to boost our children's listening skill. This step enhances your child's listening skills by helping him not only recall what he heard but also identify from everything he heard the most important ideas to remember.

I was thirty thousand feet in the air flying to Atlanta to give a teacher seminar when I realized just how significant it is to teach children to listen effectively. I had grabbed any reading material I could find; it turned out to be a business magazine called Success, *and the article titled "How You Can Be a Success" instantly caught my attention. The interviewer had asked ten high-achieving, wealthy entrepreneurs what they considered the most important qualities for success. All ten interviewees gave the same number one response: the skill of listening! Each entrepreneur felt that possessing effective listening skills is critical for succeeding in today's business world and is pivotal in getting interviews, winning jobs, and working your way up the corporate ladder.*

The next day, I shared what I had learned with the high school teachers at my workshop. I explained that although I had always felt that listening skills are critical for student success, I had never realized how valuable the skill was for job attainment! Obviously those teachers recognized its value: by the first break, I was swarmed with participants concerned by how many of their high school students' listening abilities were so inferior. They knew these students' school and life successes would be greatly hindered. Their concerns were justified: their students' grades were suffering because they frequently misinterpreted directions and did assignments incorrectly. Their test scores were lower because they were not hearing core parts of lectures. And conflicts among peers were escalating, often because of simple misunderstandings.

That day those teachers unanimously agreed that listening skills were becoming a lost art with their students, and they convinced me that kids must learn listening skills at a younger age. I've been their most ardent advocate ever since, and in every workshop I present, I implore teachers and parents to enhance children's listening skills.

Four Ideas to Help Kids Listen for the Main Idea

Here's a quiz: What is one of the most important study skills your child needs to be successful in school? The answer: learning to sort out from everything she's heard the most important ideas and to remember them. As your child gets older, she'll need to learn to write down only those most important facts and study them. They are the items most likely to be on the test. The result: her grades will dramatically improve! These four ideas help kids remember the most important ideas they have heard so as to enhance their learning successes.

1. **Teach the acronym SOLER.** I was observing a dynamic high school history teacher recently, and noticed the acronym SOLER on his chalkboard. He explained that many students are losing important pieces of information in his lectures because they aren't practicing good listening behaviors. SOLER is his acronym for the five behaviors he wants his students to demonstrate whenever they listen—whether it be to his lectures, a class video, or to one another:

> S—*Sit* upright.
> O—*Open* your mind and show your interest.
> L—*Lean* in.
> E—Make *eye contact* with the speaker and nod.
> R—*Review* in your mind: "What did I hear?"

You may want to make a SOLER chart and post it as a reminder of effective listening behaviors for the whole family.

2. **Remember your "keeper."** After students have viewed a video or heard a lecture, Dr. Spencer Kagan, an educational consultant, asks them

to say or write the most important thing they want to remember. He calls it a *keeper*. This is a great tip for helping your child remember key ideas. After your child finishes listening or reading, ask, "What's your keeper?" and then help him decide what the most important idea is. If you use the word often enough, children not only start listening for keepers but also try to beat you in saying, "So what's *your* keeper?"

3. **Learn dinner-hour paraphrasing.** This game enhances children's ability to listen attentively to the exact words of speakers around the dinner table. Each family member takes a turn briefly describing something that's happened to her during the day. The next speaker must correctly restate the previous speaker's ideas, before contributing his experience. To make it challenging, after everyone has had a turn, see if anyone can identify one important idea from each person's conversation.

4. **Make one-fact note cards.** You need a few index cards or 3" × 5" pieces of paper, a pen or pencil, and any nonfiction reading material. Read the selection aloud together and stop at the end of every paragraph or so to ask, "What's the most important idea you heard?" Help your child draw or write down one fact or idea on a card. When you are finished reading, help your child review the card facts and show him how to store them in a small recipe-size box so that he can study them again on his own. You've just taught your child a great way to review for tests, take notes, and tune into the main ideas.

STEP 4: PROVIDE OPPORTUNITIES TO USE COMMUNICATION SKILLS

Telling your child about communication skills or even demonstrating them to her doesn't necessarily mean that your child knows how to use them. Learning these skills takes practice and more practice before she can use them on her own. This final step helps you establish family meetings and home traditions that provide opportunities for your child to practice a wide range of communication skills at home, enabling her to get her point across more confidently in the real world.

SUCCESS TIP
Helping Children Remember What They Hear

In the 1960s, Mary Budd Rowe, a noted educator, recognized that students in some classrooms were engaged in more sophisticated discussions than students in other classes—even though they were all using the same lessons. Rowe noticed that the more successful students' teachers were doing only one thing differently: whenever they asked a question, they waited a minimum of three seconds for students to think before they called on the students to respond. The result was profound: these students' test scores and confidence improved, and their verbal responses were significantly lengthier. Rowe concluded that children need "wait time"—or simply more time to think about what they hear—before speaking. So whenever you ask a question, remember to *wait at least three seconds* for your child to think about what she heard. She will absorb more information and probably give a more sophisticated answer.

When I was a teacher, I would always start Monday mornings with a "class meeting." We'd begin with a "compliment circle"—each student would quickly say something kind to the person next to him—then discuss our weekly schedule, and address any special student concerns. The students knew my rules: no interrupting or put-downs were allowed, everyone's idea was important, and decisions were determined by majority rule. This was also the time I'd teach students problem solving and communication skills as well as nurture a supportive atmosphere.

I never realized how powerful those class meetings were until one day when I arrived late and found an unexpected sight: my students were seated in a tight circle engaged in a serious discussion. Off to the side I saw one student, Angela, crying while two girls sat trying to comfort her. Fascinated, I tiptoed in to listen and learned that Angela had been teased unmercifully by a few students in another class. When my students found out, they decided to hold an emergency meeting to help Angela. And those next few minutes proved to be one of my proudest teaching memories: I watched my students discuss a serious issue, listen respectfully to each other's views, and come up with a solution to solve their classmate's problem. At that moment I also recognized how critical it is teach children these success skills and then provide practice opportunities so that they would be able to use them in real-life situations. I also became convinced that the class or family meeting is one of the most powerful methods to help children learn those skills.

Five Principles of Effective Family Meetings

Class meetings came out of the family council model designed by Rudolph Dreikurs, a psychiatrist, in the 1950s to help families work out problems democratically. The family council, or family meeting, is a great way for kids to practice communication skills, learn to assert themselves, hear different points of view, experience problem solving and consensus making, and share ideas, as well as learn many other skills important for succeeding in life. The family meeting is also a wonderful way for families to get together at regularly scheduled times and talk about common problems in an equal, cooperative, supportive atmosphere.

There are many possible topics for your family meetings. You can use them to set television or bedtime hours; plan vacations; announce family activities or menus; settle conflicts; handle repetitive problems or inappropriate behaviors; celebrate positive happenings for individual family members; voice concerns; and establish or revise family rules, curfews, computer times, chores, and allowances. You can begin meetings by announcing any special upcoming family events—game times, field trips, test dates, doctor's appointments, parties, or school projects—and clarifying everyone's schedules. Many families set aside a small box for suggestions from members regarding family issues or topics they'd like to address at the next meeting. Here are the five most important principles of successful family meetings; do modify them to fit your family's needs.

1. **Make it democratic.** The goal of the family meetings is get your kids involved, so it's important to make sure they feel their ideas count. This is a time to encourage your children to speak up, while you hold back

your judgments. During family meetings each member's opinion is considered equal, everyone has a right to be heard, and anyone can bring up any sort of problem or concern.

2. Determine decision making. Usually decisions are based on a majority vote, though some experts feel there should be unanimous agreement. Any decisions made in the meeting must be kept at least until the following meeting, where they can be changed.

3. Hold regularly scheduled meetings. Most experts suggest holding weekly meetings lasting twenty to thirty minutes for younger kids and slightly longer for older. Post a meeting reminder on your refrigerator or bulletin board and mandate everyone's attendance.

4. Rotate your meeting roles. One way to help kids take an active part in meetings is to assign different roles that can be rotated weekly. A few possible roles might be that of chairperson (starts and stops meetings and keeps everyone to the agenda), parliamentarian (makes sure rules are followed), meeting planner (posts the meeting date and time), and secretary (keeps meeting notes). Younger kids can use a tape recorder to record the meetings.

5. Create a fun meeting spirit. A strong suggestion is not to hold meetings just to hash out problems; after a while kids will dread coming. Instead, try to keep meetings fun and upbeat. One family from Orlando told me they always start their sessions by having family members take turns complimenting each other's good deeds during the week. End your meeting on a fun note: serve a dessert; have a family game of cards, Monopoly, volleyball, or football; or even rent a great family video to watch together.

Four Traditions to Help Kids Gain Confidence in Speaking Out

The greatest way to help your child learn communication skills is by making good communication a top priority in your family. Here are four ways to help your child get his point across in the comfort of his home so that he can assert himself more confidently in the real world.

1. Set up "Do Not Disturb" signs. One mom from Sacramento told me she was so frustrated from always being interrupted in the middle of

SUCCESS TIP
The Best Communication Tip:
Teach Kids "I Messages"

Dr. Thomas Gordon, author of *P.E.T.: Parent Effectiveness Training,* developed one of the easiest and most powerful communication skills: the use of the I message. It's a great way for kids to communicate their frustrations and anger to their offender. A message starting with "You" puts the recipient on the defensive because of its critical tone: "*You're* such a pest." "Don't *you* ever think what you're doing?" "*You* make me so mad when you grab take my stuff." Teach your child that instead of starting a message with the word "You," begin with "I" and then simply tell the other person how some unacceptable behavior makes her feel. The I message focuses on the troublesome behavior and doesn't put the recipient down: "*I* get really upset when you take my stuff." "*I* don't like to be kicked. It hurts." Here are the three parts of sending an I message:

1. Start your statement with "I am . . ." You could also say, "I'm . . ." or "I feel . . ."
2. Tell the person how you feel: "I am mad . . .," "I'm upset . . .," "I'm sad . . .," or "I'm hurt . . ."
3. Tell the person what he or she did that made you feel that way. You could add what you want the person to do instead: "and I want you to . . ." "I'm mad because you took my pencil without asking, and I want you to give it back." "I am upset because you pushed me down, and I want you to stop."

conversations with her kids that she found a "Do Not Disturb" sign. Now whenever a child starts a conversation that needs tuning into, she and her child go to her bedroom, hang the sign on her doorknob, and talk uninterrupted. Family members know that if the sign is up, no interruptions are allowed except in extreme emergencies. If you have younger children, you may need to schedule talking appointments for when another adult is home to watch your younger kids.

2. **Mandate family dinners.** If your home is anything like ours, sports, church groups, music lessons, and play practices constantly appear on the

calendar, taking away from your "together time." We finally sat down and figured out the times no one had anything scheduled, and those were mandated for family dinners. If your family schedule is this hectic, you may want to set aside specific weekdays for your family dinners. Don't let anything interfere with your plan: family dinners still are the greatest place to learn communication skills.

3. **Start a talking candle.** One of my children's favorite nighttime traditions was to light our old hurricane lamp, sit on the rug, and talk and read. My boys called it our Talking Candle. The rules were simple: I'd always be the one to light it, slip the hurricane over the candle, and put it on the mantel so that it couldn't tip. The boys always thought it was a "campfire"—I thought it was absolute heaven! It was our uninterrupted time to listen, enjoy each other, and create cherished memories. You may want to start a Talking Candle tradition: use any candle or even a flashlight; curl up with your kids, a great book, and fabulous talks.

4. **Turn off the TV.** Did you know that children in the United States rank number one in the world for the percentage of thirteen-year-olds who watch five or more hours of TV every day? During the time kids are glued to the screen, there is little opportunity for them to practice communication skills. The solution is simple: turn off your TV—or at least limit viewing to predetermined hours—and use those times to talk to your kids.

SUCCESS TIP
Did You Know?

In their book *Raising Self-Reliant Children in a Self-Indulgent World*, H. Stephen Glenn and Jane Nelsen point out that in 1930 children spent three to four hours a day personally involved with members of their extended families. Today's typical family interactions are cut to only a few minutes a day—most of which are not positive interchanges but are instead one-way monologues of negative parental warnings or criticism for misbehavior. We all need to buck this trend by providing uninterrupted quality time with our kids and enhancing their communication skills.

WHAT ONE PARENT DID

Yuval's mom listened to her son's teacher and knew he was right: her son really had listening problems. He seemed always to get directions mixed up, and lately was getting in trouble because he misunderstood what he heard. What the teacher said made sense: "It's almost as though he doesn't know how to listen." And that's where Yuval's mom decided to begin: by teaching him exactly what to do when listening.

That night after dinner, she and Yuval had a long talk. "I notice you are having problems listening," she said. "If we practice listening each night, school will be easier and you'll even have more friends. Kids really like to be around kids who look interested in what they say." The last comment really seemed to get his attention, so she began helping him learn the skill.

The first thing she did was to make sure Yuval knew what listening looked like. She sat facing her son—almost knee to knee—and said, "Tell me anything you did today. I'm not going to say anything, but my body will show you I'm listening." While Yuval described his basketball game, his mom deliberately exaggerated good listening behaviors: she nodded her head, smiled, looked at Yuval eye to eye, leaned forward, and didn't interrupt. When he finished she said, "What did you see my body doing that showed I was listening to you?" She and her son made a chart listing listening behaviors and hung it in his bedroom as a reminder. His mom also knew her son would need lots of practice as well as her support to be a better listener, so every day she found a simple way to help him learn the skill.

While driving to school, they played the List Game: she'd name a few animals—or foods, flowers, cars, or other simple things—and Yuval would try to repeat them. At dinner time, she helped Yuval remember to listen without interrupting and join into discussions only after waiting his turn. At bedtime, she worked on Yuval's conversation skills: she'd ask open-ended questions about things Yuval did during the day: "What was the most interesting thing that happened?" or "What did you do during recess?" She encouraged him to answer in complete sentences instead of his usual one-word responses. And day or night she'd point to her eye as a private signal to help Yuval remember to look interestedly at whoever was talking. Gradually, Yuval's mom noticed two changes in her son: his listening skills were improving, and his confidence was growing.

FINAL THOUGHTS ON ENHANCING COMMUNICATION SKILLS

Until recently, enhancing children's communication skills has been largely ignored as a success booster. But now many experts confirm that teaching this third skill of success is essential for helping kids get along in life. Knowing how to listen and to make yourself be understood opens doors to new relationships and enriches countless experiences. Effective communication skills enhance our children's school successes and life successes by making it easier to gain knowledge and understand other people's views. We also know that learning these skills does not happen by chance. In fact, when left to chance, most children will not develop the techniques so needed to attain successful and fulfilled lives. You are your child's best communications instructor. Just remember, it's never too early—or too late—to enhance this third critical skill of success.

POINTS TO REMEMBER

- Teach your child to express his feelings through words—never through violence.

- Use active listening skills to keep the lines of communication open between you and your child.

- Remember that what your child needs most is for you to listen—really listen—to her thoughts and concerns. You are your child's best instructor in learning how to communicate effectively.

- Encourage your child to speak up—to air his views, ask questions, participate in conversations, and ask for assistance. Help him understand that his thoughts and opinions count.

Parents Do Make a Difference

- Help your child learn to communicate effectively in a variety of circumstances—with teachers and adults, with new and old friends, in class, on the phone, with the elderly, with younger children, at the dinner table, and so forth.

- Establish family listening opportunities—the dinner hour, evening walks, family meetings, no-TV times, before-bed huddles—where family conversations are given top priority.

RESOURCES FOR FURTHER ACTION

For Parents

Between Parent and Child, by Haim Ginott (New York: Avon, 1972). This classic is rich with helpful ideas showing the difference between destructive and constructive communication.

Helping the Child Who Doesn't Fit In, by Stephen Nowicki Jr. and Marshall P. Duke (Atlanta, Ga.: Peachtree, 1992). Excellent guidance for parents and teachers on helping children learn the skills of nonverbal communication.

How to Talk So Kids Will Listen and Listen So Kids Will Talk, by Adele Faber and Elaine Mazlish (New York: Avon, 1982). A practical, highly readable volume for helping parents learn to communicate more effectively with their kids.

How to Talk to Your Kids About Really Important Things, by Charles E. Schaefer and Theresa Foy DiGeronimo (San Francisco: Jossey-Bass, 1994). A fabulous source for helping parents answer some of their child's most difficult questions.

P.E.T.: Parent Effectiveness Training, by Thomas Gordon (New York: Signet, 1975). Every parent should have this book on her bookshelf. Gordon's book describes a proven method to help enhance the communication between parents and their children.

Raising Kids Who Can: Using Family Meetings to Nurture Responsible, Cooperative, Caring, and Happy Children, by Betty Lou Bettner and Amy Lew (New York: HarperCollins, 1992). A simple guide to help parents use the principles of family meetings with their children.

What to Say When You Talk to Your Kids, by Shad Helmstetter (New York: Pocket Books, 1989). A wonderful resource for ways to improve communication with your children.

For Children Ages Three to Seven

The Cat Who Wore a Pot on Her Head, by Jan Slepain and Ann Seidler (New York: Scholastic, 1980). This humorous gem depicts a kitten who always seem to mix up directions and listen incorrectly because of the pot she wears on her head. It isn't until she takes the pot off her head and tunes into what people are saying that "life becomes fun again."

The Conversation Club, by Diane Stanley (Old Tappan, N.J.: Macmillan, 1983). Overwhelmed by his friends' Conversation Club, where each member speaks at the same time, Peter Fieldmouse forms a Listening Club.

Even That Moose Won't Listen to Me, by Martha Alexander (New York: Dial, 1988). A little girl tries various means to get rid of a giant moose in the garden after she repeatedly warns her of pending problems.

Nobody Listens to Andrew, by Elizabeth Guilfoile (New York: Scholastic, 1967). A classic and still a gem. Andrew tries to tell everyone there is a bear in his bed. The problem is, no one listens.

The Way It Happened, by Deborah Zemke (Boston: Houghton Mifflin, 1988). A wonderful example of how rumors can start and blow way out of proportion if no one listens.

For Children Ages Eight to Twelve

Nothing but the Truth, by Avi (New York: Orchard Books, 1991). A unique novel dealing with issues of respect, freedom, and patriotism and with what can happen because of miscommunication.

What Do You Do When Your Mouth Won't Open? by Susan Beth Pfeffer (New York: Dell, 1981). Eighth-grader Reesa has just won an essay contest at her school, which she must now deliver in a speech. Her problem is a severe fear of speaking in front of others. This book is packed with effective ways to reduce such fears and with actual tools to enhance public speaking.

Parents Do Make a Difference

Videos for Family Viewing

Close Encounters of the Third Kind (RCA/Columbia Home Video, 1977). A Steven Spielberg film about the arrival of spaceships in a small community. The way the humans finally develop a communication system with the aliens is unique and opens up wonderful doors for discussion.

Doctor Dolittle (20th Century-Fox, 1998). A skilled physician has long suppressed a talent he possessed as a child: the ability to communicate with animals.

E.T. the Extra-Terrestrial (MCA Home Video, 1982). A ten-year-old boy befriends a creature from another planet who has been stranded on Earth. Despite their language barriers, the boy and E.T. find a way to communicate by "reading one another's emotions," and true empathy evolves. Just plain wonderful! (PG)

The Miracle Worker (MGM/UA Home Video, 1962). The powerful true story of Helen Keller, born deaf and blind, who is completely unable to communicate with the world until she encounters Anne Sullivan, who becomes her teacher and lifelong companion.

Websites

"Children's Literature Web Guide" [http://www.asc.ucalgary.ca/~dkbrown/index.html]. A huge archive of Internet resources to help you locate the perfect read-aloud books for your family.

"Family Resources" [http://einet.net/galaxy/Community/Family.html]. A great new way to gather your family together and talk—around the computer! A compilation of resources for families.

"International Kids' Space" [http://www.kids-space.org]. A site for kids to use with other kids around the world. The PenPal box is a messaging area for kids to talk to other kids and is divided into different age groups.

"Kids Domain" [http://www.kidsdomain.com/]. A site where your child can review new software and explore ways to communicate on the computer.

"Not Just for Kids" [http://www.night.net/kids/index/html-ssi]. A collection of stories and poems for children that parents can read with their kids while talking about how to explore the Web together. You'll even find information about real kids who were adopted from China.

Problem Solving

Knowing How to
Find Solutions and
Resolve Conflicts

Eight-year-old Derrick sits at his desk waiting for the dismissal bell with growing tension. If today is like all the other days this week, Jeremy and Devon will be waiting around the corner for him. How will he face their taunting and name-calling again because of the color of his skin? He's already thinking how he can pretend he's sick so that he can miss school tomorrow. Right after dinner he'll tell his mom he has a headache and a sore throat. His coach probably will kick him off the team for missing practice again, but anything is better than facing the teasing. Derrick can't think of any other way to deal with his problem; staying home will have to do.

Ten-year-old Cassidy looked sadly at her science report about cats. It was due tomorrow, and her baby sister had ripped up half the pages she'd spent all night working on. In an hour her foster mom was coming to take her to dinner for her birthday. Not only would she miss her birthday outing, but she would

84

probably get a bad grade. Cassidy shook her head. "There's got to be something I can do." She knew she didn't have time to redo the whole report, so she thought of other options, then started in. She quickly removed the report's ripped page and grabbed an old coloring book. Next she traced cat pictures from the coloring book and glued them on the front of a folder to make a new cover. Then she reprinted the pages she'd typed yesterday on her computer and stapled them inside her cover. She was so glad she'd remembered to save them on the computer! After an hour, Cassidy stood back and smiled: her report looked almost as good as new! She was still smiling as she drove off with her foster mom to celebrate her birthday; she was so glad she'd thought of a solution!

No parent wants his children to suffer heartaches and disappointments. Our first parental instinct is to try to protect our kids from frustrations and solve their problems for them. Doing so, however, deprives them of opportunities to develop the very skills they need to deal with the multitude of issues they will inevitably face the rest of their lives. And the kinds of problems our children face are enormous and frightening.

Just this week I sat in the pediatrician's office absorbed in a *Parents* magazine article. The opening had me hooked: "Have you talked to your child about what to do in case you are carjacked?" Not only had I never discussed the issue with my kids—I hadn't even thought about doing so. Then I thought of a few horrific events our kids have been exposed to in the last few years: bombings, hate crimes, and the massacre of children by children in our schoolyards. SuEllen Fried and Paula Fried, authors of *Bullies and Victims: Helping Your Child Through the Schoolyard Battlefield*, cite these troubling new trends concerning the state of our children: a 1998 study by the Centers for Disease Control and Prevention found that one in five teenagers in our country carries a weapon and one in ten has attempted suicide. And a recent government survey on American children found an increase in drug use: more teens are using marijuana at an earlier age. Sexual experiences are common at much younger ages. Whether or not our kids must personally deal with such problems, don't think even for a minute that they aren't aware of them. Growing up in America can be frightening.

But let's take a moment and realize that the problems our children face just aren't on the nightly news: they are in our neighborhoods, schools, and even our homes. Adjusting to new family relationships and coping with such problems as divorce, sibling conflict, and moving are critical issues for a growing child. Being rejected by friends, dealing with academic and youth sport pressures, and having to face prejudice, bullying, and harassment are all too common. Classmates are increasingly exhibiting troubling character problems—cheating, stealing, and lying. Add to these the everyday frustrations of just growing up, and it's easy to see why researchers tell us there is a sharp increase in the number of children experiencing stress and anxiety.

To succeed in this world, our kids need a repertoire of skills to help them solve whatever obstacles—big or little—face them. The fourth success skill, problem solving, teaches children to be resourceful so that they learn to stand up for themselves and solve their own problems, whatever they may be. The earlier our children are exposed to these problem-solving steps, the greater the chances that they will make more responsible decisions. It's the best way to help our kids learn to handle *whatever* problem comes their way.

WHAT YOU WILL LEARN IN THIS CHAPTER

The techniques in this chapter will enhance your children's potential for success by helping them learn to rely on themselves to solve their problems and make wiser and more responsible decisions. You'll learn how to:

- Teach your child strategies to calm down so that he can focus on dealing coolly with any difficulty.

- Help your child learn how to identify his problem so that he has a starting place to develop a solution.

- Teach the rules of brainstorming so that your child can think of many possible solutions in a short space of time.

- Help your child learn to think through the possible outcomes of decisions and narrow them down, allowing him to choose the wisest and safest solution.

- Enhance your child's awareness that problems don't need to stop him from succeeding; he just needs to think of alternative solutions to roadblocks that seem insurmountable.

HOW IS YOUR CHILD DOING NOW?

The statements below describe behaviors usually displayed by children who have developed strong problem-solving skills. To evaluate your child's strengths in this fourth success skill, write the number you think best represents your child's current level on the line following each statement and then add all the scores to get her total score. If your child scores 40 to 50, she's in great shape with the skill. If she scores 30 to 40, she could benefit from skill enhancement. A score of 20 to 30 shows signs of potential problems. If your child scores 10 to 20, consider getting help to increase this skill.

5 = Always 4 = Frequently 3 = Sometimes 2 = Rarely 1 = Never

A child with strong problem-solving skills: My child

Rarely repeats the same errors or problems.   _____

Depends on herself to make her decisions; rarely looks
   to others for rescue.   _____

Is decisive and is willing to make her own decisions. _____

Carefully thinks through possible outcomes of a
   decision before making it.   _____

Can easily put into words a problem that's bothering her. _____

Rarely gives up when faced with a problem.   _____

Considers several alternatives before making a decision.   _____

Doesn't get upset or tense when confronted with
   problems; stays cool and calm.   _____

Makes decisions that are wise, safe, and responsible.   _____

Evaluates the good and bad points of ideas before making
   a decision.   _____

Total Score   _____

FIVE STEPS TO DEVELOPING PROBLEM SOLVING

There are five steps to enhancing your child's problem-solving capabilities. To help children remember these critical problem-solving steps, I teach them to use the acronym *STAND*. Each letter in the word represents one of the five problem-solving steps and helps children recognize that obstacles don't need to stop them from succeeding.

The first step is the most important part of "taking a STAND": the *S* reminds your child first to *s*top, calm down, and tune into his feelings. Once the child is in control, he can learn the second problem-solving step. The *T* reminds him to *t*ell what the problem is in his own words so that he can begin the process of solving it. The third step, *A*, reminds the child to think of all the possible *a*lternatives by brainstorming ways to remedy his dilemmas. Once he has alternatives to consider, the fourth step, *N*, reminds him to *n*arrow the solution possibilities by eliminating any ideas he doesn't feel comfortable doing or that he feels aren't responsible. The fifth and final step, *D*, reminds the child to *d*ecide on one solution and *d*o it. The sooner we teach children these five steps, the sooner our kids will understand that they can survive setbacks by figuring things out for themselves.

Step 1: *S—Stop,* Calm Down, and Identify Your Feelings
Step 2: *T—Tell* What the Problem Is
Step 3: *A—Ask,* "What Are My *Alternatives?*"
Step 4: *N—Narrow* the Choices
Step 5: *D—Decide* on the Best Choice and *Do* It

STEP 1: STOP, CALM DOWN, AND IDENTIFY YOUR FEELINGS

The first step in problem solving is for your child to calm down and tune in to her feelings. The reason is simple: it's impossible to think about how to solve a problem when you are upset. When you are really angry, usually your heart is pounding so hard and you are breathing so quickly that you can't think about solutions: your body won't let you. Once you calm down, you can begin to figure out rationally why you're upset and then find an answer to your dilemma. The activities in this section help your child learn the first step to solving problems: staying in control by understanding how he is feeling. Then he can begin to do something about his dilemma.

Our children are facing much more pressing types of daily stresses than most of us ever dealt with in our childhood. Just think of the kinds of horrific images our kids are exposed to on the nightly news: riots, hate crimes, random shootings, bombings, kidnappings, senseless murders. We're also seeing a troubling increase in bullying, name-calling, and prejudicial slurs among schoolchildren. Do these issues affect our children? You bet they do! The single greatest trend I've seen as a consultant to hundreds of schools over the past ten years is the marked increase in anxiety and anger in our children. We shouldn't kid ourselves: the steady onslaught of stress and violent images is taking a major toll on our children's emotional well-being.

Kids need to stay in touch with their feelings and know how to calm down. That's the first step to solving *any* problem, big or little. It's a step our children must know how to do to increase their chances for success both now and forever. The sooner we teach this skill, the sooner our kids will be able to practice making "calming down" a healthy habit that will last a lifetime.

How Does Your Child Deal with Problems?

Four-year-old Blanca rushed to get her sweater, but it wasn't on the hook. Her mom would be at the day-care center any minute to pick her up. Blanca's heart started to pound. "Oh, no," she thought. "Where is it?" She was breathing so quickly she couldn't think where it might be. By the time her mom walked in, Blanca was so upset, she was sobbing. It took almost ten minutes for her mom to calm her down enough for Blanca to be able to say why she was so distraught.

Seven-year-old Lee didn't realize he was so late. The bus would be there any second. He grabbed his backpack, ran for the door, and then came to a screeching halt. "I don't have my library book!" He told himself, "If I don't have it today I can't go on the field trip." He took a slow, deep breath to calm down and then thought hard. And an image came: the laundry room! He raced quickly, grabbed the book from the counter, and headed out at full speed just in time to catch the bus.

Blanca and Lee obviously react to problems differently. On the one hand, Blanca seems to unravel at the first sign of a dilemma, which hinders her from dealing effectively with even the smallest concerns. Lee, on the other hand, has learned that the best way to solve a problem is by first calming down. Then he can think of his alternatives. How these children deal with smaller problems now will more than likely be the same way they deal with larger problems later. It's easy to recognize which child will be more successful in handling the more difficult issues inevitable in life.

Take a minute to think about how your child typically reacts to a problem. Here are a few behaviors to review: Does he stay calm, or does his body tense up? Does she confront the problem, or does she walk away? Does he coolly try to solve the problem or become so anxious that he needs help calming down? If your child usually reacts to dilemmas in a calm and cool manner, he's well on the way to developing strong problem-solving skills.

The more common approach used by many kids these days is to handle difficulties by becoming increasingly anxious and frustrated. The result: their problem-solving abilities are greatly hindered. They aren't calm enough to think through what's bothering them or to figure out what they can do to resolve the issue. The first step to solving any problem is to stop and calm down.

SUCCESS TIP
A Calm Down Poster

Help your child see that there are dozens of ways to calm down: make a poster of possibilities. The poster could include pictures, words, and magazine cutouts. Here is a list of ways to calm down that my family created one year:

Do jumping jacks or an exercise.	Think of something pleasant.	Read.
Hum or sing.	Take a walk.	Talk to someone who calms you down.
Draw a picture.	Ask for a hug.	Say to yourself, "Cool it!"
Shoot baskets.	Listen to soothing music.	Count to ten.

Five Ways to Help Kids Stay Cool

These next activities teach your child the first step to solving any problem: learning to stay cool and in control so that she can think about how to begin fixing what concerns her.

1. **Model coolness when facing problems.** Showing you can keep your cool, even in crisis, is an important way to help your child learn to problem-solve. You send a clear message: "It may look like a crisis, but by staying cool I'll be in a better position to solve the problem." Example is always the best teacher: "I need to take a deep breath and stay cool before I call the bank. I can't understand how my account is so overdrawn!"

2. **Convey the importance of staying calm.** You will use a balloon for this fun way to help your child understand the importance of staying calm. Say to your child, "We all get angry sometimes, especially when things aren't going the way we plan." Hold up the balloon and slowly blow it up halfway, then stop and pinch the tip to keep the air in. Say, "When we're upset, anger inside us can blow up very quickly. Watch what happens." Continue blowing the balloon to full size, then pinch the balloon to hold the air and say, "When there's so much anger in you, it's hard to

think. Your heart is pounding, your palms may be sweaty, and you are breathing faster. This is when you can make poor choices and get into trouble." Quickly let go of the balloon so that it flies around the room. Say, "See how it spins out of control all over the place? That's what happens when you don't get rid of the anger." Ask your child to take a slow, deep breath. Place your child's hands on his stomach for him to "feel" his breaths. Too often kids try to take quick, fast breaths from their chest instead of their stomach—it doesn't work! Say, "Taking a slow, deep breath is an easy way to calm down. It lets the anger out so that you can start to think about how to solve your problem."

3. **Identify anger warning signs.** Cut a large piece of paper into the shape of a big stop sign and print the word *ANGER* inside. Explain to your child that we all have little signs that warn us we're getting angry. Guide your child to think of ways her body feels when she's angry, such as, "I talk louder, my cheeks get flushed, I clench my fists, my heart pounds, my mouth gets dry, my palms start to sweat, and I breathe faster." Help your child print or draw a few of her physical anger signs on the paper. Now write a large *D* in front of *ANGER* so the word now spells *DANGER* and say, "Remember, anger is just one letter short of danger. Listen to the danger signals your body sends you. They'll help you learn to stop and calm down so that you can figure out what's bothering you."

4. **Teach a calm down formula.** The most effective strategy I've ever used with children to help them calm down is called "1 + 3 + 10." I introduce the formula by printing "1 + 3 + 10" on large pieces of paper and hanging them around the room. Then I tell kids how to use the formula. You can say the same thing to your child: "As soon as you feel your body sending you a warning sign that says you're losing control, do three things. First, stop and tell yourself, 'Be calm.' That's 1. Second, take three deep, slow breaths from your tummy. That's 3. Now count slowly to ten inside your head. That's 10. Put them all together, it's 1 + 3 + 10, and doing it helps you calm down." I knew my kids had mastered the technique when all three of them chimed in one day, "Looks like you need a 1 + 3 + 10, Mom." Were they right!

5. Use affirmations to stay calm. At four, our youngest child went through the predictable fear of darkness. Each night it was a major feat just getting him to his bedroom. Nothing seemed to work until one night my husband decided to pretend he was afraid of the dark, too, and show our son another way to deal with his apprehensions. As he walked down the hall with Zach toward the bedroom, my husband started murmuring, "I'm calm and in control." I'm sure that Zach, following close behind, wondered what his father was up to. My husband just kept slowly repeating the message, each time deliberately saying the words more confidently. By the time they reached the room, Zach was saying the same words under his breath. Over the next few days his dad helped Zach remember the words until he could say them by heart. Slowly, his fears faded as he began to believe the message. Soon he was walking calmly to his room by himself. It had worked!

Zach's dad taught him an affirmation—a simple, positive message he could purposely say to himself to build confidence. Other affirmations kids can say to themselves to help them calm down are "Stop and calm down," "Take a deep breath," or "I can handle this." The more your child practices it, the greater the likelihood she will use it during a real time when she needs to calm down. You might post the words throughout the house as a reminder.

STEP 2: TELL WHAT THE PROBLEM IS

The second step in problem solving is for your child to tell himself what the problem is. As soon as children can name what the difficulty is, they can begin to solve it. It sounds so simple, but time and again I've seen kids so overwhelmed with a problem that they can't tell what's troubling them. When I sit with them a few minutes to help them figure out what's bothering them, they are always relieved. Many times just naming the problem is enough to "make the problem better." Instead of acting out in frustration, the child now has a starting place to remedy her troubles.

SUCCESS TIP
Teaching Kids an Emotion Vocabulary

Knowing both how you feel and how the other person feels about an issue helps you make better decisions. How well your child can identify feelings depends in part on whether she has an accurate emotion vocabulary. To enhance your child's emotion vocabulary, together make a list of feeling words and post it. Use the words to help your child tune into feelings with such questions as, "You seem [tense, anxious, worried] about something. What's the matter?" or "Your friend seems really [unhappy, angry, upset]. What do you think is bothering her?" Once she develops an emotion vocabulary ask, "How does he feel?" "How do you feel?" or "How did that make you feel?" Here are a few words to get you started:

Happy	Satisfied	Pleased	Excited
Elated	Proud	Angry	Sad
Frustrated	Disappointed	Upset	Ashamed
Tense	Anxious	Worried	Concerned
Irritated	Calm	Scared	Enthusiastic

Angela ran into the house and slammed the door. "I hate school," she told her father.

"What's really troubling her?" wondered her father. But Angela was so distraught she could barely think. Her father helped her calm down and then asked, "What happened that makes you hate school, Angela?"

"I don't know," she said. "Nobody's nice. Why did we have to move here anyway?"

Her father thought maybe that was what was bothering her: kids weren't being nice to her. But he needed to find out more: "Tell me about someone who isn't nice to you."

"Rose's not nice at all. She never lets me sit with her at lunch," she explained.

"Do you want to eat lunch with Rose?" he asked. "Is that what is the matter?"

"No," she explained. "I want to sit with Nancy and Dee, but Rose won't let me."

"So, not everybody is mean. What do you think is the real problem, Angela?"

"I guess it's Rose," Angela admitted. "She's always telling the other kids not to play with me because of my limp. She says I walk funny, and the rest of the kids do what she says. I don't know how to get her to stop being mean."

Her dad realized that Angela had every right to be upset. She was born with one leg slightly shorter than the other and did have a slight limp. But it had never caused a problem with her friends before. He also noticed that his daughter seemed much calmer as soon as she was able to put her problem into words. The next step was helping Angela figure out how to deal with a bully.

Helping your child figure out what specific issue is troubling her means she is closer to solving it. This is a process that can take some time and patience—especially if your kids are used to having someone solve their problems for them. The more practice they have putting their problems into words, the better prepared they will be to face the inevitable more difficult dilemmas of adolescence and adulthood. So the next time a problem comes up, stand back and use the moment as an opportunity to help your child figure out, "What's the problem?"

Three Ways to Help Kids Identify Their Problems

Here are three ways to help children learn to put their problems into words.

1. **Identify problems in books and movies.** Almost any children's book or movie deals with characters who face problems and have to figure out how to solve them. Use those moments as opportunities to help children, especially younger ones, identify problems. Here's an example: while watching or reading *The Wizard of Oz* together, stop and ask, "What is Dorothy's problem?" Then help your child name the dilemma: "She wants to get back to Aunt Em and doesn't know how."

2. Work the problem backward. Some problems are complicated and involve more than just one simple issue. Identifying in sequence everything that happened that led up to the problem can be difficult, especially for younger children. An easier approach is to ask your child to work the problem backward starting with the *last* thing he remembers. Here's how a mother used this idea when her son came home with a black eye and couldn't put into words what caused the fight.

Mother: *Tell me what happened, Jose—backward. What's the last thing that happened?*

Jose: *I ran home. Johnny hit me.*

Mother: *And what happened just before he hit you?*

Jose: *I told him he was stupid.*

Mother: *And the reason you told him he was stupid . . . ?*

Jose: *Because he grabbed my baseball.*

Mother: *Why did Johnny take your baseball?*

Jose: *Because I took his the day before.*

Mother: *And why did you take his baseball the day before?*

Jose: *Because I didn't have one.*

By reviewing in reverse the chain of events that led up to the fight, Jose's mother was able to help him think through what caused it. She also recognized that hitting wasn't the only issue she needed to work through with Jose: taking things that don't belong to him and name-calling were two other problems that needed to be addressed.

3. Rephrase what your child says. Because older or more verbal children have stronger language and cognitive abilities, a simple prodding question, such as "What's the matter?" is usually all they need to identify the problem. Younger children often need more coaxing to help them put their problem into words. Sometimes rephrasing children's own words back to them helps them stop and rethink the dilemma and then reword it.

Parents Do Make a Difference

Parent: *What's the matter, Shawna?*

Shawna: *Debby's mean to me.*

Parent: *Debby's not being nice to you.*

Shawna: *Yes! She won't let me play with her.*

Parent: *Debby doesn't want you to be with her. So tell me your problem.*

Shawna: *I want to play with Debby, and she won't let me.*

SUCCESS TIP
Questions to Help Identify the Problem

Whenever your child confronts a problem, use these questions to help your child identify what's troubling him. They're all different ways of saying, "What's the matter?"

"What's the first thing that happened?"
"What's the last thing you remember?"
"What happened next? . . . Then next?"
"What would somebody else say happened?"
"Here's the problem as I see it. How do you see it? What can we do about it?"

STEP 3: ASK, "WHAT ARE MY ALTERNATIVES?"

Successful children rely on themselves to solve their problems. Dependent kids lean on us to make their decisions. These next ideas teach children the third problem-solving step by helping them learn to ask themselves, "What are my alternatives?" so that they realize they always have options.

"Ari! I just read this note from your teacher," his mother began. "She says you're disrupting the class by always clowning around and making the kids laugh. Is that right?"

Ari slowly nodded his head. "I guess so."

"Well, I can't imagine why you have to be such a clown, but this has got to stop or you'll be grounded," she said. "I don't want to ever get another note like this."

Ari walked sadly to his room. He always clowned around because he wanted the kids to like him. The problem was, he didn't know any other way to get kids to talk to him.

To succeed in school and in life, children must understand there are solutions to problems. Jumping too quickly to solve our kids' problems robs them of the chance to use the skills of problem solving and figuring out for themselves, "What can I do to make things better?" It also cheats our kids of opportunities to develop the healthy self-esteem that comes from knowing they found the solutions all by themselves. Our children need to develop the personal resourcefulness necessary for dealing confidently with the multitude of issues and problems they will face throughout their lives. So whenever your child is confronted with a problem, step aside and ask, "Looks like you have a problem. What are all the ways you could solve it?"

The Mirror Box Story

A foster parent shared with me the unique way she helps her children recognize that every problem has solutions. Each time a new child comes to live with her, she tells "The Mirror Box Story" to help him understand that the best place to find solutions is to look within. Here's her story, which you can also tell your own child.

I met the most interesting person, who just happens to be a famous inventor. Her latest invention is so powerful, it's going to change the world, because it can make most problems fade away like magic. When I told her about you, she got so excited, and said I had to share the invention with you. She swears that once you know about it, you'll never forget it, and you'll be able to use it for the rest of your life. She let me borrow it just for today, but made me promise you'd keep the information a secret. I swore you'd do that. Do you think you can keep a secret? Take a quick peek inside the box so that you can see the solution to every problem. [Open the box so the child can see herself in the mirror.]

Do you see the answer to solving problems? It's you! Remember, every problem has a solution. All you need to do is ask yourself, "What else could I do instead?" That's the secret!

SUCCESS TIP
Making a Mirror Box

To make a mirror box to use when you tell the story to your child, glue a mirror or piece of aluminum foil to the inside lid of a box. After telling the story, save the box. Each time she attempts a problem-solving step, write the effort on a slip of paper and store it in the box. Every so often, open the lid to show your child just how capable a problem solver she's becoming and keep encouraging her endeavors.

Four Ways to Teach Kids Brainstorming

The best way I've ever found to help children think of alternatives is to teach them brainstorming. It's a simple tool that helps them think of many possible solutions to a problem in a short space of time. I make paper hats with big cardboard lightning bolt shapes for younger kids to wear whenever we brainstorm ideas. The kids love them because the hats help them remember to "storm their brains" for solutions. With older students, we make colorful posters with the brainstorming rules and hang them around the room. Whether your child is a preschooler or an adolescent, the basic rules for brainstorming are the same and are easy to teach. Once she learns them, she'll use them in every arena of life.

1. **Explain brainstorming.** You might say, "Every problem has a solution. The trick to getting unstuck from a problem is to 'storm your brain' of every possibility you can think of to make the problem better. Brainstorming is a tool you can use to help your brain think of alternatives to your problem. There may be dozens of ways to solve your problem, but

unless you have the courage to say them, you may never know all the possibilities for making your troubles better."

2. **Go over the brainstorming rules.** Next, teach your child the four rules of brainstorming. As you explain the rules, print them on a poster to help your child remember. (See the Success Tip that follows.) Say, "Brainstorming helps you think of all the different choices you can use to solve your problem. You start by naming your problem and then asking, 'What are my alternatives?' The rules help your brain think of lots of alternatives or choices; then you choose the one you like best."

3. **Practice brainstorming.** As they do when learning any skill, children need lots of repeated practice before they can confidently use brainstorming on their own. So anytime the opportunity arises when your child is confronted with a problem, help her use brainstorming as a way to solve her problem. Suppose your child comes home from school upset because a classmate has teased her. Instead of offering her suggestions, help her brainstorm ways she could deal with it. Say, "Let's brainstorm what you can do if she teases you again. You just name any idea that comes to you, and I'll write them down. Then you can choose one to try."

Your child might say, "I could tell the teacher or get other kids to stop playing with her. I could tell her to stop." Remember not to judge any idea, and if your child stops brainstorming, simply say, "Anything else?" Your child might add a few more ideas. "I could walk away or pretend it doesn't bother me." It's best to write your child's ideas down; you can read the ideas back to her and say, "Is there one you'd like to try?"

4. **Zap put-downs.** Usually the hardest brainstorming rule for kids to follow is not putting down anyone's idea. The fastest way I've found to reinforce the rule is to ask the children to create a word—or even a sound—to send to the put-down offender. One year my class developed a word signal: "Evaluative!" The next year's group discussed the destructiveness of criticism. They came up with a rattlesnake sound as their signal, "Ssssss!" because they thought put-downs were so deadly. My own kids decided to just use the word *Zapper!* as our family signal, and it came

in handy. One year my boys were quite dissatisfied with their required chore list. To stop their grumbling I decided to have them brainstorm a new chore list. I was noting their ideas, and all was well until one of my kids suggested vacuuming the car as a possibility—which for some reason has always been on the top of my middle son's "least favorite chore" list. "That's a dumb idea," that brother predictably responded, and the rest of us quickly turned on him yelling simultaneously, "Zapper!" We all laughed, and the offending brother apologized. The signal served as a funny reminder that when we brainstorm, no criticism is allowed.

 ## SUCCESS TIP
Brainstorming Rules

Here are the four rules for brainstorming. You might want to post them in your home to remind everyone to "storm his brain" to find options.

1. Don't put down or judge any idea. No criticism is allowed!
2. Piggybacking onto ideas is fine. You may change or add onto anyone's idea at any time. It is now a new idea.
3. The more ideas the better! Go for quantity. Say the first thing that comes into your mind. Don't worry if it doesn't seem practical or realistic.
4. Never limit your thinking! Turn your brain power on, and let your mind go.

STEP 4: NARROW THE CHOICES

In my work in schools, I see too many children rushing to make decisions only to regret their choices later. We need to help our children learn to slow down and think through all the possible consequences that might result from their choices. Once your child has looked at all the possibilities, he is ready to begin the process of elimination. This process is immensely valuable, because it helps him think through what the outcomes might be if he puts his plan into place. It prevents him from making rash decisions that

SUCCESS TIP
Play the Solution Game

The Solution Game is a fun way to help your child practice brainstorming. It's especially fun to do with a group of kids or as a family, and the best part is that you can do it *anywhere*. Explain that the object is to come up with as many solutions to a problem as possible in a short amount of time. Tell kids, "Don't worry how silly your idea sounds. Say it, because it may spin off another idea." Comments such as, "What's another idea?" "What else could you do?" or "That's one way, now think of another!" encourage kids to think of more ideas. Here are a few problems for kids of varying ages:

- Every day a boy throws sand at you because he doesn't like the color of your skin.

- You want to give your friend a birthday present, but you have no money.

- You overheard the school bully say he is going to fight a classmate after school.

- Your calculator is missing, and you see a classmate using a model just like yours.

- You find out a friend is using drugs.

- Every day two kids tease you about your family being poor, and you don't like it.

- You want to play ball, but the kids say you can't play with them because you stutter.

- A few of your classmates are always taunting you about the way you talk.

- You know a student is sneaking money from another classmate's desk.

could haunt him the rest of his life. The fourth step to problem solving is to narrow the options down to a few choices so that your child is closer to making a wiser and safer decision.

Myna walked home shaking her head. She couldn't understand why Mrs. Byers would accuse her of stealing her rake. She'd been raking her neighbor's leaves for months without a problem. "I have to do something," she sighed, "or she'll tell the other neighbors, and I'll never get another job." And Myna thought through her options. "If I do nothing, she'll probably think I took it," she began. "I could ask around to see if anybody knows who took it, but I probably won't find anything out." Through a process of elimination, Myna finally decided she had only one choice: "I'll just go talk to her tomorrow and try and convince her I didn't do it. I've got to make her believe me." She felt better just knowing she had a plan.

Three Ways to Help Kids Narrow Their Choices

Here are three ways to help your child learn to narrow her choices so that she's one step closer to making the most reasonable decision.

1. **Recall the solutions.** Before your child is ready to make a final decision, you may need to remind her of the solutions she has generated. It is a way to help your child organize her thoughts so that she can narrow the choices. You might ask, "What were those ideas you thought of again?" Whenever convenient, write down solution possibilities as your child says them. You can then reread them to help her choose the best idea: "Kara, you came up with a lot of different ways to act when Sophie teases you. You said you could tease her back, tell the teacher, walk away, ignore her, walk to another group of kids, or pretend you're looking at someone else. Which choices do you want to eliminate?"

2. **Make cross-offs.** Together, list the possible choices on paper. Tell your child to "cross off" with pencil any selection that he doesn't feel comfortable doing. Emphasize to your child that if he feels he can manage the consequences of his choices, it's probably safe to keep it on the list. Any decision that he can't live with should instantly be crossed off.

Suppose your child is invited to a party he desperately wants to attend, but it's at the same time as his soccer game. If his coach finds out he's at the party he'll be kicked off the team. He's brainstormed these options: (a) tell the coach I'm sick; (b) go to the party and then go to the game late; (c) play, then go late to the party; (d) don't go to the party. Now is the time to guide your child in thinking about consequences. Reread each choice and say after each one, "What would happen if you chose that?" It may take time the first few go-rounds, but it's worth it. Your child will more likely start thinking through choices and recognizing that his decisions have consequences.

3. **Predict the outcome.** A large part of making responsible choices is thinking about the immediate as well as long-term consequences of decisions. Predicting how decisions will turn out is not easy for many adults, let alone children. A way to help your child narrow her choices and think about possible outcomes is to ask after each selection, "If you pick that choice, do you think you'll still feel OK about it tomorrow?" "What about next week?" Remind your child that if she ever feels she may later regret making a particular decision, she should eliminate the choice.

STEP 5: DECIDE ON THE BEST CHOICE AND DO IT

The teachers in Hong Kong taught me the Chinese ideogram for *crisis.* It consists of the Chinese characters for *danger* and *opportunity.* I remember thinking how appropriate to problem solving the ideogram is. Our children are confronted with so many complex problems and possible solutions. To succeed in school and in life, they will need to learn how to choose the most responsible choices leading them toward opportunity and the farthest from danger. The final step helps our kids learn how to make the best decision by thinking through the consequences of their choices.

Rita read the news article about the rise of cigarette smoking among school-age children. She never thought her twelve-year-old son would smoke, but she also knew you can't be too sure about anything. She decided to discuss it with Josh and help him think through what to do if someone asked him to smoke. "I was reading the newspaper about how many kids your age are smoking," she began. "Do any of your friends smoke, Josh?"

"Yeah, some," he admitted. "But I'm not going to because it can make your body really sick like what happened to Uncle Harry."

His mom smiled. "I'm glad you know how sick it can make you. But someday a friend may offer you a cigarette, and turning down friends can be hard. Brainstorm a minute for ideas you could try if a friend really pushes you to smoke."

"I'd just say no," Josh told her. "Or maybe I'd say I don't want to get sick."

"Those are two possibilities. Anything else?"

"I could just walk away or tell him he shouldn't do it," Josh replied. "Maybe I could tell him it makes your breath smell bad."

"Those are some pretty good ideas," she admitted. "Think about what would happen if you tried them. Which ones wouldn't work?"

"Walking away wouldn't work. He'd just follow me. And he'd tell me to use a mint to make my breath feel better," Josh answered. "I don't know if he'd listen if I told him it would make him sick. He'd probably just do it anyway."

"So let's see what's left. You could just say no or tell him you don't want to get sick. Which is the best choice for you?" she challenged.

"I guess a little of each," Josh said. "I'll tell him no; I don't like smoking because I don't want to get sick."

"You really thought through your choices," his mom said. "I'm glad we talked."

As our kids get older and problems get more complex, we need to teach them how to decide among their various possible choices and anticipate what each outcome might be. These skills aren't learned by chance: our kids need to practice the entire problem-solving process under our guidance, until it becomes almost second nature.

Four Ideas to Help Kids Reach a Decision

Even young children usually have little difficulty generating strategies to solve problems. The challenge is for us to guide them so they know how to make the best choice. By helping them recognize that each decision has a consequence and both good and bad points, they will soon learn to consider what might happen if they were to pick each possibility. These next ideas help children learn to choose the most reasonable choice from the few remaining ideas.

1. **Model your decision-making process.** During the course of a typical day, dozens of opportunities come up where we must weigh choices and make decisions. When you make an important decision, such as changing jobs, buying a new car, or remodeling a room, let your child hear how you made your choice by reviewing your problem-solving steps out loud. It helps her understand all the things you considered while making your decision: "I thought a lot about whether to take the job. It would give us the extra money we needed, but I also knew it would mean I'd have to give up time with my family. I finally decided that there were only two hours each day when you'd be by yourself, and during those hours you usually were in after-school sports or at a friend's house. So I took the job."

2. **Teach decision vocabulary.** Using decision vocabulary words with younger children, such as *choose, decide, prefer, pick,* and *select,* helps them learn to use the words in their own conversation. Give children frequent opportunities to make choices, starting with simple decisions that involve only two options: "Do you prefer the blue dress or the pink one?" You can work up to more sophisticated problems later: "Which college will you choose?"

3. **Compare the remaining solutions.** A family brainstormed possible vacations they would like to take that summer and narrowed down to two choices, camping at a beach or lake, but couldn't decide between the two. So the father showed them how to make a decision by comparing the choices: "If we went to the beach, Ian could learn to surf. We'd be able to go deep-sea fishing, but only once because it's so expensive. If we went to the lake, Ian couldn't surf, but he could learn to water ski. We could fish every day because it wouldn't cost anything." Once the family compared their choices, they chose the lake. Teaching your child to compare the good and bad points of the remaining two or three solutions helps her learn to make reasonable choices.

4. **Ask, "What might happen if . . ."** You can help your child think about the consequence of his remaining choices by asking, "What might

happen if you tried that?" Another way to help kids decide on the best choice is by helping them weigh the pros and cons of each remaining possibility: "What are all the good and bad things that might happen if you chose that?"

SUCCESS TIP
The Benefits of Teaching Problem Solving

One of the most widely respected children's problem-solving programs, I Can Problem Solve (ICPS), was developed in the 1970s by Drs. George Spivack and Myrna Shure. With over twenty-five years of research on the program's effectiveness, the psychologists found that children as young as three and four years old can be taught to think through their problems. They also discovered that children skilled in problem solving were less likely to be impulsive and aggressive when things didn't go their way, tended to be more caring and less insensitive, were better able to make friends, and tended to achieve more academically. Spivack and Shure's research and many other studies confirm that learning problem-solving skills greatly enhances our children's chances for success.

WHAT ONE PARENT DID

Carol was exhausted; it seemed that all she did lately was arbitrate her stepchildren's conflicts. She knew that if her daughters were to learn to be problem solvers, she would have to step aside and let them work through their own conflicts. Within moments her older stepdaughter, Kim, ran to her yelling, "Mom, Andrea took my book!" Andrea followed her looking every bit as upset as her sister. Carol figured now was as good a time as any to let them resolve their own disputes.

"I can see the two of you are having a problem," she began. "Stop and take a deep, slow breath. Now that you're calm, what happened?" And both girls started talked at once. "No," Carol said. "We're going to work through your problem differently. Here are the rules: you must listen respectfully while

you tell each other what happened: no interrupting! And from now on, you're going to solve your own problems. Kim, you go first. Use an I message to tell Andrea how you feel and what happened to make you feel that way. And Andrea, you remember to listen respectfully."

Kim began, "I'm really mad, Andrea, because you grabbed my book. I don't like it when you take my stuff without asking!"

"OK," said Carol. "Now it's your turn, Andrea. Tell Kim your story and how you feel."

"Well, I'm angry that you never play with me, so I took it," she replied.

Carol tried to stay neutral. "It sounds as though each of you feels hurt. Andrea, can you think of a different way to let your sister know you want to play with her without grabbing her book?" she asked. "And Kim, Andrea feels sad because you won't play with her. I know you want to have time to yourself, but is there some time you can play with Andrea?" The girls slowly nodded their heads. "Good," said Carol. "Both of you are to help each other brainstorm friendlier ways you could solve your problem and then choose the one idea that you think will work best. I'm sure you can solve this, but if you really need me I'm in the kitchen."

Carol walked uncertainly to the kitchen but kept the door open so she could still hear. It was quiet for a very long time, then suddenly she heard them thinking up solutions. She chuckled when they had to remind each other to "listen respectfully." Ten minutes later they ran to find her, yelling, "We did it, Mom!" and each explained her plan. "I'm going to try to ask Kim when she wants to play with me," explained Andrea. Kim nodded and said, "And I told Andrea I can't play all afternoon, but I'll play every day for at least half an hour after school." And the two girls ran off.

Carol smiled. She knew it would take a while before her kids really felt comfortable solving problems on their own. But for a first try they did pretty well. The best part was Carol's deciding to step aside and let them talk through their problem on their own. That really was the only way they would learn to solve tougher problems that were bound to come up.

Parents Do Make a Difference

SUCCESS TIP
Helping Kids Solve Problems Together

Once you have taught your child the problem-solving steps, she can use them to solve *any* problem by herself or with other children. Here are a few guidelines to help kids solve problems together:

- Adele Faber and Elaine Mazlish, authors of *Siblings Without Rivalry,* say it's helpful for you to ask each child to say what happened; summarize each view, and end with, "What can you do now to solve this problem?" Stay neutral and make suggestions only when your kids seem stuck.
- Set guidelines for talking it out: No interrupting, Treat each other respectfully, and the like.
- *Do* intervene when emotions are high, before an argument escalates. "I see two angry kids who need to cool down. You go to your room, and you to the other room until you can talk calmly."
- To keep kids focused, tell them they must come up with three different solutions before you will return.
- Give children the option of writing or drawing their solutions instead of saying them to each other. It often keeps the session calmer and is helpful for younger or less verbal children.
- Set a timer and say, "Let's see if you can work this through calmly for three minutes. Then I'll return." Stretch the time depending on the children's ages and problem-solving skills.

FINAL THOUGHTS ON ENHANCING
YOUR CHILD'S PROBLEM-SOLVING SKILLS

Today's children are experiencing violent media images and daily stresses on a much greater scale than we care to admit. Statistics tell us that children in the United States today are living in a society that is substantially more violent than *any other Western democracy.* On a day-to-day basis, the problems our kids face are tough: peer pressure, bullying, sexual harassment, drugs, gangs, school violence, childhood smoking, racism, bigotry, lying, cheating—in addition to plain old meanness and just trying to get along.

Although the issues facing our kids are complex, the fourth skill of success will help our children deal more effectively with *whatever obstacle* comes their way. Each of the five steps—stopping to identify feelings, naming the problem, considering the alternatives, narrowing the options, and evaluating the consequences until deciding on a well thought out plan—needs to be reinforced again and again. We can't protect our children from problems, frustrations, and heartaches, but we can arm them with tools to handle those challenges better. The more you can encourage your child to practice these five problem-solving steps, the greater the likelihood she will develop into a self-sufficient and resourceful adult confidently able to "take a STAND" on any issue she is dealt.

POINTS TO REMEMBER

- Be a model of calmness in the face of panic. Showing you can keep your cool, even in crisis, is an important way to help your child learn to problem-solve.

- Avoid rescuing your child by solving his problems for him, which only robs him of opportunities to develop self-sufficiency. Reassure your child that you are nearby, but challenge him to solve problems himself.

- Take time to help your kids consider all the options they have for dealing with any issue that concerns them.

- Whenever you have a problem, talk through the steps you are taking to remedy a dilemma. Kids learn best through example.

- Don't be too quick to judge your child's solution; instead teach your child to evaluate the consequences of her decisions. Asking "What might happen if . . ." helps your child think through the outcomes of her decisions and anticipate what might happen if she chose a specific response.

- Your home is the best place for kids to learn by trial and error how to deal with problems. Keep reinforcing the problem-solving steps until your child is confident doing them on her own. She will use them for life.

RESOURCES FOR FURTHER ACTION

For Parents

Raising a Thinking Child, by Myrna B. Shure (New York: Henry Holt, 1994). A valuable resource full of ideas for teaching problem solving to children three to seven years of age.

Stress-Proofing Your Child, by Sheldon Lewis and Sheila Kay Lewis (New York: Bantam, 1996). This guide provides specific ways to help your child handle stress and cope with difficulties more confidently.

Teaching Your Child to Make Decisions: How to Raise a Responsible Child, by G. P. Miller (New York: HarperCollins, 1984). A wonderful explanation of decision-making techniques and how parents can teach this important skill to their children.

Teach Your Child Decision Making, by John F. Clabby and Maurice J. Elias (New York: Doubleday, 1987). A valuable resource filled with dozens of techniques to help children learn problem-solving skills.

For Children Ages Three to Seven

Angel Child, Dragon Child, by Michele Maria Surat (New York: Scholastic, 1983). A Vietnamese youngster has just arrived in the United States and is mocked by others, especially by one boy. The school principal helps the children get along and solve their problem together.

The Blanket That Had to Go, by Nancy Evans Cooney (New York: Putnam, 1981). Susie is traumatized to learn that when you go to kindergarten you don't bring your blanket! She finds a way to solve her problem.

Ira Sleeps Over, by Bernard Waber (Boston: Houghton Mifflin, 1984). Ira is invited to spend the night at Reggie's house. His problem: Should he or shouldn't he bring his teddy bear?

Swimmy, by Leo Lionni (New York: Pantheon Books, 1963). A fish learns the value of working together with others to solve problems.

For Children Ages Eight to Twelve

Hatchet, by Gary Paulsen (New York: Puffin, 1987). Twelve-year-old Brian is stranded in the Canadian wilderness and is confronted with a multitude of problems. He solves them all!

Save Queen of Sheba, by Louise Moeri (New York: Turtleback/Demco, 1994). Travel on the Oregon Trail is dangerous and creates endless problems, especially if you are twelve years old and have to take care of a little sister with whom you cannot get along.

The Trouble with Tuck, by Theodore Taylor (New York: Avon, 1981). When a young girl's beloved pet becomes blind, everyone advises her to put the dog to sleep. This is a solution she cannot tolerate, so she must find an alternative. She does!

The War with Grandpa, by Robert Kimmel Smith (New York: Turtleback/Demco, 1991). Peter is thrilled that Grandpa is coming to live with his family, until Grandpa moves into Peter's room and forces him upstairs. Peter must figure out a solution.

Videos for Family Viewing

Apollo 13 (Universal Studios, 1997). The exhilarating story of the ill-fated Apollo 13 moon mission and how the heroic work of the three astronauts on board and the incredible problem-solving capabilities and persistence of the mission control crew in Houston brought the crew safely home. (PG-13)

Babe (MCA Home Video, 1996). A wonderful family film based on the book by Dick King-Smith about an orphaned pig taken in by a farmer and how the farm animals join together to solve Babe's crisis. (G)

Davy Crockett, King of the Wild Frontier (Walt Disney Home Video, 1955). This story of a real American frontier hero who has to deal with continuous problems makes for great home viewing. I still remember sitting in front of my television as a kid, wearing my coonskin cap, and cheering for Davy. My three sons did the same thing during their childhood. (G)

The Dog Who Stopped the War (HBO Video, 1984). This French-Canadian film won international acclaim as one of the best antiwar films of its time. It is the story of a group of children who decide to spend their holidays playing "war games" and divide into two armies throwing snowballs back and forth. Eventually they come to see that even snowball fire can cause hurt feelings, but the true lesson is revealed when an innocent person is injured.

Never Cry Wolf (Walt Disney Home Video, 1983). A Canadian naturalist-scientist who has been dropped in the middle of the Arctic to determine why the caribou are decreasing must now survive. A native man and the wolves help him learn to deal with the problems he faces. Watch it with your children; there are a few scary scenes.

The Rescuers Down Under (Walt Disney Home Video, 1990). Mice detectives Bernard and Bianca form the Rescue Aid Society and travel to Australia to help a young boy in trouble. (G)

The Swiss Family Robinson (Walt Disney Home Video, 1960). A shipwrecked family encounters problem after problem in their struggle to survive. In spite of their difficulties, the family prospers and grows. (G)

Organizations and Agencies

Educators for Social Responsibility (National), 23 Garden Street, Cambridge, MA 02138. Telephone: (800) 370-2515. A national nonprofit organization supporting schools, teachers, and parents with professional development programs and instructional materials in conflict resolution, violence prevention, intergroup relations, and character education.

Kids Without Violence Program, P.O. Box 487, 35 Benton Street, Eureka Springs, AR 72632. Informs parents, teachers, and children about how kids are socialized to violence and offers a clearinghouse of information and workshops on the issue of youth violence.

National Association for Mediation in Education (NAME), 205 Hampshire House, Box 33635, University of Massachusetts, Amherst, MA 01003. Telephone:

(413) 545-2462. Promotes the development and implementation of school- and university-based conflict-resolution programs and curricula.

RCCP National Center, 163 Third Avenue, Suite 103, New York, NY 10003. Telephone: (212) 387-0225. A school-based conflict-resolution and inter- group relations program that provides a model for preventing school vio- lence and creating caring learning communities.

Websites for Kids

"Beakman's Electric Motor" [http:/fly.hiwaay.net/~palmet/motor.html]. Step- by-step instructions to help kids build the simple electric motor featured on television's *Beakman's World.* Only a few materials are needed. A great first step for problem solving.

"Camp Internet" [http://www.intercamp.com/]. An on-line site, organized like a summer camp, offering a variety of activities kids can do at home.

"Demo of the Day" [http://nyelabs.kcts.org/demo/demo.html]. Every day, this site features a different interesting project you can do with your child. A great way to practice the problem-solving steps.

"4Kids" [http://www.4kids.org]. A great way for your child to practice problem solving: the 4Kids Detectives site offers a weekly contest based on the 4Kids feature in the newspaper. If she answers correctly, your child becomes a 4Kids Detective.

"Kids' Contests" [http://www.huronline.com/kids.htm]. Lists contests, spon- sored by commercial companies, that are related to or about kids. Many give away free items in drawings. A fun way for your child to enhance her cre- ativity by practicing brainstorming.

"Lego" [http://www.lego.com]. Pictures and fun ideas for creative kids who love building with Legos.

"Who Cares: A Journal of Service and Action" [http://www.whocares.org]. An on-line journal that offers ways to solve society's problems through volun- teering and activism.

Getting Along

**Learning How to Make Friends,
Be a Friend, and Deal with
Stormy Relationships**

Five-year-old Dominick sits on the bench watching his classmates play in the sand with toy cars. Every day he puts his car in his pocket in case one of the kids invites him to join them. He knows it probably will never happen. Once he thought about asking if he could play, but he quickly talked himself out of that idea. "What do I say?" he asked himself. "Anyway, they'll probably tell me no." At last the bell rings to go back to class. Dominick has just spent another recess with no one to play with. His stepdad and mom and his teacher aren't aware of how lonely he is, thinking he would just rather be by himself. If they only knew how sad he feels.

Though five-year-old Danny transferred to the school just a few weeks ago, he has already made a number of new friends. As soon as it's recess, Danny yells to Shawn, "Come on, let's go!" and Shawn and a few other boys follow Danny's lead to the sandbox. When Charlie builds an impressive sand castle, Danny quickly compliments him: "That really looks neat." When Danny notices one of the boys without a car, he digs into his pocket and pulls out another, says, "I have an extra car. Want to use it?" and shares it with him. When Shawn's castle caves in, Danny comforts him: "Oh, too bad. Want me to help you build a new one?" They work hard creating a new construction, until the bell rings. Then the boys skip back to class arm in arm, as Danny confirms what the rest of them feel: "It's great having friends!"

Dominick and Danny are both healthy, bright kindergartners, raised in happy homes with adoring parents. But at age five there's already a significant difference between them that researchers predict will have a long-range impact on the quality of their lives. Danny, on the one hand, is successfully developing the skills of social competence. He knows how to join groups, encourage others, share, cooperate, and get along. Dominick, on the other hand, doesn't know how to make friends or be a friend. It's all too easy to figure out which boy has more confidence and higher self-esteem. How will the difference affect their lives later? Let's look ahead.

Some researchers have studied children with poor friendship-making skills to see what happens as they grow up. They discovered just how much social competence matters. They found that children with chronic friendship difficulties are prone to have poor self-esteem and become low achievers. As adolescents they frequently have drug and alcohol problems and are more likely to drop out of school and to be identified as juvenile delinquents. As adults they have problems in relationships and are more inclined to experience mental health problems. Of the two boys, Danny clearly has a significantly greater chance of living a more contented, fulfilled, and successful life—all because he knows how to get along.

Our real parenting goal is not to produce popular kids but to help them gain the confidence they will need to deal successfully with any situation involving people. That's a major part of what life is all about. Teaching this fifth success skill to your children will contribute greatly to improving the quality of their lives and will enhance their social behavior at home, in school, and beyond!

WHAT YOU WILL LEARN IN THIS CHAPTER

The best news is that the skills of social competence are *learned,* and the best place to learn them is *in the home.* This chapter has dozens of simple techniques and activities to help kids get along. You'll learn how to:

- Identify your child's potential friendship-making problems and correct them.

- Teach your child any social skill she lacks so as to increase her social competence.

- Increase your child's social confidence by teaching her how to join groups and make new friends.

- Enhance your child's social etiquette by nurturing common courtesy and good manners.

- Learn techniques to help your child respond effectively to meanness, bullying, and teasing.

- Enhance your child's social interactions by teaching her how to encourage others and use the rules of good sportsmanship during games as well as with friends.

HOW IS YOUR CHILD DOING NOW?

The statements below describe behaviors usually displayed by children who get along well with others. To evaluate your child's strengths in this fifth success skill, write the number you think best represents your child's current level on the line following each statement and then add all the scores to get his total score. If your child scores 40 to 50, he's in great shape with the skill. If he scores 30 to 40, he could benefit from skill enhancement. A score of 20 to 30 shows signs of potential problems. If your child scores 10 to 20, consider getting help to increase this skill.

5 = Always 4 = Frequently 3 = Sometimes 2 = Rarely 1 = Never

A child with strong social competence:	My child
Is sought out by others; has many friends.	_____
Cooperates; knows how to get along with others.	_____
Is polite and well mannered; always says "please" and "thank you."	_____
Is socially sensitive; has a lot of empathy for others' feelings.	_____
Relates well to others; socializes a great deal with kids.	_____
Willingly joins in; is actively involved in group activities.	_____
Feels that others like and value him.	_____
Acts as the diplomat when disputes arise.	_____
Patiently waits for his turn; does not interrupt others.	_____
Encourages and supports others.	_____
Total Score	_____

FOUR STEPS TO ENHANCING SOCIAL COMPETENCE

There are four steps to helping children become socially competent. The first step helps you identify your child's social strengths and weaknesses so that you'll understand the best way to improve her abilities to get along with others. Experts point out that a wide range of social skills are needed to establish and manage social relationships, so the second step shows you how to teach your child critical friendship-making skills. Because many studies find that well-mannered children are more popular and do better in school, the third step helps tune up your child's manners and enhance her social reputation. The last step helps your child deal with one of the most difficult parts of growing up: teasing, bullying, and meanness. Following are the four steps to increasing your child's social competence so that she can get along confidently and successfully with others:

Step 1: Identify Your Child's Social Strengths and Weaknesses

Step 2: Teach Your Child How to Make Friends

Step 3: Nurture Good Manners and Common Courtesy

Step 4: Learn Ways to Deal with Teasing, Meanness, and Bullying

STEP 1: IDENTIFY YOUR CHILD'S SOCIAL STRENGTHS AND WEAKNESSES

The first step to increasing your child's social success is not to teach him a new skill but to assess what his interpersonal strengths and weaknesses are right now. The better you understand how your child gets along with others and can identify the social skills he lacks, the more you'll be to help your child become socially competent.

Seven-year-old Hiro ran into the house and slammed the door. It was obvious from the look on his face that he'd had another bad day at school. "What's wrong? You look so sad," asked his father.

"Nobody likes me. They never want to play with me, because they say I look different," the seven-year-old cried. And before his father could say a word, Hiro bolted to his room and locked the door. It was the fifth time that week he'd come home upset, and his father felt like crying himself. He knew the move would be hard, but he never expected it to be this difficult. The Asian father also knew assimilating into a new culture would be tough. If only his son could find a friend.

Feeling rejected has to be among the most painful experiences for children as well as parents. Research tells us sobering facts about children who experience social rejection: aside from feeling lonely and tending to have lower self-esteem, they also are two to eight times more likely to drop out of high school and are at a much higher risk for using alcohol or drugs. Luckily, psychologists tell us there is a lot parents and teachers can do to help kids fit in and get along. Here's how to get started enhancing your child's social interactions.

Getting Started: Observing Your Child's Social Interactions

The next time your child is around other kids, bring a newspaper or book to pretend you are reading while you really watch to see how your child interacts. The Success Tip that follows lists the warning signs of friendship problems. Are any of these behaviors hindering your child from having positive social interactions? Once you have identified the social skills you think your child needs, the second step shows you how to teach them.

STEP 2: TEACH YOUR CHILD HOW TO MAKE FRIENDS

The ability to make friends involves a number of skills that can all be learned. This step helps you teach your child a few simple skills that are critical in enhancing social competence.

Some kids just seem to make friends easily. They're invited to all the birthday parties, attend the sleepovers, are chosen first for teams, and are sought after as everyone's friend. If we could peek into their future, we'd see them continuing to succeed socially throughout their school years, as well as for the rest of their lives. Child psychologists find that popular kids have one thing in common: they have learned the skills of social competence at an early age. Like most skills, the skills of friendship are refined through trial and error. So the more opportunities kids have to try out what works with others and what doesn't, the greater the likelihood that they will develop social competence.

Kids who hang back and are shy, kids who haven't had many social experiences, kids who never learned these first critical friendship-making

SUCCESS TIP
Warnings Signs of Friendship Problems

Here's a list of behaviors often displayed by children needing a boost in friendship-making skills. Check areas that concern you and discuss your notes with other adults who know your child well.

- ❍ Doesn't take turns.
- ❍ Doesn't have a friend.
- ❍ Acts like a poor loser.
- ❍ Rarely cooperates.
- ❍ Shows little empathy for others' feelings.
- ❍ Lacks the skills to play the game.
- ❍ Doesn't enjoy socializing with other kids.
- ❍ Acts too competitively.
- ❍ Acts too immaturely for the group.
- ❍ Acts too maturely for the group.
- ❍ Hoards toys and doesn't share.
- ❍ Acts discourteously.
- ❍ Always makes excuses when losing.
- ❍ Stands too close to or too far from kids.
- ❍ Acts bossy: always wants his own way.
- ❍ Uses a sulky, unhappy expression.
- ❍ Uses a whiny, unfriendly, or loud voice.

- ❍ Criticizes too often.
- ❍ Interrupts; never listens to others.
- ❍ Barges into an activity too quickly.
- ❍ Doesn't know how to initiate or end a conversation.
- ❍ Doesn't know how to maintain a conversation.
- ❍ Doesn't know how to join a group; hangs back.
- ❍ Manages conflicts inappropriately.
- ❍ Plays too aggressively.
- ❍ Never compromises.
- ❍ Is too argumentative.
- ❍ Doesn't apologize or make amends.
- ❍ Doesn't pay attention to the group.
- ❍ Doesn't use eye contact.
- ❍ Quits before the game is over.
- ❍ Switches rules midstream.
- ❍ Gets upset or becomes angry easily.

steps, or kids who have poor social models to copy are kids handicapped in developing the skills of social competence. Not knowing how to join a group or meet new friends will haunt them the rest of their lives. As well-liked kids continue practicing their social skills, kids lacking the skills will continue to lag behind socially. Finally, the pain of social rejection will set in. The good news is that social skills can easily be taught. Teaching them can do nothing but enhance children's social confidence and expand their potential interpersonal fulfillment. The next step shows you how to teach your child *any* skill you think she needs to enhance her ability to get along with others.

Four Ways to Help Kids Learn Friendship-Making Skills

Zoe's father volunteered to go on the class field trip to see for himself whether the other kids really were as mean to his daughter as she said. Just sitting in the back of the bus and watching how Zoe interacted with the other girls convinced him he wasn't hearing the whole story. He instantly saw how bossy she was and how she always bulldozed herself into groups without watching to see what the other kids were doing. She was obviously turning the other girls off. Now that he knew her problem, how could he help her change?

Child development experts Sherri Oden and Steven Asher worked for years with children who had problems fitting in. They discovered that these children's social successes dramatically improved when they were taught specific friendship-making skills. You can use the same steps, based on Oden and Asher's research, to help your child learn *any* social skill. By teaching your child one new skill at a time and practicing it over and over until he can use it on his own, you can help your child make new friends and improve his social confidence. Here's how Zoe's father taught his daughter new social skills.

1. **Focus on a skill your child lacks.** Look over the warnings signs of friendship problems from the first step and choose one skill your child lacks. Choose the easiest one to teach!

Zoe's father knew his daughter needed to learn many skills: she was bossy, used a loud voice, argued frequently, didn't take turns, and played too aggressively. The first thing he needed to help her learn, though, was to wait and watch the group before barging in.

2. **Coach your child in this skill.** Find a private moment to model the new skill to your child. Talk with her about why the skill is important and then be sure she can show you how to do the skill correctly. It is helpful to go with your child to a public place such as a playground or schoolyard so that she can observe other kids actually using the skill. Seeing the skill in action helps your child copy and try it on her own.

Zoe's father took his daughter to a park pretending he wanted to play ball with her. He really wanted to point out how kids joining new groups watch before barging in. He found a spot to throw her the ball near a group of kids playing baseball. As soon as a new child walked up to their group, he quietly said, "Hey, Zoe, see the girl with the braids over there? She looks like she's trying to play ball with the group." When he had Zoe's attention he added, "Watch her to see what she does first; it looks like she's waiting before barging in." Zoe paused to watch. Her father added, "Wow, she's still standing there. I guess she's waiting for the end of the inning before asking if she can play. That's a great idea, because kids don't like to be interrupted during a game."

3. **Provide opportunities to practice the skill.** Just telling your child about the skill is not enough. Your child needs to try out the skill with other children. The best kids for your child to practice with are kids she doesn't already know and who are younger or less skilled. Then keep the practice session short and stand back at a comfortable distance! If your child is having problems in the group, offer suggestions only privately—*never* in front of other kids.

The next day Zoe went straight to the baseball diamond with her dad. Her father figured this would be a good place for Zoe to practice waiting before barging in, since she didn't know the girls and was a pretty good baseball player. If the kids let her on the team, Zoe would feel comfortable playing. "Remember what you're going to do, Zoe," said her dad. "Yeah," Zoe said, "I'm first going to watch what the kids are doing and see which side's not winning, because they'll probably need me most. I'll wait until the end of an inning before asking."

"Sounds good," her father said. "Why don't you try it? The worst that can happen is they'll say no. If they do, just walk away without saying anything."

4. Review the practice and offer feedback. Child development experts Oden and Asher discovered that a critical part of teaching social skills is evaluating the child's performance with her. As soon as you can, discuss how the practice session went, asking such questions as "How did it go?" "What did you say?" "How do you think you did?" "What would you do differently next time?" Don't criticize what your child didn't do; instead praise what your child did right. If she wasn't successful, talk through what didn't go well so that she can try it differently the next time. As soon as your child feels comfortable with the skill, you're ready to teach another one. Gradually your child's social competence will grow.

Zoe stuck to their plan and was asked to play second base. When the game ended, she and her dad went for ice cream and reviewed how things went. "Looks like you had a good time, Zoe. How do you think it went?" her dad asked.

"Pretty good," Zoe admitted, "but it was hard waiting that long."

"Yes, but you did it, Zoe. Kids like it more if you don't barge in on them when they're already playing a game. Next time we'll practice saying nice things to the kids while you're playing. Kids like that, too."

Four Ideas to Help Children Gain New Friends

The four ideas that follow are what experts recommend as the first steps to help your child make new friends.

1. Arrange one-on-one play opportunities. Dr. Fred Frankel, author of *Good Friends Are Hard to Find* and developer of the world-famous

SUCCESS TIP
A Hint for Helping Shy Children

Dr. Philip Zimbardo of Stanford University, the world's expert on shyness, discovered that pairing an older "shy" child with a younger or less skilled child is an excellent technique for helping reticent kids practice learning new social skills. Your child will feel much more confident practicing any new skill with someone less skilled than himself. A younger sibling, cousin, neighbor, or even one of your friend's younger children is always a safer partner than a more self-assured, skilled, older child.

A father in Albany, New York, shared a unique way he used Zimbardo's advice to help his shy twelve-year-old daughter. He found her an after-school baby-sitting job with the next-door neighbor's six-year-old. She not only earned money but also practiced the social skills—starting a conversation, using eye contact—that she was shy about trying with kids her own age.

UCLA Social Skills Training Program, suggests one-on-one play dates as the best way for children to build new friendships. This is a time when your child invites only one child over for a couple of private play hours to get to know one another and practice friendship-making skills. Provide snacks and then try to keep interruptions to a minimum: siblings should not be included, and television viewing should not be a play option.

2. Match your child's interests with group activities. Experts say that those pairs of children who become friends and who stay friends—for at least some period of time—are especially likely to share similar activities, styles, interests, and values. So provide opportunities for your child to find friends who share his interests. The trick is to match your child's strengths with the same kind of group activities that nurture his interests. If your child's strength is singing, you might look for a choir for him to join. If soccer is her passion, find her a soccer team to join. If he's a chess whiz, search for groups of kids who love to play chess. You'll be enhancing not only your child's natural talents but also his social skills.

3. Provide interactive toys. Some toys lend themselves to interactive play and can be great icebreakers to start kids talking. Instead of playing alone, a child with a ball can ask, "Want to play catch?" The UCLA Social Skills Training Program notes that the best interactive toys are ones that require at least two people to use, have simple rules, are inexpensive, don't encourage aggression, and are fun by kid standards. Board games, marbles, ball games, pretend figures, and dolls are appropriate. Visit your child's schoolyard or a nearby park to see what kinds of outdoor games are current. Ask other parents and toy store owners for names of the hottest indoor toys for your child's age—besides video games, which are anything but interactive. Try to match the activity to your child's interests and then spend the next days teaching your child how to play the game. She doesn't have to be great; she just has to know the rules. Once she's learned the game, she'll be in better shape to use the skill to try to join others.

4. Teach conversation openers. Make a list with your child of easy conversation openers he can use: what he could say to someone he already knows, an adult he hasn't met, a friend he hasn't seen in a while, a brand-new student at a school, or a child he would like to play with on the playground. Keep in mind that kids rarely start conversations with other children by shaking hands and issuing formal introductions. The more common approach is just to walk up and say, "Hi, I'm [name]. Can I play?" "Is it OK if I play too?" or "Do you need another guy on your team?" Write down ideas for conversation starters and take turns rehearsing them together until your child feels comfortable trying them on his own.

Three Ways to Help Kids Learn the Importance of Encouraging Others

Dr. William Hartup, from the University of Minnesota, found through extensive observations that the most well liked children often praise, encourage, and cooperate with others. Children who didn't cooperate or who ridiculed, ignored, or put down others were most likely to be disliked by classmates. Kids just like to be around kids who accept them and build them up. That's information our kids need to hear. Here are three quick ways to help your children learn the importance of encouraging others.

1. **Make a list of encouragers.** Tell your child that one of the secrets of people who get along is that they frequently encourage others. Brainstorm a list of supportive statements that build others up, such as "Great idea!" "Super!" "Nice try!" "Good shot!" "Good answer!" and "Great game!" Now post the list and say the encouragers frequently so that your kids will "catch them" and start using them with their peers.

2. **Teach the Two Praise Rule.** Anytime your child is going off to a group activity—a team game, a scout meeting, a friend's house, or even school—remind him to praise the other kids at least two times. In our house we call it the Two Praise Rule. The number just is a simple way of helping my kids remember the importance of praising others.

3. **Practice family praising.** A mom in Colorado Springs shared an easy way she increases praising in her home: she purchased a little ornamental magnet for each family member and stuck them on her refrigerator with pencils and paper nearby. Family members were encouraged to write notes complimenting one another for deserving deeds and to clip them to the person's personalized magnet: "Bill, thanks for cleaning your

room. It looks great!" or "Andy, good luck at your game!" As everyone began to practice praising, her home in no time became a more encouraging place.

STEP 3: NURTURE GOOD MANNERS AND COMMON COURTESY

This third step shows you how to increase your children's social competence by nurturing the skills of courtesy and polite behavior. Using good manners will enhance your child's reputation in all arenas—home, school, and the community. Besides, kids like to be around other kids who are courteous and nice.

Three days ago, during an airplane flight, I sat totally mystified as I watched a flight attendant become ecstatic while passing out snacks. I have to admit, it's a behavior I don't typically see thirty thousand feet off the ground. The cause of her exuberance was even more astounding: she had just served an eleven-year-old a can of soda and was absolutely amazed that the child had responded with the words, "Thank you." "Wow," she told the child's mother. "I'm not used to kids with such incredible manners. He put me in shock!"

I sat in disbelief. Have good manners become so obsolete that when a child says thank you, everyone is stunned? I thought a minute and realized how often I've heard the same kind of response from hundreds of teachers I've worked with just this past year. "What behaviors concern you about your students?" is always one of the first questions I ask before starting a workshop. No matter where I work, "disrespect and lack of manners" is always among educators' top responses. I knew that the flight attendant's behavior was probably an all-too-common reaction—polite kids are becoming a scarce commodity. What a sad commentary on the state of our kids and our society.

And courtesy does enhance children's success! Many studies find that well-mannered children are more popular and do better in school. Notice how often they're invited to others' homes? Kids (and their parents) like to be around kids who are nice. Listen to teachers give them accolades. Courteous children have an edge later in life, too: people in the business world clearly tell us that their first interview choices are those applicants displaying good social graces. Polite people also get more "second" job interviews, and usually even the job. You just can't help but react positively to people who are polite and courteous. By making polite behaviors a priority with our children, we can enhance their social competence and give them a boost toward success.

SUCCESS TIP
A Sad State of Affairs

A recent survey conducted by *U.S. News & World Report* found that nine out of ten Americans believed that the breakdown of common courtesy has become a serious problem in this country. Of those polled, 78 percent said that manners and good social graces have significantly eroded over the past ten years and that this erosion is a major contributor to the increase in violence as well as the breakdown of our values in this country. So be sure to emphasize common courtesy and good manners with your child.

Five Ways to Help Kids Learn Good Manners

Good manners are one of the simplest success skills to teach children because they are expressed in just a few very specific behaviors. We can instantly point out good or poor manners to our kids: "Wow, nice manners! Did you notice the smile on Grandma's face when you thanked her for dinner?" or "Starting to eat without waiting for the others to sit down wasn't polite." We can modify our children's manners: "Next time, remember to say 'excuse me' when you walk in front of someone." And we can always tune them up: "Before you ask for the dish, say 'please.'" Here are five simple ways to enhance your child's good social graces.

1. Model good manners. All three of my sons attended a wonderful cooperative nursery school in Morgan Hill, California, led by an incredibly caring teacher, Jeanette Thompson. The first impression I had of the school was of how well-mannered the children were. And, through the years as I put in my "co-op" hours, I understood why Mrs. Thompson's students were so polite: Mrs. Thompson never taught manners at a special time; instead she taught students manners all day long through her own example. Every sentence she ever uttered included *please, thank you,* or *excuse me.* It was impossible for her students not to be polite. She would always tell parents, "Manners are caught, not taught." Was she ever right! Ask yourself, By watching my manners today, what did my children catch? The first step to teaching kids good manners is to make sure you model them yourself.

2. Point out the value of manners. Discuss with your children the value of good manners. You might say, "Using good manners helps you gain the respect of others. It's also a great way to meet new friends. Polite people just make the world a kinder place." Once kids understand the impact good manners have on others, they are more likely to incorporate courtesy in their own behavior.

3. Teach a manner a week. When my children were young I taught them a jingle: "Hearts, like doors, will open with ease, if you learn to use these keys." We'd then print a manner a week on a large paper key and tape it on our kitchen door as a reminder. Every child in the neighborhood could not only recite our jingle but also name the manners that are the "keys to opening hearts. "Of course, "catching" new manners doesn't happen overnight: it takes consistent effort on our parts. So how about teaching a manner a week? Write the manner on an index card, post it on your refrigerator, and then hold a contest to see how many times family members hear another member use the word. Here are a few to get you started: *Please, Thank you, May I? Excuse me, I'm sorry, Pardon me, I'm glad to meet you, You go first,* and *May I introduce . . . ?*

4. Correct impoliteness immediately. When your child makes an impolite comment, immediately correct the behavior by using the "three

B's" of discipline: *Be* brief, *be* private so that no one but you and your child is aware you are correcting him, and *be* specific.

Here is how two parents used the three B's: Juan's mom waited for a private moment to point out his poor manners to him: "Starting your dinner without waiting first for Grandma to sit down was impolite. Being polite means always respecting older people." Waiting for the right time when only Juan could hear his mom's correction preserved Juan's dignity but still let him know his behavior was unacceptable. When Kevin used a racist comment, his father immediately used the three B's to let him know it was unacceptable: "That was a bigoted comment and could hurt someone's feelings. Please don't ever use that word again."

5. **Practice table manners.** A friend of mine who really wanted to make sure her children "caught" good manners started a unique family tradition: once a month she asks her children to help her plan a party. The children plan the menu, set their table—with only their "company" dishes—arrange a centerpiece of hand-picked flowers, and then sit in their "Sunday best." The party is just for their family, and it's the time my friend helps her children practice table manners, such as "please pass," "Thank you," and "May I be excused?" (as well keeping your napkin on your lap, chewing with your mouth closed, waiting for others to speak, and learning which fork to use with each course). Yes, it takes a lot of work, but she swears it's worth it, especially when so many people comment on how well-behaved her children are.

STEP 4: LEARN WAYS TO DEAL WITH TEASING, MEANNESS, AND BULLYING

Childhood isn't easy; for many kids it's downright painful. Do any of these comments sound familiar?

"Jade is so mean. I'll never invite her over again as long as I live."
"I tried to tell him to stop, Dad. He just laughed at me and pushed me
   down."

SUCCESS TIP
Acknowledge Others with Handwritten Notes

Another sign of good manners and common courtesy is to acknowledge others with handwritten notes. Opportunities for written gestures are endless: I'll miss you, Congratulations! Happy Birthday! I'm sorry, I hope you feel better, Thank you, and Good luck. You might set aside a box of art supplies filled with colored ink pens, stickers, crayons, stencils, glue, scissors, and colored paper your child can use to create his own personalized stationery. A few envelopes and stamps could be included, as well as a sample showing your child the proper way to write letters and address envelopes. When he finishes a note, help your child mail or present it to the deserving recipient.

"Roberto called me Four Eyes, and the other kids laughed. I'm not going on that bus."

"Kara invited every girl in the class to her birthday except me. She says I'm too dumb!"

"Mom, don't you get it? I can't go to the park. The kids are just waiting to beat me up."

One of the universal dreams we parents have is that our kids will have friends and get along with others. The alarming rise in bullying has turned many of our dreams into nightmares: all too commonly our kids are verbally, emotionally, or physically abused by other children's hurtful behaviors. There seems to be an epidemic these days of mean-acting kids. Consider these alarming statistics:

- The National Education Association estimates that 160,000 children miss school every day due to fear of attack or intimidation by other students.

- A national study found that the amount of childhood teasing and being mean to others has significantly increased since the mid-1970s.

- In a study conducted by John H. Hoover, Ronald Oliver, and Richard J. Hazler, 76.8 percent of students in a midwestern study reported that they have been bullied, and 14 percent of those students indicated that they experienced severe reactions to the abuse.

One thing is certain, all kids are bound to be teased. Although we can't prevent the pain these experiences can cause, we can lessen our kids' chances of becoming victims. Studies say the best way to do that is by empowering children with strategies to effectively handle bullying, name-calling, meanness, and turbulent relationships. This fourth step shows you how to teach your kids those bully-proofing strategies so that they have more success getting along with peers.

 SUCCESS TIP
Common Mistakes Parents Make About Bullying

According to Elin McCoy, author of *What to Do . . . When Kids Are Mean to Your Child*, here are three of the most common mistakes experts say parents make about bullying:

1. Not taking their children's complaints about bullying seriously. Any bullying threats should be taken seriously—your child could be hurt. It's the one time to step in and contact the school.
2. Telling the child, "Just tell him to stop." Bullies rarely just go away; children need to learn ways to deal with them and stop their abuse. (See the section following this Success Tip for anti-bullying techniques.)
3. Telling the child to hit the bully back. Experts tell us that aggression among kids can escalate very quickly. In this day and age, children are getting seriously hurt over very minor issues, and too many kids *at every grade level* are carrying weapons. Kids needs to learn alternatives to hitting.

There are times when we should not put all the responsibility on a child to stop a bully. Adult intervention may be the *only* way to handle the situation. Use your instinct so that your child does not get hurt. If there's ever the possibility your child could be injured—step in.

Three Ways to Help Kids Respond to Teasing

Julie's mom watched her daughter get off the bus and instantly knew the other kids must have teased her again about her new glasses; her tears were hard to miss. By the time she walked in the house, Julie was sobbing. For the fourth day that week, her mom tried to calm her down. "Did they make fun of your glasses again, Sweetie?" her mom asked.

"Yeah," sobbed Julie. "They just never leave me alone. I tell them to stop, but they won't. I told them they were stupid and I was going to tell the teacher, but they laughed even more and called me a tattletale. I'm never going to school. I hate them!"

Have you noticed how some kids just never seem to end up as the bully's targets, whereas others become easy prey? The reason: they've learned how not to let a bully get to them. Let's look at three strategies Julie's mom could teach her daughter to deal with bullying that you can also teach your child. Not all techniques will work for all kids. The trick is to match the technique with what works best with your child's temperament.

Anti-Bully Technique 1: Stay Calm and Don't React

Bullies love power. They love knowing they can push other kids' buttons. The way Julie responded was exactly what her tormentors wanted: she let them know they upset her. By name-calling back and saying she was going to tell the teacher, Julie fueled the bullies even more. The secret is for her not to cry and let the teasers know how upset their taunting is making her but to stay calm and *not react*. She'll then be able to respond more effectively. Here are two ideas to help kids stay cool when they are teased.

1. **Count backward slowly.** I used to tell kids to count to ten to help them calm down. I find it's more effective these days to have the child count backward slowly from twenty. Because he has to really think about the counting sequence, the child takes his mind off the teaser temporarily— just enough that he can calm down.

2. Use self-talk. Teach your child to say a statement inside her head as a reminder to stay calm and not react whenever she's teased. Julie's mom taught her to say to herself, "Chill out, Julie, calm down." She practiced it so many times, she finally was able to do it when her emotions were really high.

Anti-Bully Technique 2: Ignore It

Bullies love to know their teasing upsets their victims, so a second technique is to teach your child to ignore the tormentor. Ignoring a teaser isn't easy; it takes lots of practice and encouragement from parents for kids to learn this skill. I asked a group of eleven-year-olds how they handle teasing, and they unanimously said the worst thing to do is let the bully know the teasing bothers you. Here are their suggestions on how to ignore teasers: pretend they're invisible; walk away quickly without looking at them; quickly look at something else and laugh; look like it doesn't bother you; stay quiet; and look completely uninterested.

Julie's mom taught her to think about something else when she was being teased. They brainstormed a few ideas, and Julie decided that the next time she was teased she would think about the time she hit the winning home run, and then while thinking about it, she would walk away and ignore her teaser.

Anti-Bully Technique 3: Use Comebacks

I think one of the most effective responses to a teaser is using a comeback—a simple, one-line comment that the victim says with a calm, straight face to his teaser. It usually works, because the response is not what the teaser expects, and it puts him off guard.

When Julie's teaser says, "Hey, Four Eyes, those glasses make you look so ugly," Julie might calmly say with a deadpan face, "Gcc, I never thought of that," and walk away. Another variation of the technique is for the victim simply to agree with the teaser: "Yeah, so?" or "Somebody already told me, thanks."

Julie and her mom brainstormed a list of possible comeback lines like the ones listed in the next Success Tip and chose one she was most comfortable saying. Her mom helped her rehearse the line by pretending to be the teaser, giving Julie opportunities to practice saying the line confidently. After a few days, Julie came home all smiles. It worked!

SUCCESS TIP
Comeback Lines

Comeback lines work best for children in at least the second grade. The trick is for the child to practice the line so that he can deliver it assuredly to the bully. Tell your child to use these rules: stay calm, keep a straight face, say the comeback assertively, and walk off. And emphasize that your child may not tease back or aggravate the bully. "Just answer every tease with a comeback." And don't forget: comebacks should *never* be used where physical aggression or serious threats are at stake.

Here are a few comeback lines to get you started:

"Tell me something I don't already know." "So?"

"You don't say." "And your point is?"

"Thanks for telling me." "Really?"

"Can't you think of anything else to say?" "I heard that one in preschool."

WHAT ONE PARENT DID

Jordan's father watched his son from the baseball stands and sadly shook his head. His son was a great little baseball player, but he was also a very poor sport. During the game Jordan argued the rules, made excuses for his strike-outs, and blamed everyone else for losing. If he kept this up, nobody would want him on any team.

That night, Jordan's dad dusted off their old checkerboard and called his son to come join him in a game. For the next hour they played checkers; the dad's real goal was to help his son learn the rules of good sportsmanship.

Parents Do Make a Difference

They started the game by first reviewing the rules. When Jordan said he understood them, his dad told him they had to stick by them: "Good sports don't argue the rules. They agree to them at the beginning and don't change them unless everyone agrees to. They also take the game seriously and don't quit. Let's agree to play until one of us wins. Want to shake on it?"

As they played, Jordan's dad deliberately made a few bad moves. Instead of making excuses he said, "Wow, I wasn't thinking on that one" or "You got me there!" Instead of criticizing his opponent, he praised Jordan a few times using a warm voice tone and straight eye contact: "Good move!" and "Great idea!"

That night, Jordan's father lost his first checker game—on purpose, of course—but he was subtle enough not to let Jordan know. He used the moment to show his son how to lose gracefully: "Good game, Jordan. Let's play again tomorrow," he said, and shook his son's hand. For the next few nights Jordan and his dad played checkers. Not only did Jordan's checker game improve—he also learned an even better game: how to be a good sport.

FINAL THOUGHTS ON ENHANCING SOCIAL COMPETENCE

Friends play an enormous part in the development of children's self-esteem. If we want our kids to become their personal best, it's essential to improve their ability to get along with others. Although many children are academically competent, their interpersonal incompetence may hinder their chances of success. The skills of social success are some of the most critical skills we can ever help our children learn; they are also some of the easiest skills to teach. Enhancing this fifth skill of success will boost our children's potential in every arena of their life—in school, at home, and in the community. It's a skill no child can afford to leave home without.

POINTS TO REMEMBER

- Manners are best caught—not taught. Tune up your social graces and make courtesy a priority in your home. Polite kids are well liked and have an edge on success.

SUCCESS TIP
The Basic Rules of Good Sportsmanship

There are six rules of good sports that help kids get along, adapted from Fred Frankel's book *Good Friends Are Hard to Find*. One of the best times to model them is when you play board games with your kids. Here are the rules Jordan's dad modeled:

1. Find out your friend's interests and choose a game you both can agree on.
2. Decide on the rules before the game starts and stick by them: no changing rules midstream.
3. Take the game seriously and play the best you can—no goofing around or silly stuff.
4. Play until the game ends—don't quit unless you both agree. For younger kids or children with short attention spans, set an oven timer for a specific play time, and play until the buzzer goes off.
5. Encourage your teammates and try to praise your teammates at least twice before the game ends. Don't criticize or coach: if you can't say anything nice, just don't say anything.
6. Always end the game on a positive note with a handshake or by saying, "Good game" or "Let's do it again." Don't be overly concerned about winning or losing—just have a good time.

- Reduce the time your child spends on activities that don't promote positive interaction—video games, television, and aggressive toys—and increase those that nurture social interchanges: organized group activities, scouts, team sports, and park programs. Get involved with your child!

- Identify one social skill at a time to teach your child. Tell him why it's important, show him what it looks like, give him opportunities to practice using it, and then review his performance. Gradually your child's social competence will blossom.

- Do not tolerate any form of bullying: name-calling, put-downs, teasing, meanness, physical aggression, or sexual harassment. Take an active stand in bully-proofing your school, neighborhood, and community. Teach your kids that cruelty is *never* acceptable.

- Emphasize good sportsmanship skills in your child—they are the same skills that nurture friendships.

- Build your child's self-esteem; it protects your child from resorting to bullying behaviors as well as from becoming the victim.

- Teach kids to "use their words" to express themselves, instead of using their fists.

- Encourage your child to encourage others. Kids like to be around kids who build them up.

RESOURCES FOR FURTHER ACTION

For Parents

Gang Free: Friendship Choices for Today's Youth, by Valerie Wiener (Minneapolis, Minn.: Fairview Press, 1995). If you are concerned about your child's selection of peers or gang involvement, this is a must-read.

Good Friends Are Hard to Find, by Fred Frankel (Pasadena, Calif.: Perspective Publishing, 1996). Written by the director of the UCLA Parent Training and Social Skills Programs, this guide is especially valuable. It lays out step by step how to help five- to twelve-year-olds make friends, solve relationship problems, and deal with issues of teasing, bullying, and meanness.

How to Raise a Child with a High EQ (Emotional Quotient), by Lawrence E. Shapiro (New York: HarperCollins, 1997). A practical guide to helping children master the social and emotional abilities that allow them to be happy and well adjusted.

More Than Manners! Raising Today's Kids to Have Kind Manners and Good Hearts, by Letitia Baldrige (New York: Rawson Associates, 1997). A road map for guiding kids to succeed in life by enhancing decency, kind hearts, and great manners.

The Shy Child: A Parent's Guide for Overcoming and Preventing Shyness from Infancy to Adulthood, by Philip Zimbardo and Shirley L. Radl (New York:

Doubleday, 1982). An outstanding resource for helping children overcome shyness before it becomes a lifetime handicap.

Teaching Your Child the Language of Social Success, by Marshall P. Duke, Stephen Nowicki Jr., and Elisabeth A. Martin (Atlanta, Ga.: Peachtree, 1996). Easy-to-use guide includes ways to help kids improve their nonverbal skills to enhance relationships with others.

What to Do . . . When Kids Are Mean to Your Child, by Elin McCoy (Pleasantville, N.Y.: Reader's Digest, 1997). Dozens of strategies for helping kids get along and deal with teasing and bullying.

Why Doesn't Anybody Like Me? A Guide to Raising Socially Confident Kids, by Hara Estroff Marano (New York: Morrow, 1998). Helpful hints on fostering traits of popularity in children of any age.

For Children Ages Three to Seven

Cap It Off with a Smile: A Guide for Making and Keeping Friends, by Robin Inwald (Kew Gardens, N.Y.: Hilson Press, 1994). Simple, practical ideas for building friendships.

How to Lose All Your Friends, by Nancy Carlson (New York: Viking Penguin, 1994). This hilarious tale offers advice on the kinds of things to do if you don't want to have any friends.

Lilly's Purple Plastic Purse, by Kevin Henkes (New York: Greenwillow Books, 1996). Lilly sends a mean note to her teacher and then is sorry; she writes a sincere apology note.

Manners, by Aliki (New York: Greenwillow Books, 1990). An assortment of different manners are cleverly illustrated.

Swimmy, by Leo Lionni (New York: Pantheon Books, 1963). A wonderful tale vividly describing the concept of "we sink or swim together."

Together, by George Ella Lyon (New York: Orchard Books, 1989). Here's a delightful picture book that can be used for all ages (including adults!) describing in rhyme the value of working together.

For Children Ages Eight to Twelve

Bridge to Terabithia, by Katherine Paterson (New York: Avon, 1979). A sensitive character portrayal of a friendship between a boy and a girl. Newbery Award winner.

The Sign of the Beaver, by Elizabeth George Spears (New York: Dell, 1983). A story of survival in the wilderness. Twelve-year-old Matt is rescued by an Indian chief and his grandson, and a powerful friendship emerges.

Teammates, by Peter Golenbock (Orlando, Fla.: Harcourt Brace, 1990). Powerful text describes the racial prejudice experienced by a black player in major league baseball.

Videos for Family Viewing

Honey, I Shrunk the Kids (Buena Vista Home Video, 1989). The comedy of four kids accidentally reduced to microscopic size by a ray gun, who find themselves stranded across the yard from their home. They must now work together to solve a wide array to problems before they can finally make it back to true size and home. (PG)

Little Women (MCA/UA Home Video, 1933). Based on the classic by Louisa May Alcott. Four devoted sisters face obstacles with love and courage. The story is rich with lessons in caring, courtesy, and morals. (PG)

Pride of the Yankees (Key Video, 1942). One of the best baseball films ever made portrays Lou Gehrig and his teammate Babe Ruth and their long-lasting feud that finally ended the day Gehrig retired.

Sarah, Plain and Tall (Republic Pictures Home Video, 1990). A Hallmark Hall of Fame production set on the Great Plains in 1910, where a prospective wife and later stepmother must somehow help two kids and their father overcome loneliness and get along.

Table Manners for Kids (Public Media Video, 1993). A detailed narration of everything kids need to know about proper table manners.

Websites for Kids

"Berit's Best Sites for Children" [http://www.cochran.com/theodore/noframe/ksites.html]. An index of children's websites and links where your child can meet other children on the Net. Also includes activity centers, games and toys, and family and kids' home pages. Great for ages nine and under.

"Children's Page" [http://www.comlab.ox.ac.uk/oucl/users/jonathan.bowen/children.html]. A site for every member of your family; there are jokes, calendars, sound clips, movie clips, and games.

"Kidlink" [http://www.kidlink.org]. A site for older children (ages ten to fifteen) all over the world to talk to one another on the Net. Supports a number of different languages.

"KidsCom Home Page" [http://www.kidscom.com/]. A place your child can find an e-pal, play games, and talk about her favorite things in French, German, Spanish, or English.

"KidsGames" [http://www.shastahome.com/kids/kidgames.htm]. A wealth of descriptions of fun childhood games.

"Kids Space" [http://www.kids-space.org]. Scores of activities just for kids: pictures, stories, pen pals, and kid Web pages. A great place for your child to interact with other children.

Goal Setting

Targeting What You Want and Taking Action to Achieve It

Nine-year-old Kara sits at her desk wiping away her tears. It's already nine o'clock, and she still has more homework! Any minute her foster mom will tell her to turn the lights off and go to bed. Tomorrow when her teacher discovers she didn't finish her work, she'll probably have to work in the classroom and miss all her recesses again. She shakes her head unhappily, realizing she has been at her desk for at least two hours. It seems all she can think about when she sits down is how much work she has to do. Somehow she never finishes what she starts. "I'll probably spend the rest of my life missing recess," she sobs. "Why can't I ever get my work done?" She looks up sadly when she sees her foster mom. It's time to go to bed, and once again she's only half done with what she set out to do.

Tyrel finished his dinner and went straight to his room. His science project was due the next day, and he knew it would take several hours to finish. Tyrel was determined to get an A on his project. He began by sitting at his desk and making a list of everything he needed to do to finish the assignment. Next to each item, Tyrel wrote the time each task would take. Then he gathered all the materials he would use for the project. For the next few hours, he stuck to his plan. Each time he completed a task, Tyrel checked it off. When he finished several hours later, Tyrel was satisfied he had done the best he could do. Two days later, his teacher gave out the grades. Tyrel wasn't at all surprised that he earned an A. After all, that had been his goal, and he had worked hard to achieve it. He had planned his success and succeeded.

Last year I was presenting my "Raising Successful Kids" workshop near my hometown of Palm Springs, California, and was dumfounded to see one particular father in the audience. There were two reasons I was surprised. First, the father had seven children. I was amazed he found time to be there. Second, everyone in the community knew that his kids were quite successful in school as well as in life. His children earned well-deserved academic accolades and were hardworking. They were also likable, courteous, and responsible. He raised the kind of children parents hope for. His children were solid in character, and great human beings.

I finished the session and went straight over to talk with him. "Look," I said, "You've obviously done something very right as a parent. You've raised seven children you should be enormously proud of. Do you remember anything special you did that might explain why your kids turned out so successfully?"

The father paused a minute and then explained, "Well, there is one thing I remember doing since my kids were young. Once a month, I'd ask each child, 'What goal do you have for yourself this month?' I'd try to help them think of what they wanted to achieve. Then we'd talk a few minutes about what they could do to attain it. Every few days I'd ask how they were doing and whether they needed any help. As they got older, my children started coming to tell me their goals. The little talks helped my kids stay focused on what they wanted to achieve, and usually they were successful. I guess it really helped them become self-motivated."

What valuable advice! Dozens of studies validate what the father told me: goal setting is a critical success skill. He also proved how easy goal setting is to teach. You can help your children learn this fundamental success skill. Teaching goal setting enhances your children's potential in every area of their lives. I know that's a big assertion, but that's how important this skill is for your kids to learn.

WHAT YOU WILL LEARN IN THIS CHAPTER

Goal setting is a powerful skill that can enhance your child's chances of success in school and beyond! This chapter describes dozens of simple techniques and activities to increase this sixth success skill. Teaching your child these strategies will enhance her inner motivation, improve her personal planning skills, help her manage her time more effectively, and enhance her confidence as she sees herself as capable of achieving her goals and dreams. You'll learn how to:

- Help your child recognize where to direct his energy, and develop a clearer understanding of what he needs and wants to do to achieve success.

- Increase your child's awareness that goal setting is a valuable skill that can increase his chances of success.

- Teach your child a simple goal-setting formula so that he can learn to use the skill on his own.

- Expand your child's time management and planning skills by teaching him how to decide what's most important and to prioritize.

HOW IS YOUR CHILD DOING NOW?

The statements below describe behaviors usually displayed by children who are successful goal setters. To evaluate your child's strengths in this sixth success skill, write the number you think best represents your child's current level on the line following each statement and then add all the scores to get her total score. If your child scores 40 to 50, she's in great shape with the skill. If she scores 30 to 40, she could benefit from skill enhancement. A score of 20 to 30 shows signs of potential problems. If your child scores 10 to 20, consider getting help to increase this skill.

5 = Always 4 = Frequently 3 = Sometimes 2 = Rarely 1 = Never

A child with strong goal-setting traits:	My child
Easily develops a start-to-finish plan for completing a project.	_____
Recognizes where to direct her energy in a project.	_____
Is able to name the steps needed to complete a task.	_____
Can say what she wants to achieve or improve.	_____
Once she sets a goal, she sticks to it until she succeeds.	_____
Is self-motivated and wants to "keep trying" on her own.	_____
Can prioritize what is important to do when completing a project.	_____
Can answer, "What do I want to do now?"	_____
Sets realistic time lines for completing what she wants to achieve.	_____
Can break down tasks into smaller parts.	_____
Total Score	_____

FOUR STEPS TO ENHANCING GOAL SETTING

There are four steps to helping children become successful goal setters. The first step is perhaps the most important lesson of all: explaining to your child why goal setting is useful. The second step is to guide him in pinpointing what he wants to do and where he wants to go, so that he is clearly focused on his objectives. The third step helps your child learn skills to plan how he will successfully achieve his goals. The more specific his plans, the greater his chances of success will be. The final step is to celebrate your child's goal successes. Whether the success is big or small, each achieved goal is a victory that nurtures your child's self-confidence.

Step 1: Teach the Meaning and Value of Goals
Step 2: Decide on a Goal Direction
Step 3: Plan and Guide the Route to Success
Step 4: Celebrate the Arrival

SUCCESS TIP
What Research Says

Stanford professor Lewis Terman studied fifteen hundred gifted children for several decades and found that high intelligence was a poor predictor of success. Only a small portion of the highly intelligent group did succeed. What did those who succeeded have in common? They had all learned goal setting before they left high school, and regularly used the skill to help them succeed. Make a commitment to teach your child this sixth success skill and then help him practice it. Goal setting will become a habit he will use the rest of his life.

STEP 1: TEACH THE MEANING
AND VALUE OF GOALS

In our efforts to help kids learn new skills, we often overlook the most valuable lesson of all: telling them why the skill is important. Wouldn't you put more effort into learning a skill if you knew it would help in your own life? This first step helps your child recognize the merit of using goal setting, which will encourage him to incorporate the skill into his own life.

A teacher in San Diego told me how he helps his students understand the value of goal setting. One of his first assignments requires students to find newspaper or magazine articles about individuals who use goal-setting principles. Students share the articles and then hang them on a bulletin board. By the end of the week, the board is covered with goal-setting examples. He says the simple activity convinces students that the skill is important. The following week, he teaches students how to set their own goals. "Students are always more willing to try skills if they recognize they are important in real life. If I'd taught goal setting without showing my students how people benefit from the skill, they wouldn't be nearly as willing to try it. Discussing how the skill is used by successful people in the world helps my kids realize goal setting can also help them. By the end of the month, almost all my students are setting daily goals. Hopefully, they'll use the skill the rest of their lives."

The teacher's lesson was valuable: clearly he helped his students understand how goal setting enhances their success potential. It's a lesson we need to teach our own kids. Keep in mind that the easiest way for your kids to recognize the value of any skill is by telling them why you feel it's important. Your own stories about how you have successfully used goal setting are usually the lessons your kids remember most.

Four Ways to Help Children Understand the Meaning of Goals

Studies prove goal setting can help your child gain the sense of discipline it takes to stay motivated to complete the tasks he has set for himself. When he has learned the skill it shows: you'll see your child start a school project—without waiting until the last minute—and finish it. You'll find your child doing his chores—without your nagging—because he knows he has to do them in order to start on his homework. You'll see your child thinking through the jobs he needs to do for the week and making plans to complete them. You'll also see your child's confidence grow as he achieves the goals he has set for himself. These four activities are simple ways to help kids understand what goals are and why using them can enhance their chances of success.

1. **Define "goal."** One of the easiest ways to explain goals is to link the term to a sport children are familiar with, such as hockey, soccer, or football. You might say, "A goal is like a target or something you shoot for. A

football player is aiming for a touchdown. A hockey or soccer player is shooting for a goal. Goals aren't just for sports. Goals in life are something you shoot for to be more successful. People set goals for things they want to achieve or get better at. Planning what you need to work on is called goal setting. It's a skill that will help you in school, at home, with your friends, or later in your job or as an adult. It's a skill that helps you succeed."

2. Make a goal poster. Explain that goal setting is so important that your family will be learning about the skill for the next month. On large paper boldly print the word *GOAL*. Family members can decorate the poster with colorful drawings, words, and magazine cutouts of goals they would like to achieve. You might include the definition of a goal: "A goal is something you shoot for to be more successful." Hang up the poster to remind everyone of the skill's importance.

3. Talk about personal goals. To help children feel comfortable talking about goals, we parents need to share our own aspirations. You might explain, "Goals very often start as 'wishes.' If we want a wish to come true, we have to work hard to make it happen. When we decide to work on the wish and to plan how to make it come true, it's called goal setting." Then take time to share a few of your dreams and wishes.

4. Look for real goal setters. Put your family on the alert to look for real people using goal-setting principles. The sports page and front newspaper section are usually filled with examples of goal setters. Encourage your children to share their discoveries at the dinner table.

Purposefully Modeling Goal Setting

One of the easiest ways for your child to learn the skill of goal setting is to watch you model it. In fact, modeling is such a simple way to learn the skill, why not model goal setting "on purpose"? This learning technique is called purposeful modeling. All you need to remember is the simple formula for setting goals: *I will + what + when.*

Goals usually start with the words *I will* and have two parts: a *what* and a *when*. The *what* explains what you want to accomplish. The *when* tells when you intend to accomplish it. Whenever an appropriate moment arises, put your goal into the language of the goal formula and purposefully model it so that your child sees the goal formula in operation. Here are a few examples of how you can purposefully model the goal formula in real moments with your child:

- You walk into the laundry room and find it piled high with dirty laundry. It's a perfect opportunity to model the goal formula. Tell what you hope to do, using goal language to your child: "I will get these clothes washed and dried by three o'clock."

  what = washing and drying the clothes + *when* = by three o'clock

- Explain a goal you've planned to achieve that day: "I will call Sally and thank her for taking you home, the minute I get to the office."

  what = call Sally to thank her + *when* = as soon as I get to the office

- A shopping outing can be a perfect opportunity to teach children long-range planning. You might use an example of something you're saving for. "We need a new refrigerator. I will start saving money each week so that we can afford one by February."

    what = saving for a new refrigerator + *when* = by February

SUCCESS TIP
Reading About Goal-Setting Characters

Books can be a wonderful tool to help your child understand goal setting. It's also a great way to review the goal formula: I will + what + when. The Resources for Further Action at the end of this chapter include several selections. As you read about goal-setting characters, ask your child a few of these questions to help spark great discussions about the value of using the goal formula.

"What was the character's goal? What was he shooting for?"

"When did he want to achieve it?"

"What did he do to solve any problems that might have stopped him from reaching his goal?"

"Pretend you're the character. Say your goal using the goal formula: I will + what + when."

STEP 2: DECIDE ON A GOAL DIRECTION

Would you ever begin a long journey by just getting in your car, closing the door, and driving off into the unknown? The majority of us would answer, "Of course not!" Without knowing where we're going, we would probably spend hours wandering around or even get hopelessly lost. Usually we plan how to get to our destination. Goal setting works with the same premise.

Goal setting is like planning a road trip: first you plot the places you'll go on a map to help you chart your course, step by step. The clearer our children are about what they want to do and where they want to go, the greater their chances of achieving their dreams. Goals are like a compass. They help steer you in the right direction and keep you on the path pointed toward success. The word *compass* will help you remember seven key questions to help your child map an effective goal course.

C—Clear	Can my child clearly picture exactly what he wants to accomplish?
O—Owned	Is this something my child really wants to "own" and take responsibility for achieving?
M—Measurable	How will my child measure his progress and success?
P—Positive	Will this plan help my child and others grow positively?
A—Achievable	Can my child actually achieve this now?
S—Specific	Can my child explain the specifics of his plan to someone else?
S—Sensible	Does it make sense to do this?

Three Ways to Help Children Create Their Own Goals

Children are empowered when they recognize the control they have over creating their own successes. These three activities nurture "I did it" feelings in your child by helping her learn to turn her dreams into goals.

1. **A dream list of goal possibilities.** Tell your child that goals start with dreams. You might say, "Dreams are something you wish would happen. Goals are something you make happen." Provide paper and colored marking pens for each family member. Take turns writing or drawing dreams of what they wish they could achieve or have or improve. Reread the list and help your child select only a dream that he can turn into a reality through his own effort. Ask family members to circle the one dream they care the most about.

2. **Dream clouds.** Encourage a younger child to draw her goal choice from the last activity on large white paper. Cut the drawing into a big cloud shape and glue on a few cotton balls for fun. Hang the cloud on the ceiling over her bed to keep her dreams alive.

3. **"You're in the driver's seat."** Remind your child that goals must be those he can personally command. You might say, "Remember, you're in the driver's seat, and you have to steer yourself to success. Nobody else should take over the wheel and drive for you." If your child chooses an unrealistic goal he cannot personally control, ask, "Do you have power over that? A goal must be something you can control yourself. Let's think of another one."

SUCCESS TIP
Fifteen Goal-Setting Possibilities

Help your child recognize that goal possibilities are endless. Here are fifteen categories of goals for children to consider.

Grades	Free time	Reading
Hobbies or interests	Savings	Behavior
Friends	Sports	New skills
Exercise	Homework	Chores
TV viewing	School	New learning

Four Ways to Help Your Children Write Goals

Once your children have chosen realistic goals toward which they are willing to work, help them put their goals in writing. Take a minute to quickly review the goal formula, I will + what + when, with your children. You might want to write the formula on a large piece of paper and post it on the refrigerator as a reminder. You are now ready to teach your children how to write their goals using the goal formula.

1. **Goal formula strips.** Cut a 3" × 12" paper strip for each child (longer for younger kids). Fold the strip into three even sections. In the first section, boldly print the words *I will*. In the middle section print *what*, and in the final section print *when*. Now help your child set a goal using the goal

formula. First ask, "What do you want to have, be, or do?" Help your child print or draw his goal in the middle section. Now ask, "When will you try to reach your goal?" In the last section of the strip, write or draw when your child hopes to accomplish the goal. Help him reread his goal and hang it in a special place. Here are a few examples using the goal formula:

"I will get eight out of ten spelling words right on my spelling test."
"I will be one pound lighter on Tuesday."
"I will learn five math facts in fifteen minutes."
"I will read ten pages in thirty minutes."
"I will clean my room in forty-five minutes."
"I will do twenty-five sit-ups in one minute."

2. **Goal picture reminder.** Tell your child the old proverb, A picture is worth a thousand words. Explain that the more we see our goal, the more we'll remember to work toward achieving it. Help your child write or draw his goal using the goal formula on several index cards. Tape the cards in special visible places around the house, such as on the refrigerator, at his desk, on the bathroom mirror, on his bed, and even on the ceiling. Have fun and be creative.

3. **Twenty-one days of sunshine.** Help your child stay focused on the same goals for at least twenty-one days. Research says it generally takes at least three weeks for new skills or behaviors to be learned. On the first day, provide drawing paper and yellow, orange, or red marking pens or crayons. Tell your child to draw a four- or five-inch circle—a "sun"—in the middle of the paper. Ask your child to close her eyes and picture herself as if she had already achieved the goal. Tell her to draw that picture inside the sun to remind her of what the success will look like. Help her write or dictate her goal using the goal formula, "I will + what + when," somewhere on the paper. Hang it up in a special place.

Each day your child makes an effort toward achieving her goal, add a sun ray on the paper—a line from the circle toward the edge of the paper. Explain, "The more you try to succeed at your goal, the brighter the sun will shine!" At the end of twenty-one days, the sun should have at least twenty-one sun rays, and your child should be much closer to reaching her goal.

4. **Set monthly family goals.** One parent told me a wonderful way her family learned the goal-setting formula. On the first day of each month, the family members hold a goal-setting session and share their goal dreams. Each member selects one goal and writes his goal using the goal formula: I will + what + when. They post their goals on the refrigerator with magnets. The mother says that the goals are almost always attained, because all month long the family members work on them and keep encouraging one another to succeed.

 SUCCESS TIP
Helping First-Time Goal Setters

First-time goal setters need to see some immediate success. Have your child set a goal that can be achieved within no longer than a week. Here are a few goals children can achieve in a short time: finishing a simple school project, reading a book, losing one pound, writing thank-you notes, cleaning a closet, raking the leaves on the front lawn, and learning how to address an envelope. Some children need to set even shorter goals: ones that can be achieved by the end of the hour or the day. Set the amount of time allowed to correspond to what you think your child needs to succeed.

STEP 3: PLAN AND GUIDE
THE ROUTE TO SUCCESS

One of our most important tasks as parents is to help our children become self-motivated. Although we may relish the role of cheering our kids on to success, in the end our kids have to be their own cheerleaders and learn to motivate themselves in life. Goal setting helps children put their energy into what they want to achieve and keeps them focused until they are successful. Once our children learn how to choose what it is they want to achieve and recognize how to write down specific plans to make their goals possible, their lifelong journey toward success is far more likely.

How can we encourage children to respond to an inner drive rather than depend on external rewards? The easiest way to self-motivation I know is through goal setting. These next activities help children learn one of the greatest secrets of success: how to plan their route to accomplishment. You'll find simple ways to help your child develop successful goal-setting techniques and develop strategies to make his dreams come true.

Helping Kids Set Goals Using the Goal Formula

Nine-year-old Tyler looked so discouraged. His soccer game was over, and again he had sat on the sidelines most of the game. His dad tried to comfort him: "Tough luck, Tyler. I know you wanted to play more. Everybody can't play all the time. I bet you'll play next Saturday." Tyler just shrugged his shoulders and quietly said, "I don't think so, Dad. I'm just not a good enough player."

All the way home, Tyler's dad kept thinking about what his son had just said. Deep down he knew Tyler was probably right. Chances were that he wouldn't play much in the next game. It wasn't because Tyler didn't have the ability—he really was a pretty good little athlete. He just didn't practice enough. Looking in his rearview mirror, Tyler's dad saw that his son was still pretty upset. He decided this was a good time to help Tyler set a goal to improve his soccer skills.

Tyler's dad recognized that his son was motivated to improve his soccer skills. He also knew his son needed to develop a plan so that he would know exactly what to do to be a better player—and the more specific the better. Here's how Tyler's dad used the goal-setting formula to help his son work out the steps to becoming an improved soccer player.

Dad: *Tyler, you had a discouraging day. What do you want to do to make things better?*

Tyler: *I want to be a better soccer player. Then the coach would let me play more.*

Dad: *OK, being a better soccer player is your goal. Let's figure out what you can do to improve your playing skills. Goals usually start with "I will," then tell what it is you want to do and when you'll do it. Let's start having you think of what you could do to be a better player.*

Tyler: *Well, I could practice kicking every day with you. Maybe I could ask the coach for extra help at each practice. I could also practice with a friend or by myself in the backyard every day.*

Dad: *Those are all great ideas, Tyler. Doing them would improve your game. From everything you said, what are you willing to do so you succeed? To make a goal, start by saying "I will," and then say what you'll do.*

Tyler: *I will practice kicking ten minutes every day with you and ten minutes by myself.*

Dad: *Super! When will you start working on your goal?*

Tyler: *I'll start tonight and keep going until the season is over.*

Dad: *That sounds good, Tyler! Let's write your goal on paper and hang it on the refrigerator to remind you of your plan. What will your goal say?*

Tyler: *I will become a better soccer player by practicing kicking ten minutes with Dad and another ten minutes by myself, starting tonight until the season ends.*

Dad: *Tyler, it seems like a great plan. Why don't you make a pledge to your goal by signing the paper. If you stick to your plan, Tyler, I know you'll be a better player.*

Tyler now had a specific plan for improving his skills that fit the goal formula. He knew *what* it was he wanted to do: "I will become a better soccer player by practicing kicking ten minutes with Dad and another ten minutes by myself." He also identified *when* he would start working on the goal: "starting tonight until the season ends."

Each night Tyler's dad helped his son practice kicking, and every day Tyler practiced dribbling, kicking, and running on his own. Progress was slow at first, but Tyler's dad kept reminding him to expect that. Any time he saw any improvements in his son's skills—however small—he pointed them out. Tyler didn't play the next three games, but his dad told him that learning new skills usually takes at least three weeks of steady practice. All the practicing finally paid off: at the fourth game, Tyler played so well his coach told him he would be playing in all the remaining games. The smile on Tyler's face was all his dad needed to see that the goal setting had really paid off.

 SUCCESS TIP
Making Sure the Goal Is Achievable

The trick is to choose goals that are challenging but still within your child's reach! These three questions help you determine if the goal is achievable for your child:

1. Does my child have the necessary skills and knowledge to achieve the goal?
2. Does my child need much help from others to succeed at the goal?
3. Does my child have enough time to achieve the goal?

If you answered no to any of the three questions, you might want to help your child choose another goal. Remember: the goal must be within your child's ability and should always be realistic.

Four Ideas to Help Kids Plan Their Goals

The more your child can think through her goal and identify what she needs to do to achieve success, the greater the chance she will succeed. These four ideas help children learn to plan the steps they need to take to achieve their goals.

1. **Identifying the first step.** Give your child a large piece of paper and help him trace around his shoe with a crayon or marking pen. Help him cut out the shoe shape. Then ask, "What's the first step you'll need to take to get started on your goal?" Help your child identify the first step and then draw or write the plan inside the shape. Continue helping your child as he writes the next step—and the next and the next—to be successful with his goal.

2. **Listing what needs to be done.** Achieving goals sometimes seems overwhelming. Listing what needs to be done in a sensible order makes goals more manageable. Here's how to help your child learn this planning skill. Provide several paper strips cut into 1" × 8" lengths. Ask, "What are all the things you need to do to achieve your goal?" Help your child write or draw a different task on each strip. When finished, reread the tasks and put them in order, asking, "What should you do first . . . , second . . . , third . . . ?" Keep arranging the strips in sequence, then staple the packet together. Encourage your child to use the packet as she works on her goal. Each time a task is finished, your child tears off a strip until no more remain!

3. **Gathering your resources.** Fold a piece of paper in half. On the top of one side, write *People,* and on the top of the other side, write *Things.* Ask your child, "Who or what do you need to help you succeed in your goal?" Help your child list all the needed resources under the correct category. Suppose your child wants to increase his running time. On the People side, he might list a coach to talk to about running techniques, his dad to help him practice running, and his mom to drive him to the track. On the Things side he might include an alarm clock to remind him to wake up earlier to get to the track, a stopwatch to time himself, and graph paper to list his running times. Encourage him to hang up the page to remember his plan.

4. **Tracking progress.** Write your child's goal on paper and tack it up on the refrigerator or bulletin board. Tell your child that each time she works toward her goals, you will mark the effort on the paper. Stickers or gummed stars are always colorful incentives for younger children to stick

onto the page to mark their progress. Point out the improvements and say, "Look how much closer you're getting to your goal!" Helping our kids see their progress motivates them to keep on trying.

STEP 4: CELEBRATE THE ARRIVAL!

Nothing is more affirming to children than succeeding at goals they have worked hard to achieve. Goal victories, large or small, deserve celebrating. A celebration is the tangible proof your child interprets as, "I really did it!" It is also one of the greatest ways to nurture your child's self-confidence. When your child achieves her goal, celebrate it as a family. Then help your child set the next goal and the next and the next.

Four Ways to Help Validate Children's Goal Successes

Here are four ideas to help your family celebrate your child's goal successes. Enjoy them: you've worked hard to help your child earn her victories.

1. **Victory log.** Give your child a small notebook or journal. You might wish to write your child's name and glue his photograph on the cover. Explain that the journal will be a victory log. Each time your child achieves a goal, describe and date the success on a page. Be sure to update the log at least every few weeks. The book can become a priceless record of special achievements.

2. **Photo success image.** Photograph your child achieving her goal and frame it. If you don't have a camera handy, you and your child can still draw the moment of success. Put the framed image in a special place, such as next to her bed or right on the coffee table, to constantly remind your child, "You did it!" Change the photo or drawing as your child achieves new goal successes. Glue older photographs in a photo album created just for preserving memories of special family goal victories.

3. **Balloon pop.** Take a dollar bill or a picture of an inexpensive prize and help your child tightly roll and insert it inside a large party balloon. Blow up the balloon and knot the end. On the outside of the balloon, use

a black laundry pen to write or draw a goal your child wants to achieve. Tie string to the end and hang the balloon in a special place. Tell your child that the moment he achieves the goal, you will pop the balloon together. The prize inside will be his reward for his hard work. In the meantime, the blown balloon serves as a reminder to work hard at the goal.

4. **Victory dinner.** Here's the opportunity to take out your best dishes, dress up, and honor your child's goal achievement. Cook your child's favorite dinner, hang up balloons, and invite special guests. It's time for a deserved family victory dinner.

WHAT ONE PARENT DID

Luis was a fourth-grade boy who was failing in history and reading. His teacher explained to his mom that the child had the ability to get better grades but never finished his assignments. That night his mom helped Luis develop a goal to complete his homework on time. They decided to do three things: each night he would do his homework at the same time, he would always list his homework tasks, and his mom would help him track any signs of progress. His mom also kept a supply of long, narrow note paper on his desk for him to list the steps he needed to finish his project.

His mother said the results were amazing. The regular homework hours gave her son consistency, listing and checking off each completed assignment enhanced his confidence, and tracking his progress increased his motivation. Within a few months, her son's grades improved. When his teacher asked him what he was doing differently, he explained, "Writing down and checking off my assignments. It helps me see what I'm supposed to do."

FINAL THOUGHTS ON ENHANCING CHILDREN'S GOAL-SETTING SKILLS

One of our most important parenting tasks is helping our children become competent, self-sufficient human beings. Although we may love encouraging and guiding our children, in the end we want them to walk away capable of directing, guiding, and encouraging themselves. One of the most important reasons why we should teach goal setting is that it helps our kids become self-motivated. They will rely on themselves to direct their lives, instead of waiting for us to nag them or cheer them on.

Goal setting gives our children's lives a sense of direction; it teaches kids how to choose what they want to achieve. Goal setting enhances our children's planning skills; it helps children discover how to write down specific plans, list steps and needed resources, and decide on their priorities. Goal setting helps our kids develop resourcefulness; it helps them learn to anticipate and deal with possible obstacles. Goals help guide children toward success. As our children continue to succeed in reaching their goals, they come to see themselves as individuals capable of achieving their dreams. The steps they've learned in this sixth success skill help our kids learn how to work toward making their dreams come true.

POINTS TO REMEMBER

- Begin with the easiest goal to tackle so that your child experiences more immediate success. Select only one or two goals to work on at once: working on too many goals scatters your child's efforts and can lead to disappointment.

- Help your child list the steps to achieve the goal, then set the time length of the goal according to the time you think the child needs to achieve the goal.

- Encourage your child to name reasons why he wants to achieve the goal. Make sure your child can clearly describe the goal and tell exactly what he wants to achieve.

- Never compare your child's goal progress with the performance of others.

- Show your pride not only for an accomplished goal but also for the effort your child took to achieve it.

RESOURCES FOR FURTHER ACTION

For Parents

Kids Are Worth It! Giving Your Child the Gift of Inner Discipline, by Barbara Coloroso (New York: Morrow, 1994). A wonderful resource of parenting ideas to enhance internal motivation and create a nurturing home.

The Optimistic Child, by Martin P. Seligman (Boston: Houghton Mifflin, 1995). This book covers many important parenting premises, but the goal-setting section on pages 251–255 is particularly helpful in teaching this sixth success skill.

Punished by Rewards, by Alfie Kohn (Boston: Houghton Mifflin, 1993). Argues against raising kids on rewards and shows how it robs them of opportunities to develop strong inner motivation.

For Children Ages Three to Seven

Applemando's Dreams, by Patricia Polacco (New York: Philomel Books, 1991). Because Applemando spends his time dreaming, the villagers are convinced that he will never amount to much. In time, his dreams change the village and all the people in it.

Flight, by Robert Burleigh (New York: Philomel Books, 1991). This picture book, based on Lindberg's actual diary, describes how Lindberg set his goal to be the first human to fly solo across the Atlantic and achieved his dream.

Follow the Dream, by Peter Sis (New York: Knopf, 1991). This beautifully illustrated picture book describes the dreams, goals, and adventures of Christopher Columbus.

Someday, by Charlotte Zolotow (New York: HarperCollins, 1965). The young heroine of this tale knows that some dreams are just dreams. She also knows there are some dreams that do become realities.

For Children Ages Eight to Twelve

Dreams into Deeds: Nine Women Who Dared, by Linda Peavy (New York: Scribner, 1985). This is a collection of short biographical sketches of a few powerful women who dreamed and then acted to make their dreams become realities.

Greg Louganis: Diving for Gold, by Joyce Milton (New York: Random House, 1989). A biography of a champion diver whose goals helped him win more titles, including several Olympic medals, than anyone in diving history.

I Have a Dream, by Margaret Davidson (New York: Scholastic, 1986). The story of Martin Luther King Jr., his dream of racial equality, and his quest to fulfill his goal.

A Jar of Dreams, by Yoshiko Uchida (New York: Aladdin, 1981). Here is the first of three novels about an eleven-year-old Japanese-American girl who feels alienated because of her cultural differences.

To Space and Back, by Sally Ride and Susan Okie (New York: Lothrop, Lee & Shepard, 1986). Ride's goal was to be not only an astronaut but also the first woman in space. She achieved both her dreams.

Videos for Family Viewing

Clowning Around (Public Media Video, 1992). Sim is given up by his mother at the age of five and lives in and out of institutions and foster homes. His dream is to become a clown. The makeup and the clowning around help him cover up his lonely self and gain friends.

Cool Runnings (Walt Disney Home Video, 1993). Based on the true story of the members of the Jamaican bobsled team, who set their goal to compete in the 1988 Winter Olympics despite the fact that they had never seen snow, let alone a bobsled! Great display of goal setting, persistence, and getting along. (PG)

Hoosiers (Live Entertainment, 1986). An ex-alcoholic, has-been coach is given a last chance to coach a small-town Indiana high school basketball team in the 1950s; he gets the team to the state championship. Persistence, goal setting, getting along, communicating, and self-esteem are all addressed. For older children. (PG)

Iron Will (Walt Disney Home Video, 1994). The story of a boy who enters an arduous dogsled race between Winnipeg, Manitoba, and St. Paul, Minnesota, in the winter of 1917. The prize is $10,000, but the race is really about goal setting, perseverance, courage, and caring. Watch it with kids ten years and older. (PG)

The Karate Kid (RCA Home Video, 1984). I still love watching this with my kids! An elderly Japanese man, Miyagi, becomes the mentor to a great boy who has just arrived in a new school and faces a group of arrogant, unkind kids. Miyagi helps the boy slowly reach his dream of becoming a martial arts expert. (PG)

The Right Stuff (Warner Home Video, 1983). The true story of America's first astronauts and their quest to fly. Open up your encyclopedias and show your children the real astronauts. (PG)

Rudy (Columbia Tristar Home Video, 1992). Based on a true story of a working-class boy whose goal is to play football at Notre Dame despite his mediocre academic record and athletic ability. He makes it! (PG)

Not Giving Up

Encouraging Perseverance

Seven-year-old Kisha sits at the side of the pool watching her friends dive glee-fully off the board into the water. Each time they swim up from the water, they encourage Kisha to jump in and join them. They had all been in swimming classes together, so they know she can swim. "Come on! Just jump, Kisha!" they yell. Kisha shakes her head and points to her foot; "I can't," she says. "My foot hurts." The other girls shrug their shoulders and dive back in the water. They know Kisha's foot is just fine. It's just another one of her excuses not to try something she doesn't feel she can do well. After a while, Kisha gets up and walks home. She tells her mom, "The girls were so mean again. They never want to play with me." Kisha's mother sighs. She had heard her daughter tell the same story so many times. She wonders if Kisha will ever change.

Eight-year-old Alfredo stands watching the other boys jump off the curb on their skateboards. He's never been on a board, but he wants so badly to skate. One of the kids sees him staring and calls out, "Hey, Alfredo! Want to use my board awhile?" Alfredo doesn't hesitate a second. "Sure!" he yells back. "Thanks! Can you teach me how?" *Alfredo knows skateboarding isn't easy. He figures he'll probably fall, but he doesn't care. He wants to learn to skateboard, and he knows from experience that learning something new is tough at first. He has made up his mind that if he's going to learn, he'll just have to keep trying and not give up! By the end of the day, Alfredo is jumping off the curb like the rest of the guys, and he's already planning how to save his allowance to buy his own skateboard.*

Kisha and Alfredo deal with new experiences very differently. Kisha tends to avoid difficult tasks whenever possible. Long ago Kisha developed the perception that if she fails, others will think less of her. Failing experiences also make her think less of herself. She has decided that it's just easier not to try. That way she won't have to deal with another defeat. It would just add to the negative image she has developed about herself.

Alfredo handles challenges differently. He knows that learning something new isn't always easy. He recognizes that he will probably have a few setbacks along the way, but that's just the way it is when you try new things. After all, he feels, the only way to get better at anything is by trying.

It is rather easy to predict which child will be more successful in meeting life's challenges. Alfredo has developed an inner strength and stamina to hang tough through trying times. That attitude will help him through all sorts of ups and downs in childhood as well as adulthood. His accomplishments will steadily grow, because he's willing to try new tasks and stick with them until he succeeds. His self-confidence will continue to blossom simply because Alfredo knows he can survive setbacks. Sadly, chances are that Kisha's successes will be limited, largely because of her tendency to give up on a task at the first sign of difficulty. Unless she learns to develop a "never give up" attitude, she will be plagued with self-doubts. She also will be deprived of experiencing the exhilarating feeling that comes only after you try: "I did it!"

Perseverance often makes the critical difference between whether children succeed or fail. The old proverb "Always at it wins the day" is a telling example of how important the seventh success skill, perseverance, can be in our children's lives. It isn't just the effort kids put into learning new things but often their "stick-to-itiveness" that matters most. If our children are to survive and succeed in this competitive world, they must learn to hang in there, especially in challenging times, and not quit.

WHAT YOU WILL LEARN IN THIS CHAPTER

This seventh skill teaches children how to stick with a task *despite difficulty,* cope with setbacks that sometimes happen along the way, and recognize that hard work and an "I won't give up" attitude are the best determinants of success—both in school and beyond. You'll learn how to:

- Increase your child's potential for achieving success by learning techniques to help her cope with mistakes and see them not as signs of failure but as opportunities to try again.

- Increase your child's awareness that a large part of success depends on how much personal effort she is willing to put into the task.

- Teach your child affirmations to say to herself to rebound from defeat, expand her inner strength, and rebuild her confidence.

- Respond noncritically when your child fails so that she'll be more willing to try again.

HOW IS YOUR CHILD DOING NOW?

The statements below describe behaviors usually displayed by children who have developed a strong "never give up!" attitude. To evaluate your child's strengths in this seventh success skill, write the number you think best represents your child's current level on the line following each statement and then add all the scores to get his total score. If your child scores 40 to 50, he's in great shape with the skill. If he scores 30 to 40, he could benefit from skill enhancement. A score of 20 to 30 shows signs of potential problems. If your child scores 10 to 20, consider getting help to increase this skill.

5 = Always 4 = Frequently 3 = Sometimes 2 = Rarely 1 = Never

A child with a strong "never give up" attitude:　　　　**My child**

Willingly tries new tasks with little concern about whether
　　he will fail or make a mistake.　　　　_____

Rarely gets discouraged when he faces difficulties or
　　setbacks.　　　　_____

Needs little encouragement to complete a challenging task.　_____

Rarely becomes defensive or blames others when he errs.　_____

Is willing to try again if he is not successful with a task.　_____

Recognizes that the way to improve is by working harder.　_____

Rarely says negative self-comments when he falls short
　　of success.　　　　_____

Is not devastated if he isn't successful or doesn't get the
　　highest grade.　　　　_____

Does not become overly frustrated when something
　　becomes difficult.　　　　_____

If a task becomes too difficult, he rarely quits but instead
　　keeps trying.　　　　_____

　　　　　　　　　　Total Score　_____

THREE STEPS TO ENHANCING
PERSEVERANCE IN YOUR CHILD

There are three steps to helping children develop perseverance and stick-to-itiveness. The first step is one of the most critical lessons of success: helping your child recognize that a large part of succeeding is a matter of how much effort she chooses to put into her work. The second step helps her deal with mistakes by teaching her that everyone makes them—they are a part of learning. The final step increases your child's likelihood of achieving success by teaching her how to bounce back and not let setbacks get her down. These are the three steps your child needs to handle life's ups and downs for the rest of her life! Learning these steps expands your child's inner strength and stamina and enhances the seventh success skill—not giving up!

Step 1: Teach Your Child to Value Effort
Step 2: Erase the Idea That Mistakes Are Bad
Step 3: Teach Your Child to Bounce Back

STEP 1: TEACH YOUR CHILD TO VALUE EFFORT

This first step helps children recognize that a large part of success is controllable: it is a matter of how much personal effort and work they choose to put into a task. We can make an immense difference in our children's potential if we emphasize effort, and stress that "it's not good enough just to start; you have to finish."

One of the most fascinating recent studies on student achievement was conducted by Harold Stevenson, a professor of psychology at the University of Michigan, assisted by James Stigler. Stevenson sought to answer a question many Americans ask: "Why do Asian students do better academically than U.S. students?" Since 1979, his team of researchers conducted five intensive cross-national studies analyzing students' achievement in the United States, China, Taiwan, and Japan. After spending hundreds of hours observing students and interviewing their teachers, the researchers reached a conclusion: a critical key lies in what parents emphasize about their children's learning. Asian parents strongly stress the value of effort. Over and again they tell their children, "Work as hard as you can, and you will be successful." By expecting their children to work hard and emphasizing the attitude that "there are no excuses for failure or poor performance—you just didn't work hard enough," Asian parents nurture perseverance in their children. And the parents' expectations had a remarkable effect on their children: the researchers found that on the whole, Asian

Parents Do Make a Difference

children worked longer and harder than their U.S. counterparts because they understood that their success was based on how hard they worked.

Instead of giving priority to how much effort children put into their learning attempts, U.S. parents put emphasis on "So what grade did you get?" or "How many did you miss?" or "Did you win?" For parents in the United States, the effort a child puts into the process is not nearly as important as the end product—the grade or score. Stevenson also found that U.S. parents place a greater emphasis on their children's innate abilities. They tend to lower their academic expectations for their children if they perceive them to have lower academic abilities. An Asian parent's philosophy is different: any child can succeed regardless of his IQ score or handicap—success is all a matter of how hard he is willing to work.

Just think for a minute about the long-term effect that stressing effort could have on our children! Our kids would learn from an early age that there's nothing that can stop them from succeeding if they put their heart and soul into their endeavors. They would see mistakes or failures just as temporary setbacks instead of as excuses to quit. If they just keep on trying and use their mistakes as learning clues, they will ultimately achieve their goals!

Five Ideas to Help Kids Recognize the Value of Effort

I walked into a classroom at William F. Davidson School in British Columbia and instantly knew the teacher was emphasizing perseverance. A large hand-printed sign greeted her students with Thomas Edison's quotation, "Genius is 1 percent inspiration and 99 percent perspiration." The teacher told me, "You know, I never dreamed that poster would be so effective. I put it up weeks ago and told my students that the best way to guarantee their success is by working hard and not giving up. The amazing thing is, now any time a student is frustrated with a task, I hear another student tell them, '99 percent perspiration—you can do it—don't quit!'" The teacher's method of stressing stick-to-itiveness was effective. By continually emphasizing the importance of perseverance, her students "caught" her message and incorporated it into their own lives.

SUCCESS TIP
Churchill's Most Valuable Lesson: Don't Give Up!

Many historians feel that one of Winston Churchill's greatest speeches was given at a graduation ceremony at Oxford University. England's prime minister had worked on the speech for hours. When the moment finally came, Churchill, then in his twilight years, stood up to the cheering crowd, and in a strong, clear voice shouted just three words, "Never give up!" He paused a few seconds and shouted the words again, "Never give up!" He then reached for his hat and slowly walked off the podium, satisfied that he had told the graduates the most important message they would ever need to succeed.

We need to make sure we pass on Churchill's message to our own children. Also be sure to tell your child that Churchill, one of the greatest leaders of the twentieth century, failed sixth grade, had a severe lisp, was hyperactive, and twice failed the entrance exam for the military academy. Only when children realize that success comes from hard work and not giving up until their goal is reached will they be the best they can be.

The following techniques are designed to help your child understand how critical perseverance is to achieving success. Like the teacher's technique, these ideas are simple and best mastered if you constantly reinforce the ideas for least three weeks.

1. **Define "perseverance."** Take time to explain that perseverance means "not giving up" or "hanging in there until you complete the task you started." Now use the word *perseverance* frequently to help your child understand how important the trait is in her life. When your child sticks to a task, point it out: "There's perseverance for you. You hung in there with your work even though it was hard." Make perseverance your family theme for the month.

2. **Teach "don't give up" words.** Help your child tune into the language of persevering individuals so that he can learn to use the terms in

his own life. Ask, "What are the kinds of things you hear people who "don't give up" say?" Write a list of phrases, such as, *I can do it! I'll try again, Don't give up! I won't quit! This is hard, but I'll keep going,* and *I'll give it the best I have.* Add the heading "Don't Give Up Words" and hang up the poster; encourage everyone to say at least one phrase a day.

3. Model effort. Take a pledge, especially this month, to show your child how you don't give up on a task even when things get difficult. Before starting a new task, make sure your child overhears you say, "I'm going to *persevere* until I am successful." Modeling the trait is always the number one teaching method, so consciously tune up perseverance in your behavior.

4. Start a family "Never Give Up!" motto. If you haven't already, begin using the family motto "Don't quit until you succeed." A father in Jackson Hole told me that conveying this life message to his children was so important that they spent an afternoon together brainstorming family anthems about perseverance, such as "Try, try, and try again and then you will win," "In this family, we finish what we start," "You'll never succeed if you give up," and "Quitters never win." They wrote them on index cards, and his kids taped them on their bedroom walls. Develop your own family anthem as a reminder that your family code of behavior is to never give up.

5. Create a "Stick to It" award. Ask your child to help you find a stick at least the length of a ruler to acknowledge stick-to-itiveness. A family in Seattle uses an old broomstick; another mother said her family uses a yardstick. Print "Stick to It Award" across the stick or dowel with a black marking pen. Now tell everyone to be on alert for family members showing special persistence for the next month. Each night have a family gathering to announce the names of family members who didn't give up, and print their initials on the stick with marking pen. Make sure to tell the recipients exactly what they did to deserve the award. Make it a family contest to see how long it takes to fill the stick with family members' initials. Children love to count how often their initials appear on the stick!

Emphasize with Children: "Try Your Hardest!"

Isidor Rabi, the prizewinning nuclear physicist, was one of the most incredible minds of our century. He grew up in Austria living an impoverished life. One of his most vivid childhood memories was of his mother. Every day when he came home from school, she always met him at the door with one question. "Son," she would say, "what good questions did you ask today?" Rabi swears that one of the greatest reasons he went on to win the Nobel Prize and other accolades was because of his mom. He explained that she was never concerned with "Did you get those answers right?" Instead she focused on "Did you try your best?" Because of her emphasis on trying, Rabi always felt capable of success—so long as he put all his efforts into his quests.

 SUCCESS TIP
Encouraging Kids to Try Their Hardest

The kinds of words we say to our children can help them learn the value of effort and get into the habit of completing what they start. Here are a few phrases you can use with your child to stress "Don't give up!"

"I know you can do it! Don't give up!"

"It's usually harder at the beginning."

"You'll get it. Keep at it!"

"Keep it up—don't stop!"

"You need to finish what you started."

"Hang in there. Don't stop!"

"Almost! Try again."

"The more you practice, the easier it will be."

"In this house, we follow through."

"The harder you try, the more successful you'll be."

STEP 2: ERASE THE IDEA THAT MISTAKES ARE BAD

Children cannot learn to persevere unless they learn how to deal with failure. Mistakes can be a chance to start over. These next activities help children understand the importance of failing and learning from mistakes. This step is so critical for success that we must purposefully set aside time to make sure our kids understand it.

I always loved waiting at the door for my kids to come home. One day was particularly memorable: one of my sons, who was in first grade at the time, walked into the house a little tenser than usual. I noticed he was hiding a crumpled paper behind his back. I greeted him with a big hug, trying to sneak a peek at the paper. "What could possibly be causing him such concern?" I wondered. I helped him take off his backpack and gently took the paper from his hands. When I uncrumpled the page, I was surprised to see the cause of his distress: he had missed five words on his spelling test. Large red check marks left by the teacher pointed out his mistakes.

I looked at the panic on his face and knew I needed to help him learn from this experience. After all, making mistakes is a part of life, and his life was just beginning. Searching for the right words, I began by saying, "Wasn't it nice that your teacher took the time to put these red check marks on your paper?" I ignored his skeptical look and kept on: "You know it takes a lot of time checking work to let you know which words you missed. Your teacher must care a lot about you." The look in my son's eyes clearly told me he couldn't believe what I was telling him, but I continued. "You do know why your teacher took the time to mark those words, don't you?" I watched my child, who was obviously confused with where all this was going, slowly shake his head. "Well," I explained, "She's concerned about your learning. What she wants you to do is study the words she's marked so you won't make the same mistake the next time. Wasn't that nice?"

This was a moment parents live for. My child was really thinking about everything I had said. Then I saw the light go on—his look showed me he understood what I was trying to tell him. He nodded, gave me a quick hug, and ran to his room with his world back in control.

A few weeks later, as he was dashing off to the bus, I knew my words had stuck. He was carefully holding a package. When I asked what was in it, he excitedly explained, "It's a present for my teacher. I bought her a red pencil!" I stood there with my mouth open as he added, "Now she'll always have an extra one to mark my mistakes. That way I'll never make the same ones again!"

As he hurried to get on the bus, I stood there amazed that my little lesson had worked. And then a staggering thought hit me: What if I had never told him that mistakes can help him learn? How long would it have taken for him to figure it out himself?

How often we assume that our kids understand so many critical skills! If we don't take the time to teach those skills, their chances of success may be greatly reduced. Stop and ask yourself, Have I taken the time to teach my child that mistakes can help her learn? If not, set aside time to ensure that your child understands this critical lesson of success.

SUCCESS TIP
A Lesson About Mistakes

I watched a teacher give a small wrapped present to each student on the first day of school. The children were amazed to find small erasers inside the boxes. The teacher told them, "You'll be needing these this year, because you'll be making lots of mistakes. That's how you learn. So whenever you make a mistake, just erase your mistake and try again. In this room, mistakes are always a chance to start over." The teacher's simple gift helped "erase" the idea that mistakes mean failure. Find time to tell your child the success lesson: mistakes don't mean failure; they are a chance to start again. It is a lesson she will use forever.

Four Ideas to Help Kids Learn That Mistakes Aren't Fatal

Making mistakes is how we learn. Making mistakes is especially how young children learn. Unfortunately, far too many kids (and grownups!) have never learned the value of making mistakes. And far too many don't realize that successful people don't let setbacks derail them: they just find new routes to success. Succeeding depends on sticking with our efforts and not letting setbacks get us down. This section helps children recognize that mistakes don't need to mean failure but instead can be learning opportunities in disguise.

1. **"It's OK to make mistakes."** The first step in helping kids realize that errors don't have to be fatal is simply to say, "It's OK to make a mistake." Whatever grade I taught, on the first day of school I always did one thing that never failed to produce amazing reactions from my students. I simply announced, "In this room, it's OK to make mistakes. Everybody makes them; after all, that's how we learn." Every year I would watch a few students literally wipe sweat from their foreheads in relief knowing I wasn't expecting them to be perfect. How sad that they thought that was what I would require! How can a child ever learn under such stress? We need to give our kids permission to fail, and help them see that mistakes can be positive learning experiences.

2. **Admit your mistakes.** Whether you're aware of it or not, your child sees you as all-powerful and all-knowing. Obviously we make mistakes, but too often we keep them to ourselves. Admit your errors to your child: it helps her recognize that mistake making happens to *everyone*. (Beware: she is also watching to see how you handle failure!)

3. **Show acceptance.** Whenever your child makes a mistake, show your support with both your words and your nonverbal reactions. The quickest way our kids will learn to erase the idea that mistakes are fatal is by experiencing our accepting responses to their errors.

4. **Tell how you learned.** When you make a mistake, tell your child not only what your error was but also what you learned from it. Suppose your dinner menu was a disaster: first, *admit the mistake* to your family (do it quickly before they let you know your error), and then say *what you learned* from your mistake. Here's how it would work: "I sure blew this recipe. I learned I should always read the whole recipe before adding the eggs." Or, "I was late for work because I couldn't find my keys. I learned I need to put my keys in the same place every time so that I can find them

when I need them." When your child makes a mistake, simply ask, "What was your mistake?" and then, "What did you learn?"

Twelve Famous People Who Succeeded Against the Odds

The world is filled with examples of individuals who suffered enormous obstacles and setbacks but didn't cave into disaster. Instead they looked at their problems as opportunities and kept striving toward their dreams until they succeeded. Their stories are wonderful evidence to your child that mistakes don't have to be devastating if she views them instead as just temporary setbacks! As you tell these mini-stories to your child, you might remind her, "These people all had setbacks in their lives. Many had trouble learning in school, but none of them used their problems as excuses to give up. They just kept trying until they succeeded. That's what success is all about—not giving up!"

Thomas Edison, the inventor of the light bulb, was told by his teacher that he was too stupid to learn anything.

Louisa May Alcott, author of *Little Women,* was turned down by countless publishers who told her no one would ever read her now classic children's book.

Charles Darwin, the famous naturalist and developer of the theory of evolution, did quite poorly in his early grades and even failed a university medical course.

Woodrow Wilson, a Rhodes scholar and president of the United States, didn't learn the alphabet until he was eight; he didn't read until he was eleven.

Wilma Rudolph contracted polio at age four, crippling her as a child. She was told she would never walk. She decided to become a runner and went on to win three Olympic gold medals and was named the "Fastest Woman in the World."

Albert Einstein did not talk until age four or read until age nine. He performed badly in almost all of his high school courses and failed his college entrance exams.

Abraham Lincoln began his service in the Blackhawk War as captain. By the end of the war he had been demoted to private.

Lucille Ball was told when she first started studying acting by an instructor to "Try any other profession. Any other."

Ludwig van Beethoven was initially told by his music teacher that he was hopeless as a composer.

Cher had learning disabilities as a child.

Michael Jordan was cut from his high school basketball team.

Walt Disney was fired by a newspaper editor for lacking great ideas. He went bankrupt several times and was told repeatedly to "get rid of the mouse because there's no potential in it."

A Lesson in Courage

I was observing a classroom for children with severe learning disabilities in Beaverton, Oregon, and was fascinated with the long strips of yarn tied to the students' chairs. The teacher, Maria Wickwire, explained that her students constantly faced difficulties in learning and in life, and she wanted to keep encouraging them never to give up. She began the yarn activity after she read the book Knots on a Counting Rope, *by Bill Martin Jr., to her class. It is the story of a young blind boy facing enormous physical obstacles (his "dark mountains"). He*

SUCCESS TIP
Discuss People Who Don't Give Up

I love to tell children—especially kids who are struggling—brief stories about famous people who succeeded against the odds, because their stories offer hope. Consider reading with your children a biography of someone who faced setbacks. Use these questions as springboards for discussing how persistence played an important part of the person's ultimate success.

"Which person persevered in the story?"
"What goal did the person want to accomplish?"
"What was the obstacle or problem the person faced?"
"What did the person do to overcome the problem?"
"What is one success tip we can learn from reading about this person's life?"

doesn't let his problems get in his way—he succeeds. The teacher told her students, "Everyone sometime in her life will face crossing a dark mountain. You may feel you're not going to make it. If you don't give up, get help if you need it, and try your best, you usually succeed." She then gave each student a piece of yarn and explained, "Every time you 'cross a dark mountain' and make it, tie another knot in the rope. They will be your knots of courage!"

I noticed that many of the students' strips of yarn were filled with knots. The students saw my curiosity and asked if I wanted to hear the stories of their "knots of courage." Did I! "This knot is because I was sick for a long time and afraid to come back to school, but I did!" one boy said triumphantly. "I had to give a speech in front of the class," one girl explained. "I hate giving speeches because I have a speech problem. I gave it, though," she added, proudly touching her knot. "I tied this one," said a darling red-haired child, "because I just moved here. I didn't know anybody, so they let me tie it because I made some new friends."

One by one the students explained the dark mountains they had overcome. As they touched their knots, what struck me was how their faces radiated such pride. Maria Wickwire's lesson had stuck with these kids: dark

180   *Parents Do Make a Difference*

mountains do take courage to cross, but if you persist, you will make it. Your reward is knowing you did it all by yourself. This is a lesson we need our children to know well, so that they can be the best they can be.

SUCCESS TIP
Encourage Trying Something New

Read the book *Knots on a Counting Rope,* by Bill Martin Jr., to your family and enjoy its valuable message about not giving up. Give each child her own piece of rug yarn (about a yard long) with which to tie knots whenever she "crosses her own dark mountains." Remind her that it takes courage to try something she doesn't feel confident doing. Stand by to support her triumphs—as well as her losses—they are all part of growing up.

STEP 3: TEACH YOUR CHILD TO BOUNCE BACK

All children make mistakes. The difference between successful and unsuccessful kids lies in how they view their mistakes. When a successful child makes an error, he sees the event as the problem, not himself, so he picks himself up and tries again. When an unsuccessful child makes an error, he frequently views himself as the mistake, and his confidence to try again is curtailed. "Why bother?" he tells himself. "I'll probably just fail again." This third step helps our children learn how to handle failure constructively and to rebound from errors, thus increasing their opportunities to succeed.

My son Zach's kindergarten teacher had a simple way of helping her students bounce back from mistakes. Whenever a child made an error in her classroom, she taught them to say, "That's OK. After all, nobody's perfect." I knew it was effective when one weekend I was playing with Zach and accidentally spilled a tray filled with beads. Zach didn't miss a beat. He ran over and put his hand on my shoulder, and in his most reassuring five-year-old voice he said, "That's OK, Mom. After all, even you aren't perfect."

What Zach taught himself to say whenever he made a mistake—"That's OK. After all, nobody's perfect"—is called an affirmation. Affirmations are simple, positive statements you learn to purposely say to yourself to build confidence. Children can learn to use them to bounce back from adversity. In his book *Positive Self-Talk for Children,* Douglas Bloch says that to be most effective, the affirmation must be practiced over and over. The simplest way for your child to learn the affirmation is by hearing you use it. Start saying the statement out loud whenever you've made a mistake, making sure your child can overhear it. After a while your child will begin saying the phrase inside his head and replacing the negative, defeating messages he may have said instead.

How to Respond When Children Fail

Many children cut short their opportunities for success because they give up at the first sign of difficulty. If they see errors as indications that they are failures, eventually they are likely to stop trying. The Tender Loving

---

 SUCCESS TIP
Eight Affirmations to Encourage Bouncing Back

Here are eight affirmations you can teach your child to say to help her bounce back from defeat. Select one and then help your child practice saying the same affirmation out loud several times for a few days. The more often she sees and hears it, the greater the chance she will remember it. You can write it on a card so that she can carry it in her pocket, make a tape recording of the phrase to play over and over, or turn it into a song for your child to sing.

It doesn't have to be perfect.	I can learn from my mistakes.
It's OK to make a mistake.	Everybody makes mistakes.
It's just a mistake.	I can't get any better unless I try it.
I made a mistake. Now I'll correct it.	I can turn it around.

Parents Do Make a Difference

Care (TLC) way of positively responding to your children's mistakes helps them rebound from thinking they are incompetent. The strategy also helps them figure out what they can learn from their errors so that they won't make the same errors again. Both lessons will improve their chances of success.

There are three parts to the simple strategy: first, *talk* calmly and not critically to your child about something she feels is a mistake. Next, discuss with your child what she can *learn* from the mistake. Finally, *comfort* your child by reminding her that everyone makes mistakes. Here is how it works:

T—*Talk* calmly about the mistake with your child. Try not to criticize or show anger.
> Adult: *Let's talk about your spelling paper. What do you notice?*
> Child: *I missed five of my words.*

L—Ask the child to tell what he can *learn* from the mistake.
> Adult: *What can you learn from the test so that you won't make the same mistakes next time you take it?*
> Child: *I learned I need to study my words a little every night and not wait until the last minute.*

C—*Comfort* your child by reminding him that everybody makes mistakes.
> Adult: *That sounds like a great plan! Successful people look at their mistakes and figure out what they can learn from them. That's what you're doing!*

Nine Ways to Respond to Your Child's Mistake

One of the most common questions parents ask me is "What's the best way to react when my child makes a mistake?" Here are nine affirming, noncritical ways to respond to your child's error. (The most important parenting tip is the one listed ninth.)

1. Offer support only when needed—"I'm here for you if you need help"— but avoid the temptation to do the task for your child. Your child needs to build confidence that he can figure out the problem for himself.

SUCCESS TIP
The Family Babe Ruth Award

A great example of someone who built his success from his failures is Babe Ruth, one of the greatest athletes of all time. He is best known for setting a record of 714 home runs. What is not as well known is that the year he hit the most home runs was the same year he had the most strikeouts (1,330!). Start a Babe Ruth Award for the family member who attempts something new. When someone in your family takes a risk—whether she succeeds or fails—the family commemorates the attempt by writing the person's initials on an old baseball with a black marking pen. Keep the ball in a special place until it's time to honor the next risk taker. As Babe Ruth himself said, "Never let the fear of striking out get in your way."

2. Help your child see that mistakes are chances to learn. Ask, "What did you learn so that you won't make the same mistake again?"

3. Encourage your child to give it another try. You might say, "Just because it isn't easy doesn't mean you're not good at it."

4. Stay nonjudgmental and help your child focus on what she's trying to achieve. Don't criticize, but do calmly ask, "How did you want this to turn out?"

5. Help your child recognize that you believe he can succeed in his efforts. Say, "I know you can do it. Hang in there."

6. Fight the temptation to say, "I knew that would happen" or "I told you so." Jane Bluestein, author of *The Parent's Little Book of Lists: Dos and Don'ts of Effective Parenting*, recommends instead trying, "That's interesting" or "That wasn't what you had in mind, was it?"

7. Let your child watch you do the task again and again. Some children need to learn "by seeing" how to do the task correctly instead of hearing you tell them how to do it right.

8. Don't yell, shame, criticize, judge, blame, or ridicule. Nobody (especially children!) likes to make mistakes, and everybody hates to be

reminded of making them. As Bluestein points out, "There's a difference between *making* a mistake and *being* one."

9. Stay calm, stay calm, stay calm!

SUCCESS TIP
Don't Call It a Mistake!

Studies have identified a common trait of high-achieving kids: they are not thrown by errors. In fact, they often call mistakes by other names (glitch, bug, a "temporary") so that they don't discourage themselves in the middle of their learning. Help your child come up with a word to say inside his head whenever he encounters a mistake. Any word will do—just make sure to help him practice saying it over and over so that he will remember to use it when he really makes a mistake.

A teacher in Santa Barbara taught her students to call mistakes *opportunities*. The same day of her lesson I watched a child make a mistake. Instantly the student next to him leaned over and whispered, "Remember, it's an opportunity!" The smile on the child's face was all the proof I needed that the teacher's lesson had worked!

WHAT ONE PARENT DID

Math homework was becoming a nightmare for Monica's father. As soon as she saw the assignment, his daughter would do only a few problems, then quit in tears. What was especially puzzling was that Monica had always been strong in math. A conference with her teacher confirmed what he felt: "Monica is capable of doing the work," her teacher told him. "She just gives up at the first sign of difficulty."

"She never had a problem with her math homework last year," her father pointed out. "The only difference I can remember is that there weren't so many problems on the paper. I wonder if she feels overwhelmed?"

That night Monica's father tried three things to help his daughter learn not to give up. First, he set a house rule: "In this family, we finish what we start, Monica. Each day, there will be no television or phone privileges until you finish your math." Second, her father put an oven timer on her desk and set it for ten minutes. He then explained, "Keep working until the bell goes off, Monica, then you can take a break for a minute or two. You then must set the timer for another ten minutes." Her father even encouraged her to write down the number of problems she completed every ten minutes: "Make it a contest to see how many problems you can get done before the bell goes off." Finally, he took her math assignment and folded it so that only the first row of problems showed. "Start with just these, Monica. I know you can do them. When you finish that row, just unfold another row."

It took a few nights for Monica to get into the new homework routine, but by the end of the week she was working the whole ten minutes without her dad's help. She seemed to enjoy the contest of writing down how many problems she completed each time, particularly because she saw the number increasing. Her father was amazed with the results. He recognized that although Monica was a very smart little girl, she had a very short attention span. The large number of homework problems was overwhelming her, so she probably thought it easier just to quit. By breaking the assignment into "chunks" and working for shorter periods of time, Monica didn't feel quite so overwhelmed, and her confidence grew—as did her ability to persevere.

 SUCCESS TIP
Chunk It

You can use the technique Monica's father used with her when she felt overwhelmed by "all the work on a page." Section your child's homework into smaller chunks and tell her to do "one chunk at a time." She can even take a short break after completing each chunk. Chunking assignments is often helpful for kids who have difficulty sticking to a task, have shorter attention spans, or are overly concerned with making sure "everything's right." As they successfully complete a section, their confidence will increase. Gradually they'll be able to finish larger and larger "work chunks" on their own.

Parents Do Make a Difference

FINAL THOUGHTS ON ENCOURAGING PERSEVERANCE

My twelve-year-old son, his teammates, their moms, his teacher, and I were flying home from a state History Day competition, where the team had won third place. The plane was packed with other History Day school teams. Obviously, not everyone had won a medal. The plane landed, and even from inside the plane I could hear loud applause coming from the terminal. I figured it had to be a large group of parents waiting to meet the winning teams. What I saw at the end of the jetway is a sight you don't see too often: a group of parents wildly cheering their kids, *even though their children had not won*. Each parent was holding a handmade sign with a quote about the value of trying. "The reward of a thing well done is to have done it" was written on one. Another said, "You're never a loser until you quit trying." No matter what the quote, the bottom of each poster read, "I'm so proud of you!" As the parents hugged their children, they handed their signs to them. The kids took them from the parents as though the signs were gold medals.

I was absolutely mesmerized. How often do you see parents applauding their children in defeat? How often do you hear parents cheering their children for their efforts—even though they received no medals? Those parents' reaction to their children's "defeats" was the greatest success message there is: *You're a winner because you tried*. It's certainly the best example I've ever seen of what the seventh success skill, "never give up!" is really all about.

POINTS TO REMEMBER

- Make mistakes be OK in your household. Stress that everyone makes mistakes: no one is perfect. Mistakes are how we all learn.

- Emphasize again and again, "Don't worry about your mistake. Think about what you will do differently the next time."

SUCCESS TIP
Help Your Child Learn from Mistakes

Experts tell us that some children give up because they are afraid of making a mistake. Mistakes can be valuable lessons if we help kids learn from them. Once they realize mistakes don't have to be "deadly," they will be more likely to hang in there and not give up. Here is a simple strategy to help your child learn how to figure out what to do so that he won't make the same mistake again.

1. Name the mistake.
   Adult: *What was the mistake?*
   Child: *The mistake was missing the ball with my bat.*
2. Say what you plan to do "next time" to correct the mistake.
   Adult: *What will you do next time so you won't make the same mistake?*
   Child: *Next time I'm going to keep my eyes open to see the ball coming.*

- Teach your child to cope with mistakes through your example: "Wow, I sure didn't do this right. I think I'll try it again a new way." Describe how you correct your mistake.

- When your child experiences frustrations, resist the urge to step in and do the task for her. Too much rescue will not help your child learn to bounce back from setbacks.

- Whatever idea you try to help your child bounce back, remember to practice it with your child over and over again. Learning new habits takes time and much repetition, especially a habit so strong as fearing failure.

RESOURCES FOR FURTHER ACTION

For Parents

"I Think I Can, I Know I Can!" by Susan Isaacs and Wendy Ritchey (New York: St. Martin's Press, 1989). A wealth of practical ways to nurture confidence in children.

The Parent's Little Book of Lists: Dos and Don'ts of Effective Parenting, by Jane Bluestein (Deerfield Beach, Fla.: Health Communications, 1997). A gold mine for parents; it offers simple tips on ways to build successful and confident children.

Positive Self-Talk for Children, by Douglas Bloch (New York: Bantam Books, 1993). A wonderful reference on teaching self-esteem and bouncing back through the use of affirmations.

For Children Ages Three to Seven

Fortunately, by Remy Charlip (Old Tappan, N.J.: Macmillan, 1987). This is an absolute must for young readers. It's a model on changing your unfortunates and turning them into fortunates.

Horton Hatches the Egg, by Dr. Seuss (New York: Random House, 1940). This is the classic story of an elephant who is determined to keep his word—no matter what happens!

I Made a Mistake, by Miriam Nerlove (New York: Atheneum, 1985). A young child finally realizes that it's OK to make a mistake.

Knots on a Counting Rope, by Bill Martin Jr. (New York: Henry Holt, 1987). A poignant story of love, hope, and courage. A young boy faces his greatest challenge: blindness.

My Mama Says There Aren't Any Zombies, Ghosts, Vampires, Creatures, Demons, Monsters, Fiends, Goblins, or Things, by Judith Viorst (New York: Aladdin, 1988). A young boy discovers that adults—even his mother—can make mistakes.

Nobody Is Perfick, by Bernard Waber (Boston: Houghton Mifflin, 1971). A young boy finally realizes through much trial and error that nobody is "perfick," including himself!

Nobody's Perfect, Not Even My Mother, by Norma Simon (New York: Whitman, 1981). The message comes through loud and clear in this story: it's OK not to be perfect because no one is.

For Children Ages Eight to Twelve

Be a Perfect Person in Just Three Days! by Stephen Manes (New York: Bantam-Skylark, 1991). Milo finds a book at the library on "how to be the perfect person." He follows the directions carefully and finally learns the message in the end: being perfect is boring! Besides, you are already perfect just being yourself!

Comeback! Four True Stories, by Jim O'Connor (New York: Random House, 1992). Here is the tale of four famous athletes who overcame serious injuries or debilitating conditions through effort, perseverance, and a "never give up" attitude.

Dreams and Drummers, by Doris Buchanan Smith (New York: Crowell, 1978). Stephanie is a straight-A student and seems to win blue ribbons in every contest she enters. This is a story about learning what it's like to finish second.

Mistakes That Worked, by Charlotte Foltz Jones (New York: Doubleday, 1991). A collection of short stories describing more than forty inventions that were all discovered by accident, including Silly Putty, the ice cream cone, pizza, the chocolate chip cookie, Velcro, aspirin, the Frisbee, and even the X-ray.

Perfectionism: What's Bad About Being Too Good? by Miriam Adderholdt-Elliott (Minneapolis, Minn.: Free Spirit, 1987). Designed for adolescents, this book discusses the dangers of being a perfectionist and has wonderful tips on easing up on oneself, gaining control over life, and getting professional help when needed.

Videos for Family Viewing

An American Tale (MCA Home Video, 1986). Steven Spielberg's animated feature about a little mouse named Fievel, who is washed overboard on his journey from Eastern Europe to America but perseveres.

The Autobiography of Miss Jane Pittman (Prism Home Video, 1974). Cicely Tyson brilliantly portrays a young slave girl; we follow her life story until the day in 1962 when Miss Pittman courageously makes her way to a "whites only" drinking fountain at the county courthouse and takes a sip in memory of a murdered young civil rights worker. Although fictional, the account is based on real history and is heartwarming as well as disturbing. Watch it and discuss it with your kids.

Babe Ruth: The Man; the Myth, the Legend (Fries Home Video, 1989). The biography of one of baseball's all-time greats. Key in on the part in which Ruth says, "I swing with everything I've got. I hit big or I miss big," and then explain to your kids that the year Babe Ruth hit the most home runs was also the same year he had the most strikeouts.

Homeward Bound: The Incredible Journey (Walt Disney Home Video, 1993). In this film based on the 1977 book by Sheila Burnford, three beloved household pets are separated from their human family; they set out on a next to impossible journey across the Canadian wilderness to find them, and never give up until they do. There are a few scary scenes. (G)

The Journey of Natty Gann (Walt Disney Home Video, 1985). During the Great Depression of the 1930s, a young girl journeys to join her father, who is logging in the Pacific Northwest. It's a story of hope, courage, and not giving up.

Places in the Heart (CBS/Fox Video, 1984). This film features Sally Field in an Oscar-winning role as a young widow determined to survive as a cotton farmer during the Depression. (PG)

Rudy (Columbia Tristar Home Video, 1992). Based on a true story of a working-class boy whose goal is to play football at Notre Dame despite his mediocre academic record and athletic ability. He makes it! (PG)

The Sea Gypsies (Warner Home Video, 1978). A father and his daughters start on their trek of sailing around the world but must quickly learn to survive—and not give up—when they become shipwrecked in Alaska. (G)

Young Mr. Lincoln (Fox Video, 1939). Henry Fonda portrays a young Abraham Lincoln, depicting him as a highly ethical gentleman who overcame numerous obstacles before finally becoming president of the United States. (G)

Young Tom Edison (MGM/UA, 1940). The famous inventor's early life is portrayed by Mickey Rooney. Discuss with your kids the problems Edison had growing up, and how he didn't let them get in the way of his becoming one of the most prolific inventors the world has ever known. Follow this film with *Edison, the Man* (1940), in which Edison, now portrayed by Spencer Tracy, grows up passionate about completing his inventions.

Websites

"The Giraffe Project" [http://www.giraffe.org/giraffe/]. A nonprofit organization that recognizes people for sticking their necks out for the common good and not giving up. The project's "Heroes" program helps teachers and youth leaders build courage, caring, and responsibility in kids six to eighteen years old.

"Heroes" [http://myhero.com/home.asp]. A site where kids can find out about various men and women people admire as heroes. Kids can also send in text and pictures about their favorite hero—mothers, fathers, aunts, uncles, teachers, students, and historical figures—to be added to the site.

Caring

Increasing Compassion and Empathy

Harold sat at the park watching his seven-year-old son, Austin, play ball. Austin had told him so often about how mean the other kids were, Harold decided to see for himself. Suddenly, he heard kids yelling and saw that one boy had taken a spill and scraped his knee. The other boys were trying to console him while at the same time yelling at Austin. Austin, oblivious to the other boy's injury, was trying to grab the ball from the hurt child so that he could have it for himself. The father shook his head sadly. "No wonder he has problems with other kids," he said to himself. "He has no concern for anyone's feelings but his own."

Five-year-old Jeremy's eyes were glued to the television pictures showing homes destroyed by the terrible tornado. As the reporter described the devastation, the camera focused on a young child searching through his collapsed house. Jeremy watched the child pick up the remains of a worn teddy bear and squeeze it tightly. "Oh, how sad that little boy must feel," Jeremy's mom said. Her son quickly ran to his room and came back clutching his favorite stuffed bear. "Here, Mom," he said. "Send it to that little boy. He needs Old Bear more than I do." Jeremy's mom looked proudly at her son, realizing he really had listened to her little talks about people's feelings. She knew then that her son had developed the quality she felt was most important of all: a caring heart.

Today more than ever, as our children are often exposed to an unsettling world of violence, drugs, bullying, and insensitivity, we must emphasize caring behaviors. Showing concern toward others may be the antidote that will help our kids live in a more tolerant world. The eighth skill of success, caring, builds a repertoire of connection for our children. It expands their world and helps them move from an egocentric, "always thinking about myself" attitude toward being sociocentric, or showing concern for others. Caring helps sensitize our children to different points of view and increases their awareness of others' ideas and opinions. Caring enhances the trait of empathy, the foundation of moral behavior. And caring is a trait that all our children will need to live successfully in our diverse, multicultural, twenty-first century.

WHAT YOU WILL LEARN IN THIS CHAPTER

This chapter gives you the tools to enhance caring in your child. You'll find proven, simple activities to help you develop your child's caring spirit and concern for others. You'll learn how to:

- Convey to your child how much you value the trait of caring by tuning up caring behaviors at home and volunteering in your community, thus allowing him to see real examples of compassion.

- Sensitize your child to the feelings and thoughts of others and help him recognize the positive effect caring behavior can have.

- Use techniques that help your child understand the consequences of his uncaring behaviors on other people's feelings, so as to increase his empathy.

- Nurture your child's compassion by arranging ways he can do community service projects and see that caring can make a difference.

HOW IS YOUR CHILD DOING NOW?

The statements below describe behaviors usually displayed by children who have developed strong traits of compassion and caring. To evaluate your child's strengths in this eighth success skill, write the number you think best represents your child's current level on the line following each statement and then add all the scores to get her total score. If your child scores 40 to 50, she's in great shape with the skill. If she scores 30 to 40, she could benefit from skill enhancement. A score of 20 to 30 shows signs of potential problems. If your child scores 10 to 20, consider getting help to increase this skill.

5 = Always 4 = Frequently 3 = Sometimes 2 = Rarely 1 = Never

A child with strong compassion and caring:	My child
Shows concern for others when they are in distress.	_____
Says positive, caring comments that "build up" others.	_____
Acts unselfishly and shares personal possessions with others.	_____
Shows sensitivity toward the needs and feelings of others.	_____
Displays kindness to others regardless of age, culture, or gender.	_____
Shows respect toward adults and authority figures.	_____
Delights in the opportunity to serve or take care of others.	_____
Regularly sees caring behaviors through your personal example.	_____
Acts concerned when someone is treated unfairly or unkindly.	_____
Shows a willingness to understand someone else's point of view.	_____
Total Score	_____

Caring

FOUR STEPS TO ENHANCE
CARING IN YOUR CHILD

There are four steps to building caring. Each step nurtures your child's sense of caring, kindness, and decency. The first step lays the foundation for developing caring: by modeling it in your daily life, you show your child how much you value the trait. The second step is helping your child realize the consequences of uncaring behaviors and taking a family pledge to stamp out hurtful words and deeds. The next step is encouraging your child to do caring deeds and service projects to help him recognize that he can make the world a better place. The last step provides ways to enhance your child's sensitivity to other people's feelings and needs and increase empathy. The more your child practices caring behaviors, the better he will feel about himself and the better others will feel about him.

Step 1: Model Compassion
Step 2: Stamp Out Uncaring Words and Deeds
Step 3: Encourage Acts of Caring and Service
Step 4: Build Your Child's Sensitivity to Others' Feelings

STEP 1: MODEL COMPASSION

Caring is the trait that helps make the world a kinder and gentler place, and caring can be developed and improved. Wherever your children fit on the caring scale, there is always room for improvement. This first step suggests ways you can show your child how much you value caring by tuning up your caring behaviors at home, as well as by volunteering to help others in your community. After all, the best way for your child to "catch" caring behaviors is by seeing real examples—and you are your child's first and best model of compassion.

My girlfriend's son, Colby, spent most of his senior year last fall filling out college applications. One college required applicants to write a paper about a memorable moment in their life. Colby's topic choice surprised his parents because they never realized how much the event had affected their son. One Christmas holiday ten years ago, Colby's father and two other fathers decided to have their sons put together holiday baskets and deliver them to needy families. Agencies gave them the names and addresses of a few local families as well as the ages of their children. The fathers and sons spent the day gathering toys, food, and clothes and then sorting them into boxes. Later that afternoon they drove to each family's home and delivered the filled boxes. That was the moment Colby said he could never forget.

"Every family seemed so happy to receive whatever we gave them," he wrote. "A few of the parents had tears in their eyes when they saw the toys. I guess they were the only toys their kids would get for Christmas. I'll just never forget how appreciative they were. I remember I told my dad that day I didn't want to go, but I'm so glad he made me come. By watching my dad take the time to show those families somebody cared, I learned I can make a difference in somebody else's life."

Colby wasn't the only one who learned something from the experience. His dad realized for the first time how strongly his son was affected by their mission of caring. Colby taught him that the most powerful way to convey how strongly he feels about caring is by showing his family through his own example. That was the moment he made the commitment to volunteer in the Big Brothers program. And delivering food and toys to needy families is now their yearly holiday family tradition.

When our children are grown, perhaps the greatest parenting test will be to ask ourselves, Does my adult child have a kind heart as well as a strong mind? We want our children to be compassionate, considerate, and sensitive to the feelings and views of others. We want our kids to be charitable, to champion the underdog, and to volunteer willingly to help others in need. So when can we start enhancing the trait? The latest research is making a very significant point: *it is never too early—or too late—to instill in our children the value of caring.*

In the last few years, studies have clearly shown that even young children do demonstrate sympathy and caring toward others—*especially when the traits are modeled by their parents.* Researchers have proved we can instill the trait of caring in our children through our own behavior, and our efforts can be long lasting. The first step to nurturing this skill is to model compassion yourself in your home and to volunteer your time, energy, or resources to help others in need.

Point Out Caring Behaviors

One way to help your child recognize the impact of caring is to look for caring behaviors that naturally occur during the day and to point out how they affected the recipients. Soon you will find your child pointing out caring behaviors to you! Here are a few examples of how caregivers enhanced their child's awareness of the power of caring by identifying the caring deed and then pointing out how their child's action made a difference.

Situation	*The adult says . . .*
Sarah can't find her jacket. Rebecca offers to help her look for it.	"Rebecca, that was so caring when you offered to help Sarah find her jacket. She was so upset, and you really made her feel better."
Megan just helped Matt pick up his spilled crayons at day care.	"Megan, your teacher said you were so caring to Bill when you helped him pick up his crayons. He was upset and you made him feel better."
Kelly hurt her knee at the soccer game. Polly gets a bandage for her.	"Polly, what a neat way to show you care! Kelly's knee hurt a lot, but she looked so much happier when you gave the bandage."
Marcos calls a friend at home to find out why he wasn't at school.	"Marcos, you really showed your friend you cared about him when you called and asked why he wasn't at school. I bet you made his day. Nice job!"

SUCCESS TIP
"Caring People" Watch

You can do this activity any time you are with children in a place filled with people: a store, airport, park, mall, post office, school grounds. Target a specific behavior to look for: find "people who show others they care." The object is to look for the targeted behavior, watch to see what the person did to show he cared, and discuss the observations as a group. You will find your kids focusing more on caring deeds, because you are reinforcing the trait. Here are a few behaviors my kids identified on a family outing a few weekends ago:

An elderly woman found no seats on the crowded bus. A young boy quickly offered his seat.

A woman offered to help a mother carry her baby stroller to the curb when she had difficulties.

A blind man couldn't locate the button on the elevator. One of my sons pushed it for him.

Modeling Compassion Through Volunteering

Families everywhere are taking time to volunteer their energy and resources to help make our world a better place. By watching their parents' examples, kids are realizing that their parents passionately value the trait of caring and are "catching" their caring spirit. There are dozens of ways to get involved, lend a hand, volunteer, or show you care. Here are a few ideas other parents have shared with me on how they model compassion to their children:

In San Francisco a family spends a weekend each year helping paint a shelter for battered women.

In San Jose a mom and her daughters spend an hour a week making batches of peanut butter sandwiches and then deliver them to a homeless shelter.

In Denver a father and his sons deliver meals to an AIDS hospice one Sunday each month.

In Wichita a group of families collects toys, clothes, and pennies from neighbors and brings them to shelters for battered and abused children.

In Seattle a family volunteers to work Thanksgiving mornings serving meals to the homeless.

In Atlanta the children in a family send part of their weekly allowances to a six-year-old orphan in Bombay whom they are sponsoring through Save the Children.

In Palm Springs my husband and sons spend a day in October (waking up at four in the morning) helping set up a race course through our local streets. Profits from the event go to needy children.

Volunteering your time, energy, or resources is one of the best ways to convey to your kids just how strongly you feel about caring. It's wonderful to volunteer as a family, but if you can't get everybody into the volunteer spirit, begin by yourself. Then describe to your kids what you did, how you think your actions made a difference, and how volunteering made you feel.

SUCCESS TIP
Volunteering to Show Your Kids You Care

The organizations listed here are those that usually have community programs who appreciate volunteers. There are also organizations listed in the Resources for Further Action section at the end of this chapter. To find organizations in your area, check the yellow pages of your phone book under "Social Service Organizations" and call to see how you can make a difference.

Goodwill	Salvation Army	Churches, synagogues, mosques
4-H	Braille Institute	Boys and Girls Clubs
Big Brothers	American Red Cross	Scouting

Parents Do Make a Difference

Helping Kids Recognize the Power of Caring

When children understand that caring can make a difference, they will be more likely to incorporate that behavior in their own lives. You might spend a moment defining caring by saying, "Caring means you are concerned or worried about someone, and you want to help them feel better. Caring comes from inside our hearts and makes the world a nicer, kinder place, because it makes people feel happier."

Some parents take a few minutes each night at the dinner table to share caring moments they experienced during their day, and ask their kids to do the same. You might start a care-sharing session by asking, "What caring things did you do for someone today?" "Did someone do a caring deed for you today?" "How did you think it made that person feel?" "How did you feel?" Emphasizing caring in your family helps children recognize not only how much you value the trait but also how caring actions can make our world a better place.

But kids don't learn to be caring, kind, and compassionate just by our telling them about it. They learn it best through our example. Every week or so, you might stop and ask yourself, What deeds have I done this week that show my kids I value caring? Opportunities are endless: take a batch of cookies to the new neighbor, donate old toys that the fire department can distribute to needy children, coach a sport to a group of kids, be a room parent in a classroom, bring a bowl of soup or a ready-made dinner to a sick friend, or make or purchase a baby blanket to bring to a family shelter. And always ask your child to accompany you on your missions of caring. It's the best way to convey to our kids that caring is important to us and can make our world a better place.

STEP 2: STAMP OUT UNCARING WORDS AND DEEDS

We need to teach children effective ways to deal with negative people and to combat uncaring actions. This second step teaches children to "stamp out" uncaring words and deeds and defuse negative comments before they escalate and become hurtful.

I actually remember looking forward to my turn at carpooling when my kids were in middle school. Overhearing the conversations of "just-turned teenagers" always provides stimulating material, but one carpooling day turned out to be particularly memorable. That day, I picked up my thirteen-year-old, four of his eighth-grade friends, and Zach, my eleven-year-old. For some reason, sarcasm and thirteen-year-olds go hand in hand, and this day was no exception. Within minutes, one of the boys made a cutting "You're dumb" sort of comment to Zach, but this day he wasn't going to tolerate any negative remarks. Directing his full attention to the sender, he said in a clear, assertive tone, "So validate me!" completely stunning my five preadolescent passengers (and me).

His older brother, of course, immediately asked, "What are you talking about?" Zach explained that when someone puts down another student, his teacher makes it a rule that the offender must validate the person by saying something nice. "He put me down," said Zach, "so now he has to validate me. And don't start the car until he does, Mom."

Needless to say, we didn't move until our passenger said a validation: "Hey, Zach," he said, "you're an OK kid. I didn't mean to hurt you." My carpooling went much more smoothly after Zach taught us the "no put-down" rule.

Bashing, criticizing, name-calling, and put-downs can quickly become a habit and erode the quality of any environment. The fastest way to stop such a bad habit is to draw attention to the behavior *and act fast* whenever you hear a child cutting down another child. This is the time to let your expectations be heard clearly: "Only caring and helpful behaviors are allowed." It is also the best time to help the uncaring offender realize the effect of his hurtful behavior on the recipient.

Four Ways to Stamp Out Uncaring Behaviors

Nothing can be further from the truth than the old nursery rhyme "Sticks and stones may break my bones, but names will never hurt me." One of

Parents Do Make a Difference

SUCCESS TIP
Private Reminder Code:
"No Put-Downs Allowed!"

Many children have formed a habit of making negative, uncaring comments, and they really aren't aware of how often they say them. Establish a private signal—putting your index finger on your ear, tapping your shoulder, or some such gesture—between you and your child. Whenever you and the child are in a group and you hear your child say an unkind comment, use the private signal to remind the child not to use negative comments. Suppose your child says to a friend, "That's a dumb outfit." When you have your child's attention, give her your private signal. Usually all your child needs is a silent reminder that her comment was inappropriate. If she continues saying unkind comments, quietly pull her aside and say, "You need to stop saying unkind comments, because they are hurtful. If you don't, we'll have to go home."

the quickest ways to erode the feeling of caring is to use put-downs—derogatory, negative, sarcastic comments kids say to each other—and they are on the rise. Studies tell us that kids from average families receive 432 negative statements as opposed to 32 positive acknowledgments *daily*. That is a ratio of 13.5 to 1. According to a study done by the National Parent-Teachers Organization, the national ratio of parent-to-child criticism versus praise is 18 to 1. That's 18 critical messages to every compliment! These four activities help children recognize the destructiveness of uncaring and stop it from spreading.

1. **Establish zero tolerance for uncaring.** Gather your family together and say, "In this family, put-downs are not allowed. They tear people down on the inside, and our job in this family is to build people up." Now take a vow as a family to squelch put-downs by agreeing to zero tolerance for uncaring.

2. **Make a Family Care Covenant.** Many families create a Family Care Covenant that clearly spells out in writing that uncaring words and gestures are not permissible in their family. If you would like to create one for your

home, simply gather everyone around a large piece of paper and emphasize your expectations that your family will only say and do caring and supportive behaviors. Ask for suggestions of rules for ensuring that your family adheres to a strict caring policy and vote for the best guidelines. The winning policy is written on a separate piece of paper, signed by all family members, and posted as a concrete reminder.

3. **Enforce "turnarounds."** One way to help children learn to make more caring comments is by establishing a family rule of "One put-down equals put-up." Whenever a family member makes a negative, uncaring comment, she must turn it around and say a put-up—make a positive, caring statement—to the recipient. Here's how it works: suppose I hear my child say a put-down like "My English teacher is so stupid." I say, "That was a put-down. I need a put-up statement now, please." I then expect him to say a more caring, positive statement in its place. He might say, "He's really a good teacher; I just hate all the homework he gives." A word of caution: the turnaround rule is wonderful, but it works *only* if it is consistently enforced. For some kids, putting the put-up in writing is far more comfortable than saying it. That's OK: it's a first step toward becoming more positive and caring.

4. **Put money in the jar.** One family we know has a special technique that nurtures caring as it squelches negativity. The family keeps a large glass jar on the windowsill. The house rule is, "Any family member who says a put-down—or swears—must put twenty-five cents of his or her money in the jar for each uncaring offense. Parents are included! If you're short of money, you must 'work it off.'" A list of twenty-five-cent chores is always posted on the refrigerator. When the jar fills up, the family brings it to their favorite charity.

How One Parent Broke Her Child's Negativity

Moshan's mom talked to me after my parent workshop, concerned about the change in her son's behavior. She explained that her once kindhearted eleven-year-old was becoming increasingly sarcastic and negative. She knew

Parents Do Make a Difference

these were sometimes typical behaviors of preadolescents, but lately her son's comments seemed almost hurtful and uncaring. Her biggest concern was that his new behavior would become a habit hard to break, and his reputation would suffer.

"Do you think Moshan realizes that his comments are hurtful?" I asked his mom.

"That's the biggest problem," she admitted. "I tell him all the time to stop saying negative things, and he looks at me like I'm making it up."

"Moshan doesn't realize how frequently he's saying them," I said, "because it's become a habit. The first step to helping him change his behavior is to help him recognize how often he's negative."

We brainstormed a plan, and that afternoon Moshan's mom explained it to her son. "I'm hearing you say a lot of sarcastic comments that put others down and can hurt people's feelings," she told him. "I want you to see how often you're doing it. For the next few weeks we're going to do three things. First, I'm going to keep count on a card of how many times I hear you say something uncaring, and show you every night the number of marks. Second, when we're in public, I'll pull on my ear to signal you that you said something uncaring, to remind you to stop. And third, every morning I'll give you ten pennies to put in your right pants' pocket. Every time you catch yourself saying something uncaring, move a penny to your left pocket. At the end of the day, we'll count the pennies you have left."

She did one other thing that she didn't tell Moshan she was going to do: any time her son made a positive comment, she was going to praise his effort.

I saw the mother a month later at my next parent workshop. She admitted that sticking to the plan hadn't been easy. "The first week was really hard," she told me. "Moshan didn't like the idea at all, and turned all his sarcasm on me. There were a few times I wanted to give up, but I'd always tell myself, 'Give it one more day.' I'm so glad I did!" She explained, "Last week was the first time I really did see a change. He's not nearly as negative, and he's even starting to catch himself before he says anything uncaring. I guess he finally realized he was negative, and he also knew I wasn't going to let up on him until he changed."

STEP 3: ENCOURAGE ACTS OF CARING AND SERVICE

The more children practice caring behaviors, the better they will feel about themselves and the better others will feel about them. Doing caring deeds is one of the best ways to enhance children's self-esteem. And as your child continues to do caring deeds for others, she will find she can't get enough of it: she will start going out of her way to perform more caring acts. This step offers ways to enhance your child's compassion by encouraging her to lend a hand and show others she cares.

My sons were blessed, because they had Pat Myers as their fourth-grade teacher. I get a lump in my throat just thinking of the many ways she influenced my children. One of her classroom traditions I appreciate most helped my sons recognize the joy of helping others.

Each year Mrs. Myers buys her class simple musical instruments called recorders, which students are expected to practice playing nightly. I'll admit it took me until December to figure out that the tunes my sons were trying to play were holiday songs! The children learned the songs so that during the holiday season, they could play them to elderly patients at nearby nursing homes.

"What will the old people be like, Mom?" my oldest child asked hesitantly before his first visit. He hadn't had many experiences with the elderly and was obviously uncomfortable. Any hesitancies he may have had were quickly erased in his first outing. He came home excitedly exclaiming, "They loved us!" He also quickly added, "We made them feel so good, they want us to come back!"

Mrs. Myers gave my children the opportunity to learn how great it feels to show others their caring hearts. I know they never would have learned that lesson from my lectures. They learned it through their experience of serving others.

"Straight from the Heart" Caring Gifts

The first kinds of service projects are ones your child does right at home to people he knows and loves best: his own family. This activity helps children understand that the best gifts are purchased not with money but with their time and love. It's also a perfect family gift-making activity for the holidays, for a family member's birthday, or at Father's Day or Mother's Day.

You will need drawing paper cut into pieces about 4" × 8", colored pens or crayons, and a stapler. Give each family gift-maker a few pieces of cut paper and colored pens. Ask them to choose someone to whom they will give a coupon book. On the top of each coupon page, help your child write, "Because I care about you, I will . . ." followed by a different caring chore she is willing to do for the person. Children can sign, date, and illustrate each page with drawings, cutout pictures, stamps, stickers, or stencil designs. Place the finished coupons inside a folded cover made with colored paper and staple the sides of the booklet. The book of coupons redeemable for caring deeds is ready to give to the lucky recipient. Following are a few simple ways to show others you care. They make great coupon gifts—and all come straight from the heart.

Sweep out the garage.

Let Mom or Dad sleep in one day.

Fix her breakfast in bed.

Take out the trash.

Be extra quiet when he's on the phone.

Give her full control of the remote for the evening.

Wash the car.

Pull the weeds.

Make his lunch.

Offer to help her do any chore of her choosing.

Get up early to bring in the newspaper.

Seven Ways to Start Kids Doing Service Projects

As is the case in most families, each of my children has different interests, skills, and strengths. Having all of them do the same kind of public service wouldn't have been wise. Instead, my husband and I tried to match each child's talents and interests with the right volunteer position: my son who is great with younger kids taught Bible school to five-year-olds; my science-oriented son took care of the animal exhibit at our local museum; and my sports-enthusiast child volunteered at charity track meets to raise money for needy kids. Because our kids' interests were paired with service projects supporting their strengths, they not only enjoyed volunteering but also continued doing the projects for several years.

Often the most difficult part of getting your child to volunteer is knowing where to begin. Here are a few ideas passed on from other parents on how to start kids doing service projects.

1. Identify your child's talents. The first step is helping him choose something he is good at and that he enjoys doing. To guide him in the right direction, you need to identify your child's talents and interests. Make a list of your child's skills, hobbies, interests, and strengths. Ask significant others in his life—teachers, relatives, coaches, scout leaders—for other ideas. Jot down the ways he learns best: the next Success Tip will help you evaluate your child's learning styles. Add all the ideas to your list and circle a few of his strongest talents and interests.

2. Select a project supporting your child's talents. Next, brainstorm with your child—or better yet as a family—possible service tasks that match your child's natural strengths. Look for other service prospects in the yellow pages under "Social Service Organizations." The next Success Tip offers additional volunteer possibilities. Help your child analyze the good and bad points of each possibility and then ask her to choose the project she most wants to do.

3. Contact the organization. Once your child chooses a service project, help her contact the organization by phone or in person to find out how and when she could start helping. It may be useful to write down a few questions she would like to ask the group and to help her practice them before talking to the person in charge. Before she commits herself to volunteering, visit the organization together and ask yourself, Do my child and I feel comfortable about the people involved? If you have any doubts, use your instincts and go somewhere else.

4. Enlist others in the cause. Many kids enjoy volunteering with others: a friend, you, your family, Grandma—the more the merrier—so ask your child if he would like to do his project with someone. Some kids like to form clubs, which can include neighborhood kids, classmates, members of their scout troop or church group, or just friends. If your child selects an unfamiliar organization, volunteer to go along the first time or until you feel comfortable leaving your child alone. Especially if your child is young, you may want to go along every time your child volunteers.

5. Develop civic responsibility. Once your child commits herself to volunteering, help her follow through on her obligation. Post a large monthly calendar for your child to jot down her volunteer days and times: a young child can draw a happy face or other symbols. Emphasize that she should *always* tell you her plans and *never* go anywhere unfamiliar without an adult.

6. Plan for successful sessions. Help your child plan for successful volunteer sessions. Suppose your child is tutoring a child in math; ask him, "What do you need to make the session go well?" He may want to

SUCCESS TIP
Matching Your Child's Strengths
with Service Projects

Dr. Howard Gardner, of Harvard University, has developed a theory of multiple intelligences: every child is born with a unique combination of eight intelligences and learns best when she uses her strongest intelligences. To help you determine your child's strengths, read the descriptions of the eight intelligences Gardner has identified, then try to match your child's talents with special ways she can use them to help others.

1. *Linguistic learners* like to read, write, and tell stories. They have advanced vocabularies, memorize facts verbatim, have unusual amounts of information, and learn by hearing and seeing words.
   Offer to read or write letters for people with disabilities, young kids, or the elderly.
   Become a pen pal with an orphan overseas or a patient at a nearby hospital.
   Donate used books to a library, homeless shelter, or classroom.

2. *Bodily/kinesthetic learners* handle their bodies with ease and poise for their age, are adept at using their body for sports or artistic expression, and are skilled in fine motor tasks.
   Help coach younger children in a favorite sport, dancing, gymnastics, or acting.
   Volunteer for the Special Olympics or help students with disabilities at a local school.
   Make dolls, fix or make toys for needy or sick kids.
   Mend clothes or sew blankets for a shelter.

3. *Intrapersonal learners* have strong self-understanding, are original, enjoy working alone to pursue their own interests and goals, and have a strong sense of right and wrong.
   "Adopt" someone who could use a friend, such as an elderly person; offer to call them periodically.
   Teach a special hobby—magic, juggling, art, drumming, calligraphy—to needy kids.
   Ask permission to start a food drive for the hungry in parents' workplace or community.

4. *Interpersonal learners* understand people, lead and organize others, have lots of friends, are looked to by others to make decisions and mediate conflicts, and enjoy joining groups.

   Start a club and make after-school snacks for homeless kids or soup for a shelter.

   Put together a walk-a-thon or read-a-thon and donate the proceeds to a local charity.

   Go door-to-door with a parent and friends collecting warm clothes to give to the homeless.

5. *Musical learners* appreciate rhythm, pitch, and melody, and they respond to music. They remember melodies, keep time, may play instruments, and like to sing and hum tunes.

   Offer to play an instrument at nursing homes and homeless shelters.

   Organize sing-a-longs at a shelter or senior citizens center during the holidays.

   Tutor needy younger children in how to play an instrument.

6. *Logical/mathematical learners* understand numbers, patterns, and relationships, and they enjoy science and math. They categorize, ask questions, do experiments, and figure things out.

   Tutor math, science, or computers to younger children.

   Play chess, checkers, or other thinking games with kids at a shelter or hospital.

   Make computer flyers asking for specific donations to a shelter; post them in the community.

7. *Spatial learners* like to draw, design and create things, and imagine things and day-dream. They remember what they see, read maps and charts, and work well with colors and pictures.

   Beautify any shelter: paint it or hang up hand-painted pictures.

   Make homemade holiday greeting cards and deliver them to a hospital.

   Do a favorite craft project with the elderly.

8. *Naturalists* like the out-of-doors, are curious, and classify the features of the environment.

   Pick a flower bouquet from the garden, tie it with a ribbon, and deliver it to a sick friend.

   Plant vegetables and donate the harvest to a soup kitchen or shelter.

   Help children at a shelter plant their own garden.

make a few flash cards to teach the math facts or bring cookies and juice as a treat. Set aside a large box or basket for him to put all the items he'll need for his project. Then he can just pick it up and take it with him on the planned day. It will help organize his efforts.

7. **Celebrate efforts.** Whether your child volunteers once a year or once a week, support her efforts and affirm that she's helping to make the world a better place.

STEP 4: DEVELOP SENSITIVITY TO OTHERS' FEELINGS

Empathy is the trait that enhances humanness, civility, and morality. Empathy is what moves children to be caring, because they understand other people's feelings and needs. And empathy is teachable! This last step offers ways to shift your child's attention from herself and focus it, in the form of concern, on the other person involved.

Two years ago, our youngest son brought home a note from his sixth-grade teacher asking for parent volunteers to chaperone a class field trip. His teacher was encouraging her students to give up their Saturday morning to participate in a race called Lauren's Run, sponsored by the City of Hope. The event was held in the memory of Lauren Zagoria, a three-year-old child who had recently died from cancer. Each racer would pay an entrance fee of a few dollars, and all the profits would go to pediatric cancer research. Volunteering to drive to that event was one of the easiest decisions I've made.

When we arrived in the parking lot, each child was met by an adult volunteer who thanked him for taking time to help children with cancer get better. I watched children's faces brighten as they saw that their efforts were appreciated and respected. I wished more children could have shared the experience.

The race was held and the children ran, trophies were awarded, a beautiful brunch was served, and all the children were thanked again for their time. Listening to my young passenger's conversation on the drive home was the greatest affirmation of why adults should encourage kids to serve others.

"It was fun," they said, "because we helped kids like Lauren." Another child expressed everyone's sentiments, "Maybe now other kids won't have to feel so sad and hurt so much." Before they arrived back home, they had all pledged to run again next year, and they did.

Those children exemplified what it means to be empathic: that day they were able to put themselves in Lauren's shoes and imagine how she felt. That day, the students ran not for themselves but to help Lauren. That day they won the best kind of victory: the triumph of knowing that their caring actions make a difference.

The benefits of empathy are enormous. Because empathic children have a greater capacity to recognize and understand the emotions of others, they often are more open to differing points of view and less tolerant of bigotry and racism. Because these kids are more tuned into the feelings of others, they tend to have a heightened appreciation of others' plights and engage in more prosocial, caring behaviors. Because they understand that violence can have hurtful outcomes, they are usually less aggressive and find more peaceful ways to solve problems. Empathic children are also better liked by peers and adults and have more success in school and on the job because they are more aware of the needs and feelings of others. It is not surprising that these children grow up to have more satisfying relationships with their spouses, friends, and children. Empathic children usually also grow up to become adults who find ways to make our world a better place. We owe it to our children to nurture this trait in their lives today, to ensure them a more peaceful world tomorrow.

Three Ways to Foster Empathy in Your Child

Empathy comes from the Latin word that means to "feel with." Children who are empathic can understand where other people are coming from because they can put themselves in others' shoes and feel how they feel. And because they can "feel with" someone else, they are more sensitive, tolerant, and caring. You cannot teach your child to appreciate other people's feelings and needs in a few short lessons. The development of empathy is a slow process in which your child gradually moves from an egocentric, self-centered, "always thinking about me" perspective to one in which he not only cares about the other person but also can feel and understand the other person's point of view.

Research shows that empathy is definitely a trait we can develop in our kids. These three ideas nurture children's empathy by helping them see beyond themselves and into the views of others.

1. **Point out other people's feelings.** Pointing out the facial expressions, posture, and mannerisms of people in different emotional states, as well as their predicaments, is beneficial: it helps your child tune into other people's feelings. As occasions arise, explain your concern and what clues helped you make your feeling assessment: "Did you notice Sally's face when you were playing today? I was concerned because she seemed worried about something. Maybe you should talk to her to see if she's OK."

2. **Switch roles to feel the other side.** Michael was a student who had difficulty understanding anyone's feelings but his own. One day he hurt another student's feelings with his teasing, but I just couldn't get him to understand how sad he had made the other child. I spotted a wire hanger

on the floor, quickly bent it into a large circle shape and improvised, "Michael, stick your head through the hole and pretend you're Stevie and feel just like Stevie feels. I'll be Michael." I started the role play: "Stevie, your haircut makes you look dumb. How do you feel, Stevie?" By making Michael switch places and pretend to be Stevie, he finally understood Stevie's hurt.

I used a wire hanger as a prop for Michael to use in role-playing the other child's point of view. You can help your child act out the other person's perspective using puppets, dolls, or even toy action figures. As kids get older you can just ask, "Switch places and take the other person's side. How would you feel if you were in her place?"

3. **Imagine someone's feelings.** One way to help your child connect with the feelings of others is to have her imagine how the other person feels about a special situation. Suppose your child just wrote a get well card to her grandma. Use the moment to help your child feel her grandmother's reaction when she receives the card by having her pretend she is her grandmother. "Imagine you're Grandma right now. You walk to the mailbox; when you open it you find this letter. How will you feel?" You later can expand the imagination game to include people your child has not personally met: "Imagine you're a new student and you're walking into a brand-new school and don't know anyone. How will you feel?" Asking often, "How would you feel?" helps kids understand the feelings and needs of other people.

Discipline That Builds Empathy

Barbara watched her son, Aaron, and his neighbor friend, Brent, play basketball. Just then the phone rang. Aaron ran to answer it and was back within seconds telling Brent, "Hey, Jack just called. He wants me to come over and rollerblade with him. You have to go home now."

Barbara saw her son run to grab his skates while Brent sadly walked home. Furious, she wondered how he could be so thoughtless. She turned to tell Aaron just how sad he made Brent feel, then thought differently. "That's the problem," she told herself. "I'm always telling him how he makes others feel, but he still hasn't figured out how he hurts others. I need a way to increase his empathy."

Sensitizing children to how someone else feels is a significant and serious enterprise. Children cannot do this alone—they must be supported, supervised, and encouraged to develop the skills of empathy. Parents play an important role in helping their children become more responsive to the feelings of others. The four parts in the lesson that follows help turn children's uncaring moments into teaching tools that sensitize them to the feelings and needs of others and help plant the seeds of empathy. The four parts can be remembered by the acronym CARE:

C—*Call attention* to the uncaring behavior.
A—*Ask,* "How would you feel?"
R—*Recognize* the consequence of the action.
E—*Express* and *explain* your disapproval of the uncaring behavior.

Call Attention to the Uncaring Behavior
Use this first part of the CARE lesson any time your child acts unkindly. It's an opportunity to sensitize her to the feelings of other people and to the

disastrous effect unkind actions have on others; it's the first step to developing empathy. As soon as you see an uncaring behavior, call attention to it. We're always more successful in helping children change their behavior when we "nip it in the bud," before it has a chance to escalate and become a habit. A word of caution: this is *not* the time to give a lengthy sermon on the Golden Rule (sermons generally turn kids off anyway). This *is* the time to calmly name and briefly describe the child's uncaring behavior. Here are some of examples of how to call attention to uncaring behaviors:

"Telling Brent to leave because you wanted to play with Jack was inconsiderate."
"Telling your sister she is ugly is not kind."
"Not sharing your toys with your friend was uncaring."

Ask, "How Would You Feel?"

Now that you've pointed out the unkind behavior, help your child understand why the action was unacceptable. Ideally, we want our children to think about how their behavior affected the other person, but empathy does not always come naturally. Like most skills, it needs fine-tuning and practice. A good place to begin is by asking questions that help your child think about how he would feel if someone had done the behavior to him. You might ask,

"Aaron, how would you feel if Brent told you to leave so he could play with Jack?"
"If someone said that to you, how would you feel right now?"
"Would you want to be treated like that?"

Recognize the Consequence of the Action

The third part is to help children put themselves in someone else's shoes and think how it feels to be the recipient of uncaring. Feeling from another person's perspective is often difficult for children, but by using insightful questions we can gently guide them in considering the other person's feelings—the foundation of empathy. Here are a few questions that help children realize the impact of their uncaring behavior:

"Switch places and pretend you're Brent. How do you feel right now?"
"Put yourself in his shoes. Tell me what you think he's thinking."
"What do you think the other person would like to say to you?"

Express and Explain Your Disapproval of the Uncaring Behavior

Finally, explain why you consider the child's behavior to be unacceptable and uncaring. In plain language, explain what concerns you about the behavior and how you feel about uncaring actions. This is the moment for you to make sure your child clearly understands what is wrong about the behavior and why you disapprove. You help your child shift his focus from himself to others and consider how his actions can affect other people.

"I'm very concerned when I see you treating your friends badly without considering their feelings. I expect you to treat your friends the same way you'd want to be treated."
"I am upset when you talk in that tone to me. It is disrespectful and uncaring, and I expect you to treat people with respect."

The true parenting challenge is to use those unplanned moments when a child's behavior is unacceptable as learning tools to help your child develop empathy. These are always the best lessons: they help the child discover for herself why she should be kind and allow her to see that her uncaring actions may affect others.

WHAT ONE PARENT DID

Ashley's mom left her daughter's scout meeting concerned. The troop had baked cookies for children at a homeless shelter. Ashley was the only girl who thought the idea was a waste of time. "Why do we have to take up a whole

SUCCESS TIP
What the Research Says

Martin Hoffman, a world-renowned researcher from the University of Michigan, focused one of his most influential studies on empathic children. He wanted to identify the type of discipline their parents most frequently used with them, and his finding was clear. *The most common discipline technique parents of highly considerate children use is reasoning with them about their uncaring behavior.* Their reasoning lessons helped sensitize their children to the feelings of others and realize how their actions may affect others. This is an important parenting point to keep in mind in those moments when we confront our own kids for any uncaring deed they may do.

meeting baking cookies?" she said. "They look terrible, and those kids aren't going to like them."

On the drive home, her mom decided to take a detour to the city park to show Ashley a part of life she realized her daughter didn't know existed. There, sleeping on benches, were several homeless people huddling to fight the bitter cold.

"Ashley, there really are people who would appreciate your cookies," explained her mom. "I bet some of these people haven't eaten a decent meal in days. There are a lot of people right here in this city who have no one to care about them."

Ashley didn't say much on the ride home, but her mom noticed that she wiped away a few tears. As they pulled into the driveway, Ashley confided, "I really didn't know there were people who were so hungry, Mom. Do you think there is anything I can do to help them?" Her mom smiled and hugged her. She had hoped this would be her daughter's reaction. "I know you can help, Ashley. Let's go inside and make a plan of how you can make their world a little better."

Ashley and her mom spent the rest of the evening brainstorming all kinds of ways she could help the hungry people in their city. The best idea came from

Ashley because it was something she really liked to do: she decided to plant a vegetable garden in her backyard and then donate the harvest to a local soup kitchen. She prepared the soil and planted her crops the very next day.

After school each day Ashley watered her tomatoes, zucchini, and corn. Her mom noticed how much pride Ashley had in her garden. Several weeks later Ashley delivered her first fresh-picked crops to the soup kitchen. The volunteers warmly greeted her and asked her to stay and cut her vegetables for that day's soup. Ashley and her mom spent the next hour cutting up her harvest and adding it to the large kettle. The most memorable moment for Ashley's mom was when she watched her daughter fill a bowl with the soup made from her vegetables and hand it to a homeless man. The smile on her daughter's face said it all: Ashley finally knew she could make a difference in people's lives by showing others she cared.

FINAL THOUGHTS:
WILL OUR KIDS BECOME CARING ADULTS?

The trait of caring is certainly a success builder. Visit any place where you find a gathering of children—a playground, the Girls or Boys Club, a baseball field—and within seconds you can spot the caring kids. They are like magnets. Their compassion and concern for others draws others to them. In classrooms, these are the students who share, take turns, and cooperate. As they get older, their popularity swells. Certainly, we can't credit the trait of caring as the sole determinant of these children's social successes, but it does play a large role in enhancing their potential for happiness. And it's impossible to deny that caring individuals help make a kinder, gentler, and more peaceful world.

It will take us years to know whether our children develop into caring, empathic, and compassionate adults. Although the final outcome is still years away, today we can answer whether our children are successfully taking the steps to becoming more caring individuals. Remember, it's never too late—or too early—to help our kids develop caring hearts. We owe this not only to our children but also to our children's children. How effectively we nurture this final success skill may very well determine the future of our children's and their children's world.

POINTS TO REMEMBER

- To teach children caring, you must show children caring. The best moments to teach caring are usually not planned—they just happen. Capitalize on those moments to help your child understand the power caring can have.

- Guide your child to think about his uncaring behavior. It's the most effective way to help him realize how his uncaring actions can affect others.

- If you want your child to care—expect your child to care. The easiest way to increase caring is by reinforcing caring behaviors!

- Be perceptive of the intent of your child's behavior, not just of her actions.

- Children are likely to be more caring if they understand why caring is important—and how it affects others.

- Remember: children don't learn how to be caring from reading about it in a textbook but from doing caring deeds. Encourage your child to lend a hand to make the world a better place.

RESOURCES FOR FURTHER ACTION

For Parents

Educating for Character, by Thomas Lickona (New York: Bantam Books, 1991). A call for renewal of moral education in our schools, and a precise prescription for how to bring it about.

The Moral Intelligence of Children, by Robert Coles (New York: Random House, 1997). Thorough, research-based ideas on how to raise a moral child.

Raising Compassionate, Courageous Children in a Violent World, by Janice Cohn (Marietta, Ga.: Longstreet Press, 1996). Practical ways to help children learn the qualities of kindness, courage, and decency.

Raising Good Children: From Birth Through the Teenage Years, by Thomas Lickona (New York: Bantam Books, 1983). A valuable guide to raising decent, caring, and responsible children.

Teaching Peace: How to Raise Children to Live in Harmony—Without Fear, Without Prejudice, Without Violence, by Jan Arnow (New York: Perigee Books, 1995). Ways to encourage tolerance and respect in kids.

Teaching Tolerance, by Sara Bullard (New York: Doubleday, 1996). Solid research-based suggestions for raising children to be more open-minded, tolerant, and empathic.

For Children Ages Three to Seven

A Chair for My Mother, by Vera Williams (New York: Greenwillow Books, 1982). Mom's most cherished chair burns in a fire, and the child decides to raise money to buy her a new one.

A Special Trade, by Sally Wittman (New York: HarperCollins, 1978). When the little girl was a baby, her grandfather pushed her in her stroller. Now, when the girl is five, Grandfather has a stroke, and the girl pushes Grandfather as he once pushed her.

Uncle Willie and the Soup Kitchen, by DyAnne Di Salvo Ryan (New York: Morrow Junior Books, 1991). A young boy learns the true meaning of giving when he works one day in a soup kitchen serving meals to the homeless.

A Wednesday Surprise, by Eve Bunting (New York: Clarion Books, 1989). Grandma and her granddaughter are planning a surprise for Daddy. The gift: for the first time, the grandmother reads aloud to her son. Grandma was illiterate, and her granddaughter taught her to read.

Wilfrid Gordon McDonald Partridge, by Mem Fox (New York: Kane/Miller, 1985). A young boy learns that his friend from the old people's home is losing her memory. He sets out to help her find it, and in doing so learns the power of caring.

For Children Ages Eight to Twelve

Indian in the Cupboard, by Lynne Reid Banks (New York: Avon, 1980). A toy Indian given to a young boy comes to life, and because of the Indian the boy learns the value of caring.

The Kids Can Help Book, by Suzanne Logan (New York: Perigee Books, 1992). A wonderful compilation of ways kids can volunteer and make a difference in the world.

Number the Stars, by Lois Lowry (New York: Dell, 1989). A young Danish girl sacrifices her life to save her friend from the Nazis. Based on a true story.

Stone Fox, by John Reynolds Gardiner (New York: HarperCollins, 1980). Ten-year-old Willy enters a dogsled race so that his grandfather's farm might be saved.

Videos for Family Viewing

The Adventures of Robin Hood (MGM/UA Home Video, 1939). This tale has been around since the twelfth century: Robin Hood, an exiled nobleman, forms a band to aid the poor and helpless and restore Richard the Lionhearted to his rightful place on the throne. An animated version is also available (Buena Vista Home Video, 1983).

Anne of Green Gables (Walt Disney Home Video, 1985). This adaptation of Lucy Maud Montgomery's 1908 novel is a moving account of an eight-year-old orphan, Anne, who comes to live with an old bachelor farmer and his no-nonsense spinster sister. This is absolutely wonderful family viewing, rich in values of compassion, perseverance, and love.

Charlotte's Web (Paramount Home Video, 1972). Based on the children's classic by E. B. White. Charlotte, the spider, performs a great caring deed: by weaving words of praise in her web, she saves Wilbur the pig from the slaughter.

The Little Match Girl (Family Home Entertainment, 1991). The Hans Christian Andersen tale of Angela, a homeless little girl who nearly freezes to death but is adopted by a mutt and is finally saved. Wonderful discussion possibilities about poverty, homelessness, and the need to care.

Looking for Miracles (Walt Disney Home Video, 1990). To help pay for his college education, a sixteen-year-old boy takes a job as a counselor at a summer camp, despite the fact that he can't swim and is underage. One more problem: his mother won't let him take the job unless his younger brother can come, too. It's a tale of responsibility, caring, and looking out for others. (G)

The Secret Garden (Republic Pictures Home Video, 1987). Remake of the children's classic of a ten-year-old orphan named Mary, who is sent to live with a rich but miserable widower. Though lonely, Mary develops a rewarding friendship with her invalid cousin. The message in the movie is about the power of love and kindness. (G)

Organizations and Agencies Seeking Volunteers

The addresses and telephone numbers listed here are for the organizations' national headquarters. To see if there are local chapters near you, check your phone book.

American National Red Cross, 18th and D Streets, Washington, DC 20006. Telephone: (202) 737-8300.

Boy Scouts of America, 1325 West Walnut Hill Lane, P.O. Box 152079, Irving, TX 75015. Telephone: (212) 580-2000.

Catholic Charities USA, 191 Joralemon Street, Brooklyn, NY 11201. Telephone: (718) 596-5500.

Child Welfare League of America, 440 First Street, NW, Suite 310, Washington, DC 20001.

National Network of Youth Advisory Boards, P.O. Box 402036, Miami Beach, FL 33140. Telephone: (305) 532-2607.

Points of Light Foundation. Telephone: (800) 979-5400. A free pamphlet of volunteer organizations in your area is available by calling the number.

Salvation Army National Headquarters, 615 Slaters Lane, Alexandria, VA 22314. Telephone: (703) 684-5500.

United Way of America, 701 North Fairfax Street, Alexandria, VA 22314. Telephone: (703) 836-7100.

Volunteers of America, 3939 North Causeway Boulevard, Suite 200, Metairie, LA 70002. Telephone: (504) 835-3005.

YMCA of the USA, 101 North Wacker Drive, Chicago, IL 60606. Telephone: (312) 977-0031; (800) USA-YMCA.

Websites

"American Red Cross Home Page" [http://www.crossnet.org/]. An overview of the organization; includes a list of its offices and how to become a volunteer.

"Covington's Homeless: A Documentary" [http://www.intac.com/~jdeck/cov-dex2.html]. This award-winning on-line photo-documentary portrays the lives of the homeless population of Covington, Kentucky.

"Easter Seals Online" [http://www.easterseals.org/independence.html]. Information about the Easter Seals program and how to donate and volunteer.

"Food for the Hungry: Virtual Learning Center" [http://www.fh.org/]. Describes hunger relief programs worldwide and how to sponsor a child in the Third World.

"National Coalition for the Homeless" [http://nch.ari.net/]. Kids can learn about homelessness and find out how to become involved.

Final Thoughts

Nobody said parenting was going to be easy, and the last thing I want to do is give you the impression that just doing a few quick activities will turn your child into an overnight success in all walks of life! What I can promise is that doing these activities will maximize your child's potential for living a more satisfying life. I know that's a big assertion, but hundreds of parents and teachers attest to the benefits of teaching children these skills. And regularly and consciously nurturing the eight skills of success not only helps kids become their personal best but also gives us the satisfaction of knowing we are doing what is best for our children.

The eight skills of success are not just important for parents and families. Teachers can use the ideas in classrooms, and their doing so optimizes our chances of helping even more children live more fulfilled lives. When you stop and reflect on how many hundreds of hours your child will be in school, you will realize that it makes sense for schools to reinforce the same skills you teach at home. In the five years it has taken to research and write this book, I have taught hundreds of parents and teachers how to use these skills. One of my greatest thrills has been visiting schools all over North America that have implemented them. And in those visits I have seen some of the most innovative and simple ways to teach students the skills of success:

- The student council at William F. Davidson Elementary in Surrey, British Columbia, hung butcher paper all over the hallway walls for students to write "graffiti" to one another. The graffiti were to be "nice things friends say to one another," and the project was used to introduce the student council's theme for the month, getting along.

- At Lakeview Elementary in Robbinsdale, Minnesota, at 8:30 A.M., two students were reading over the school intercom a two-minute script they wrote to reinforce the schoolwide theme, problem solving. Their topic: using brainstorming as a way to handle teasing. Each school day began with two different students reading their script.

- A large bulletin board with paper footballs covered the walls at Jefferson Elementary in Hays, Kansas. On the football shapes, students wrote out personal goals for improving their academic performance. The teachers were emphasizing goal setting that month.

- At Crest View Elementary School in Brooklyn Park, Minnesota, posters describing the skill of communicating were on the hallway walls, in the cafeteria, in the gymnasium, and in each classroom. The posters listed what you can say and do to be a good listener.

I've seen countless examples of ways schools addressed the eight skills of success, *and none of the activities took away from actual teaching time.* When natural opportunities arose, teachers found simple ways to convey the importance of the skills to their students. And the benefits were obvious! After the staff at Jefferson Elementary had taught the skills through monthly themes for one year, I surveyed them about the program. Their comments were extraordinary:

- 100 percent of the staff felt that the students were more accepting of each other, spoke more positively to one another, and were able to deal with problems more appropriately.

- 95 percent of the staff felt that the students were more cooperative with one another.

- 90 percent of the staff felt that the students were more caring and courteous.

I continued the study at two other sites: Crest View Elementary in Brooklyn Park, Minnesota, and William F. Davidson Elementary in Surrey, British Columbia. The teachers agreed to use each week at least three fifteen-minute activities that taught one of the eight skills. At all three of the pilot sites that implemented a monthly theme approach to teaching success skills, *98 percent of the staff noticed positive changes in the students at their school.* The staff at all three schools also felt that because the skills had been emphasized, their students were more confident, courteous, and respectful, and there were far fewer incidents of physical aggression, name-calling, and verbal put-downs. A majority of the staff also felt that their students were better able to solve problems and resolve conflicts. The study proved what we've known in our hearts all along: *teachers do make a difference in children's lives.* Common sense tells us that reinforcing these skills at home and at school is the best way to ensure that our kids learn the skills they will need most for living successfully.

One of the reasons these schools were so effective in helping their students learn these skills is that the whole staff agreed to reinforce one skill consistently for a month. Think about it: your child didn't learn to ride a bike or play the piano or use a computer in one day. The same is true with learning almost any new skill. So you may want to consider teaching these skills to your child using an approach similar to that of the schools: by emphasizing a different skill each month in your home.

How well I know that your time constraints are tight! And I know you're thinking, "How can I possibly teach my child these skills in addition to everything else I have to do?" Here's my answer: think about your child and choose the skills you feel would benefit her most. The evaluation at the beginning of each chapter will help you determine your child's skill strengths and weaknesses. Once you have decided which skill to work on first, enhance it any time an opportunity arises—and there are dozens:

when you are carpooling or standing in a line, during the dinner hour or at bedtime. If you keep the skill in mind, you will be more likely to find natural moments to enhance it with your child. *Besides, any time you address the skill you will be benefiting your child.* There is no limit to the power these skills can have in helping children become more competent and satisfied human beings.

I wish you all the best on your journey in helping your child become a successful human being. Although it may well be your most challenging role, it is by far your most important. After all, whether you are a parent, teacher, counselor, stepparent, coach, foster parent, or scout leader, your most critical role is to help children become the best they can be. And there is no reward more fulfilling than knowing you have made an enduring difference in your child's life. You *do* make a difference!

References

Preface

Anthony, E. James, and Bertram J. Cohler (eds.). *The Invulnerable Child.* New York: Guilford Press, 1987.

Begley, Sharon. "Your Child's Brain." *Newsweek,* Feb. 19, 1996, p. 55.

Gottman, John. *The Heart of Parenting.* New York: Simon & Schuster, 1997.

Harris, Judith Rich. *The Nurture Assumption.* New York: Free Press, 1998.

Werner, Emmy, and R. Smith. *Vulnerable but Invincible: A Longitudinal Study of Resilient Children and Youth.* New York: McGraw-Hill, 1982.

Success Skill 1: Positive Self-Esteem

Bluestein, Jane. *Twenty-First Century Discipline.* Albuquerque, N. Mex.: Instructional Support Services, 1998.

Borba, Michele. *Self-Esteem: A Classroom Affair.* San Francisco: Harper San Francisco, 1982.

Borba, Michele. *Self-Esteem: A Classroom Affair.* Vol 2. San Francisco: Harper San Francisco, 1984.

Borba, Michele. *Esteem Builders: A K–8 Self-Esteem Curriculum for Improving Student Achievement, Behavior, and School Climate.* Torrance, Calif.: Jalmar Press, 1989.

Borba, Michele. *Home Esteem Builders: Activities Designed to Strengthen the Partnership Between Home and School.* Torrance, Calif.: Jalmar Press, 1994.

Branden, Nathaniel. *The Psychology of Self-Esteem.* New York: Bantam Books, 1983.

Branden, Nathaniel. *How to Raise Your Self-Esteem.* New York: Bantam Books, 1987.

Branden, Nathaniel. *The Six Pillars of Self-Esteem.* New York: Bantam Books, 1994.

Clemes, Harris, and Reynold Bean. *Self-Esteem: The Key to Your Child's Well-Being.* New York: Kensington, 1981.

Coopersmith, Stanley. *The Antecedents of Self-Esteem.* New York: Freeman, 1967.

Covington, Martin V. *Making the Grade.* New York: Cambridge University Press, 1992.

Damon, William. *Greater Expectations.* New York: Free Press, 1995.

Kohn, Alfie. *Punished by Rewards.* Boston: Houghton Mifflin, 1993.

McKay, Matthew, and Patrick Fanning. *Self-Esteem.* New York: St. Martin's Press, 1987.

Rosenthal, Robert, and Lenore Jacobson. *Pygmalion in the Classroom.* Austin, Tex.: Holt, Rinehart and Winston, 1968.

Seligman, Martin. *Learned Optimism.* New York: Knopf, 1991.

Success Skill 2: Cultivating Strengths

Armstrong, Thomas. *Seven Kinds of Smart.* New York: Penguin Books, 1993.

Bloom, Benjamin. *Developing Talent in Young People.* New York: Ballantine, 1985.

Csikszentmihalyi, Mihaly. *Flow: The Psychology of Optimal Experience.* New York: HarperPerennial, 1990.

Csikszentmihalyi, Mihaly, Kevin Rathunde, and Samuel Whalen. *Talented Teenagers: The Roots of Success and Failure.* Cambridge, England: Cambridge University Press, 1993.

Gardner, Howard. *Frames of Mind: The Theory of Multiple Intelligences.* New York: Basic Books, 1983.

Gardner, Howard. *The Unschooled Mind: How Children Think and How Schools Should Teach.* New York: Basic Books, 1993.

Higgins, Gina O'Connell. *Resilient Adults: Overcoming a Cruel Past.* San Francisco: Jossey-Bass, 1994.

Werner, Emmy, and R. Smith. *Vulnerable but Invincible: A Longitudinal Study of Resilient Children and Youth.* New York: McGraw-Hall, 1982.

Success Skill 3: Communicating

Bluestein, Jane. "Being a Supportive Listener." *Book of Article Reprints.* Albuquerque, N.Mex.: Instructional Support Services, 1995.

Bolton, Robert. *People Skills.* New York: Simon & Schuster, 1979.

Coopersmith, Stanley. *The Antecedents of Self-Esteem.* New York: Freeman, 1967.

Dreikurs, Rudolf. *Children: The Challenge.* New York: Hawthorn Books, 1964.

Dreikurs, Rudolf, R. Corsini, and S. Gould. *Family Council.* Chicago: Regnery, 1974.

Elgin, Suzette Haden. *The Gentle Art of Communicating with Kids.* New York: Wiley, 1996.

Faber, Adele, and Elaine Mazlish. *How to Talk So Kids Will Listen and Listen So Kids Will Talk.* New York: Avon, 1982.

Favaro, Peter. *Smartparenting.* Chicago: Contemporary Books, 1995.

Ford, Edward, and Steven Englund. *For the Love of Children.* New York: Fireside, 1986.

Fuchs, Victor R. *Women's Quest for Economic Equality.* Cambridge, Mass.: Harvard University Press, 1988.

Ginott, Haim. *Between Parent and Child.* New York: Avon, 1971.

Glenn, H. Stephen, and Jane Nelsen. *Raising Self-Reliant Children in a Self-Indulgent World.* Rocklin, Calif.: Prima, 1988.

Goleman, Daniel. *Emotional Intelligence.* New York: Bantam Books, 1995.

Gordon, Thomas. *P.E.T.: Parent Effectiveness Training.* New York: New American Library, 1975.

Gottman, John. *The Heart of Parenting.* New York: Simon & Schuster, 1997.

Helmstetter, Shad. *What to Say When You Talk to Your Kids.* New York: Pocket Books, 1989.

Hewlett, Sylvia Ann. *When the Bough Breaks*. New York: Basic Books, 1991.

Kagan, Spencer. *Cooperative Learning Resources for Teachers*. Riverside: University of California, Riverside, 1985.

Mehrabian, Albert. "Communication Without Words." *Psychology Today*, Sept. 1968, p. 53.

Mehrabian, Albert. *Messages: The Communication Skills Book*. Oakland, Calif.: New Harbinger Publications, 1983.

National Center for Education Statistics. *A Profile of the American Eighth Grader*. Washington, D.C.: Office of Education Research and Improvement, U.S. Department of Education, June 1990.

Nowicki, Stephen, Jr., and Marshall P. Duke. *Helping the Child Who Doesn't Fit In*. Atlanta, Ga.: Peachtree, 1992.

Remen, Rachel Naomi. "Listening, a Powerful Tool for Healing." *Science of Mind*, July 1997, p. 18.

Rowe, Mary Budd. "Wait-Time: Slowing Down May Be a Way of Speeding Up!" *Journal of Teacher Education*, 1986, *31*(1), 43–50.

Slagle, Robert. *A Family Meeting Handbook: Achieving Family Harmony Happily*. Sebastopol, Calif.: Family Relations Foundation, 1985.

Zoglin, Richard. "Is TV Ruining Our Children?" *Time*, Oct. 15, 1990, p. 75.

Success Skill 4: Problem Solving

Achenbach, T., and C. T. Howell. "Are American Children's Problems Getting Worse? A 3-Year Comparison." *Journal of the American Academy of Child and Adolescent Psychiatry*, 1993, *32*, 1145–1154.

Adler, Jerry, and Peter Annin. "Murder at an Early Age." *Newsweek*, Aug. 24, 1998, p. 23.

American Psychological Association. *Violence and Youth*. Commission on Violence and Youth, 1993.

Clabby, John F., and Maurice J. Elias. *Teach Your Child Decision Making*. New York: Doubleday, 1987.

Cohn, Janice. *Raising Compassionate, Courageous Children in a Violent World*. Atlanta, Ga.: Longstreet Press, 1996.

Cossack, Roger. "Should We Be Tougher on Kids Who Kill?" *USA Weekend,* June 26, 1998, pp. 16–17.

Crary, Elizabeth. *Kids Can Cooperate: A Practical Guide to Teaching Problem Solving.* Seattle: Parenting Press, 1984.

De Shazer, Stephen. *Keys to Solutions in Brief Therapy.* New York: Norton, 1985.

Dreikurs, Rudolf, R. Corsini, and S. Gould. *Family Council.* Chicago: Regnery, 1974.

Elias, Maurice J., and John F. Clabby. *Building Social Problem-Solving Skills: Guidelines from a School-Based Program.* San Francisco: Jossey-Bass, 1992.

Ellis, Elizabeth M. *Raising a Responsible Child.* New York: Birch Lane Press, 1995.

Faber, Adele, and Elaine Mazlish. *Siblings Without Rivalry.* New York: Avon Books, 1987.

Fried SuEllen, and Paula Fried. *Bullies and Victims: Helping Your Child Through the Schoolyard Battlefield.* New York: Evans, 1996.

Forman, Susan G. *Coping Skills Interventions for Children and Adolescents.* San Francisco: Jossey-Bass, 1992.

Hill, Karen. "Survey: One in Five Teens Carries Weapon." *Desert Sun,* Aug. 15, 1998, p. 15.

Lantieri, Linda, and Janet Patti. *Waging Peace in Our Schools.* Boston: Beacon Press, 1996.

Prothow-Stith, Deborah. *Deadly Consequences: How Violence Is Destroying Our Teenage Population and a Plan to Begin Solving the Problem.* New York: HarperCollins, 1991.

Shure, Myrna B. *I Can Problem Solve (ICPS): An Interpersonal Cognitive Problem-Solving Program (Kindergarten/Primary Grades).* Champaign, Ill.: Research Press, 1992.

Shure, Myrna B. *I Can Problem Solve (ICPS): An Interpersonal Cognitive Problem-Solving Program (Intermediate Grades).* Champaign, Ill.: Research Press, 1992.

Shure, Myrna B. *Raising a Thinking Child.* New York: Henry Holt, 1994.

Spivack, George, and Myrna B. Shure. "Interpersonal Cognitive Problem-Solving and Clinical Theory." In B. Lahey and A. E. Kazdin (eds.), *Advances in Child Clinical Psychology,* Vol. 5. New York: Plenum, 1982.

Thornton, Stephanie. *Children Solving Problems.* Cambridge, Mass.: Harvard University Press, 1995.

Witkin, Gordon, Tharp, Mike, Schrof, Joanne, Roch, Thomas, and Scattarella, Christy. "Again." *U.S. News & World Report,* June 1, 1998, pp. 16–21.

Wood, D., J. Bruner, and G. Ross. "The Role of Tutoring in Problem-Solving." *Journal of Child Psychology and Psychiatry,* 1986, *17,* 89–100.

Success Skill 5: Getting Along

Damon, William. *The Social World of the Child.* San Francisco: Jossey-Bass, 1977.

Frankel, Fred. *Good Friends Are Hard to Find.* Pasadena, Calif.: Perspective Publishing, 1996.

Fried, SuEllen, and Paula Fried. *Bullies and Victims: Helping Your Child Through the Schoolyard Battlefield.* New York: Evans, 1996.

Goldstein, Arnold P., Robert Sprafkin, Jane Gershaw, and Paul Klein. *Skill-Streaming the Adolescent.* Champaign, Ill.: Research Press, 1980.

Goldstein, Arnold P. *Skill-Streaming the Elementary School Child.* Champaign, Ill.: Research Press, 1984.

Goleman, Daniel. *Emotional Intelligence.* New York: Bantam, 1995.

Guevremont, David. "Social Skills and Peer Relationship Training." In Russell A. Barley (ed.), *Attention Deficit Hyperactivity Disorder: A Handbook for Treatment.* New York: Guilford Press, 1995.

Hartup, William W., Jane A. Glazer, and Rosaline Charlesworth. "Peer Reinforcement and Sociometric Status." *Child Development,* 1967, *38,* 1017–1024.

Isaacs, Susan. *Social Development in Young Children.* Orlando, Fla.: Harcourt Brace, 1939.

Kostelnik, Marjorie J., Laura Stein, Alice Phipps Whiren, and Anne K. Soderman. *Guiding Children's Social Development.* New York: Delmar, 1993.

McCoy, Elin. *What to Do . . . When Kids Are Mean to Your Child.* Pleasantville, N.Y.: Reader's Digest Books, 1997.

Nowicki, Stephen, Jr., and Marshall P. Duke. *Helping the Child Who Doesn't Fit In.* Atlanta, Ga.: Peachtree, 1992.

Oden, Sherri, and Steven Asher. "Coaching Children in Social Skills and Friendship Making." *Child Development,* 1977, *48,* 495–506.

Rubin, Z. *Children's Friendships.* Cambridge, Mass.: Harvard University Press, 1980.

Smith, Charles. *Promoting the Social Development of Young Children.* Mountain View, Calif.: Mayfield, 1982.

Stocking, S. Holly, and Diana Arezzo. *Helping Friendless Children: A Guide for Teachers and Parents.* Boys Town, Neb.: Boys Town Center for the Study of Youth Development, 1979.

Zimbardo, Philip, and Shirley L. Radl. *The Shy Child: A Parents' Guide to Overcoming and Preventing Shyness from Infancy to Adulthood.* New York: Doubleday, 1982.

Success Skill 6: Goal Setting

Garfield, Charles. *Peak Performers: The New Heroes of American Business.* New York: Avon, 1986.

Murphy, Shane. *The Achievement Zone.* New York: Putnam, 1996.

Seligman, Martin. *The Optimistic Child.* Boston: Houghton Mifflin, 1995.

Shrunken, Joel N. *Terman's Kids: The Groundbreaking Study of How the Gifted Grow Up.* New York: Little, Brown, 1992.

Strayhorn, Joseph M. *The Competent Child.* New York: Guilford Press, 1988.

Success Skill 7: Not Giving Up

Adderholdt-Elliott, Miriam. *Perfectionism: What's Bad About Being Too Good?* Minneapolis, Minn.: Free Spirit, 1987.

Bloch, Douglas. *Positive Self-Talk for Children.* New York: Bantam Books, 1993.

Branden, Nathaniel. *Taking Responsibility.* New York: Simon & Schuster, 1996.

Churchill, Winston. Commencement speech, described in Glenn Van Ekeren (comp.), *The Speaker's Sourcebook.* Upper Saddle River, N.J.: Prentice Hall, 1988, p. 276.

Coopersmith, Stanley (ed.). *Developing Motivation in Young Children.* San Francisco: Albion, 1975.

Hyatt, Carol, and Linda Gottlieb. *When Smart People Fail.* New York: Simon & Schuster, 1987.

Rimm, Sylvia. *Underachievement Syndrome.* Watertown, Wis.: Apple, 1986.

Stevenson, Harold W., and James W. Stigler. *The Learning Gap.* New York: Simon & Schuster, 1992.

Success Skill 8: Caring

Coles, Robert. *The Moral Intelligence of Children.* New York: Random House, 1997.

Damon, William. *The Social World of the Child.* San Francisco: Jossey-Bass, 1977.

Eisenberg, Nancy. *The Caring Child.* Cambridge, Mass.: Harvard University Press, 1992.

Herbert, Wray, and Missy Daniel. "The Moral Child." *U.S. News & World Report,* June 3, 1996.

Hoffman, Martin. "Development of Prosocial Motivation, Empathy and Guilt." In Nancy Eisenberg (ed.), *The Development of Prosocial Behavior.* Orlando, Fla.: Academic Press, 1982.

Kohlberg, Lawrence. "Development of Moral Character and Moral Ideology." In M. L. Hoffman and L. W. Hoffman (eds.), *Review of Child Development.* Vol. 1. New York: Russell Sage Foundation, 1964.

Lickona, Thomas. *Raising Good Children.* New York: Bantam Books, 1985.

Lickona, Thomas. *Educating for Character.* New York: Bantam Books, 1991.

Mussen, Paul, and Nancy Eisenberg-Berg. *Roots of Caring, Sharing, and Helping.* New York: Freeman, 1977.

Oldenberg, Dan. "Experts Stymied by Lack of Moral Values Among Young." *Los Angeles Times,* Mar. 30, 1988.

Piaget, Jean. *The Moral Judgment of the Child.* Old Tappan, N.J.: Macmillan, 1965.

Staub, Ervin. *The Development of Prosocial Behavior in Children.* Morristown, N.J.: General Learning Press, 1975.

Index

A

Abilities. *See* Strengths, child's
Affirmations, 93, 182
Anger, 92. *See also* Feelings, identification of
Antecedents of Self-Esteem, The
(Coopersmith), 12, 63
Arrowhead, Lake, 17
Asher, S., 122
Attentiveness, 62–65
Attitude, 22–25

B

Behavior, separation of child from, 15
Birthday celebration letter, 41
Blackhawk War, 179
Bloch, D., 182
Bloom, B., 47
Bluestein, J., 184–185
Brainstorming: explanation of, 99–100;
practicing of, 100; and put-downs,
100–101; rules for, 100–101
Bridge of your nose technique, 70
British Columbia, 171, 227
*Bullies and Victims: Helping Your Child
Through the Schoolyard Battlefield* (Fried
and Fried), 65
Bullying: and comebacks, 135–136; com-
mon mistakes parents make about,
133; and techniques for responding
to teasing, 134–136; ways to deal with,
131–136

C

Calm down poster, 91
CARE, 216–218
Caring: and breaking negativity, 204–206;
encouraging acts of, 206–212; evaluation
of present success skill level in, 195; and
gifts, 207–208; helping recognize power
of, 201; and increasing compassion and
empathy, 193–221; and modeling compassion, 196–201; and pointing out caring behaviors, 198–199; and put-downs,
203; and sensitivity to others' feelings,
212–218; and service projects, 208–212;
and uncaring words and deeds, 201–
206; and volunteering, 199–200; and
ways to stamp out uncaring behaviors,
202–204
Centers for Disease Control and
Prevention, 85
Cher, 179
Churchill, W., 172, 179
Civic responsibility, 209
Comeback lines, 135–136. *See also* Bullying
Communicating: and confidence in speaking out, 76–78; and empathy, 65–66;
evaluation of present success skill level
of, 58–59; and family meetings, 75–76;
and feeling content of message, 65; formula for invitation of, 63–66; four steps
to developing strong skills in, 59–78;
and full attentiveness, 64–65; and "I"
messages, 77; and improving conversation with kids, 67; and inviting conversation, 63; and listening skills, 71–73; and
main idea, 72–73; and nonverbal messages, 66–70; and power of listening
attentively, 62–63; providing opportunities for, 73–78; and remembering, 74;
and speaking out, 60–66; and writing, 66
Comparisons, making, 13, 23, 27, 52
Compassion, 196–201. *See also* Caring
Compensation, law of, 40
Compliments, 46

Conversation, improving, 67
Coopersmith, S., 12, 63
Courtesy. *See* Good manners
Crest View Elementary School, Brooklyn
    Park, Minnesota, 3, 227, 228
Cross-offs, 103–104

D

Darwin, C., 178
Decisions: arriving at, 104–107; and
    decision-making process, 106; vocab-
    ulary for, 106
Developing Talent in Young People (Bloom),
    47
Dinner-hour paraphrasing, 73
Discipline, constructive, 14–16
Disney, W., 179
Dream clouds, 152–153
Dreikurs, R., 75
Duke, M. P., 68

E

Edison, T. A., 171, 178
Effort, value of, 170–174
Einstein, A., 179
Emory University, 68
Emotions: and emotion charades, 70; and
    emotion scrapbook, 69; and emotion
    vocabulary, 94; and guessing people's
    emotions, 69
Empathy: discipline for building of,
    215–218; and reassurance, 65–66; three
    ways to foster, 213–215. *See also* Caring
Empowering statements, 26
Encouragement, 15–16, 126–128
Englund, S., 67
Expectations: and enhancing success,
    16–19; power of, 19; questions for gaug-
    ing, 18–19; setting of, 11–16
External rewards, 24
Eye contact, 69

F

Faber, A., 109
Failure, response to children's, 182–183

Family: and development of "I can" slogan,
    21, and family Babe Ruth award, 184;
    and family care covenant, 203–204; and
    family meetings, 75–76; and mandated
    family dinners, 77–78; and praising,
    127–128
Feeling content, of messages, 65
Feelings, identification of, 89–93
For the Love of Children (Ford and
    Englund), 67
Ford, E., 67
Frankel, F., 124–125, 138
Fried, P., 85
Fried, S., 85
Friends: and conversation openers, 126; and
    friendship-making skills, 122–124; and
    group activities, 125; and interactive
    toys, 126; and one-on-one play opportu-
    nities, 124–125; teaching child how to
    make, 120–128; and warning signs of
    friendship problems, 121

G

Gardner, H., 210–211
Genetic labels, 13
Ginott, H., 63–64
Glenn, H. S., 78
Goal formula, 156–160
Goal setting: and deciding on goal direc-
    tion, 151–155; and definition of goal,
    148–149; evaluation of present success
    skill level in, 145–146; and goal formula,
    156–158; help in planning of, 158–160;
    help in writing of, 153–155; identifica-
    tion of, in books, 151; possibilities for,
    152–153; purposeful modeling of, 149–
    151; research on, 147; and route to suc-
    cess, 155–160; steps to enhancement
    of, 146–163; and teaching meaning
    and values of goals, 147–151; and
    understanding the meaning of goals,
    148–149; and validation of child's goal
    successes, 160–161
Goals: definition of, 148–149; direction for,
    151–155; and goal poster, 149; and talk
    about personal goals, 149; teaching

meaning and value of, 147–151; writing of, 153–155

Goertzel, M., 40

Goertzel, V., 40

Good Friends Are Hard to Find (Frankel), 124–125, 138

Good manners: and common courtesy, 128–131; five ways to help in learning of, 129–131; and table manners, 131

Gordon, T., 63–65, 77

H

Hartup, W., 126

Harvard University, 19, 210

Hazler, R. J., 133

Hoffman, M., 219

Hong Kong, 104

Hoover, J. H., 133

"How You Can Be a Success" (*Success* magazine), 71

I

I Can Problem Solve (ICPS) program, 107

"I" messages: three parts of sending, 77; versus "you" messages, 15. *See also* Discipline, constructive

Individuality, enhancing, 32–52

J

Jacobson, L., 19

Jefferson Elementary School, Hays, Kansas, 3, 227

Jordan, M., 179

K

Kagan, S., 72–73

Knots on a Counting Rope (Martin, Jr.), 179, 181

L

Labels: and creation of positive new labels, 14; and negative labels, 12–14

Lakeview Elementary, Robbinsdale, Minnesota, 227

Lauren's Run, 212

Lincoln, A., 179

Listening: and dinner-hour paraphrasing, 73; enhancing child's skills in, 71–73; with full attentiveness, 64; for main idea, 72–73, and observing good listening behaviors, 70; and one-fact note cards, 73; and power of listening attentively, 62–63; and remembering "keeper," 72–73; and SOLER, 72

M

Main idea, 72–73

Martin, B., Jr., 179, 181

Mazlish, E., 109

McCoy, E., 127

Mehrabian, A., 68

Mirror box story, 98–99

Mistakes: and dealing with failure, 174–176; learning from, 178, 188; lesson about, 176; and success against the odds, 178–179; value of, 176–178; ways to respond to, 183–185

Multiple intelligences, theory of, 210–211

N

National Education Association, 132

Negative labels, 13

Negative self-talk, 21

Negative voices, 21

Negatives, turning, into positives, 22

Negativity, 204–206. *See also* Caring

Nelson, J., 78

Nicknames, 13

Nonverbal messages: and bridge of nose technique, 70; and emotion scrapbook, 69; eye contact and smiling in, 69; five ways to help kids in reading of, 68–70; and good listening behaviors, 70; and guessing people's emotions, 69; and playing emotion charades, 70; sending and receiving of, 66–70; and silent movies, 69–70

Nowicki, S., Jr., 68

O

Oden, S., 122

Oliver, R., 133

One-fact note cards, 73
Oxford University, 172

P

P.E.T.: Parent Effectiveness Training (Gordon), 77
Parent's Little Book of Lists, The: Dos and Don'ts of Effective Parenting (Bluestein), 184
Perseverance: and Churchill message, 172; and courage, 179–181; definition of, 172; and eight affirmations to encourage bouncing back, 182; evaluation of present success skill level in, 168–169; and mistakes, 174–178, 183–185; and resilience, 181–183; and successes against the odds, 178–179; and teaching value of effort, 170–174; three steps to enhancement of, 169–188
Positive self-beliefs. *See* Self-belief, positive
Positive self-statements. *See* Self-statements, positive
Positive self-talk. *See* Self-talk, positive
Positive Self-Talk for Children (Bloch), 182
Potential, development of child's, 35–50. *See also* Strengths, child's
Praise: and applauding child's efforts, 48–50; and family praising, 127–128; and list of encouragers, 127; and two praise rule, 127
Private signals, 21
Problem solving: and anger, 92; benefits of teaching of, 107; and brainstorming, 99–101; and calm down poster, 91; and emotion vocabulary, 94; evaluation of present success skill level in, 87–88; five steps in development of, 88–107; formula for, 92–93; and how child deals with problems, 89–90; and identification of feelings, 89–93; and identification of problem, 93–97; and mirror box story, 98; and narrowing the choices, 101–104; and reaching decision, 104–107; and recognizing alternatives, 97–101; and solution game, 102; and STAND, 88; and ways to stay cool, 91–93

Problems: how child deals with, 89–90; identification of, 93–97; identifying in books and movies, 95; questions to help in identification of, 97; and rephrasing what is said, 97–98; reversing sequence of, 96; three ways to help in identification of, 95–97; togetherness in, 109
Progress, recording, 23, 27
Put-downs, 203

Q

Qualities. *See* Strengths, child's

R

Raising Self-Reliant Children in a Self-Indulgent World (Glenn and Nelsen), 78
"Raising Successful Kids" workshop, 144
Reassurance, 65–66
Rejection, 127
Remembering, 74
Rosenthal, R., 19
Rowe, M. B., 74
Ruth, G. H., 184

S

San Francisco, 19
Self-belief, positive: and comparisons, 23; and constructive discipline, 14–16; and developing "I can" attitude, 22–25; and effective encouragement, 16; and empowering statements, 26; evaluation of present success skill level in, 9–10; and expectations that enhance success, 16–19; and external rewards, 24; family conditions for nurturing of, 12; four steps to development of, 10–25; and internal self-beliefs, 19–22; points to remember about, 27; and seeing success, 23–24; and setting expectations, 11–16; and use of labels, 12–14
Self-fulfilling prophecies, 13
Self-image, negative, 13
Self-talk, positive, 21–22, 135
Self-statements, positive, 22
Service projects, 208–212
Shure, M., 107

Shy children, 125
Siblings Without Rivalry (Faber and Mazlish), 109
Silent Messages (Mehrabian), 68
Silent movies, 69–70
Slogan, family "I can", 21
Smiling, 69
Social competence: and acknowledging others with handwritten notes, 132; evaluation of present success skill level in, 117–118; four steps to enhancement of, 118–139; and friendship-making skills, 122–124; and identification of social strengths and weaknesses, 119–120; and interactive toys, 126; and matching child's interests with group activities, 125; and nurturing of good manners and common courtesy, 128–131; and one-on-one play opportunities, 124–125; and response to teasing, meanness, and bullying, 131–136; and shy children, 125; and teaching conversation openers, 126; and teaching how to make friends, 120–128; and warning signs of friendship problems, 121
SOLER, 72
Solution game, 102
Speaking out: and empathy, 65–66; encouragement of, 60–66; and formula that invites kids to talk, 63–66; four traditions to help kids gain confidence in, 76–78; and inviting conversation, 63; and listening with full attentiveness, 64–65; and power of listening attentively, 62–63; and reflecting feeling content of message, 65
Spivack, G., 107
Stanford University, 125, 147
Stevenson, H. W., 170
Stigler, J. W., 170
Strengths, child's: and applauding child's efforts, 48–50; cultivation of, 32–52; description of, 42; evaluation of present success skill level in, 34–35; five ways to nurture, 44–45; four keys to unlocking of, 41–42; identification of unique,

35–39; and law of compensation, 40; and learning to accept compliments, 46; list of, 38–39; and six parenting practices for nurturing talent, 47–48; and praise, 44; pointing out, 40–45; providing opportunities for development of, 46–50; recognition of, 43–44; seven ways to discover, 36–37; and talk of a winner, 51
Success: eight skills of, 5; four ways to help child in seeing of, 23–24; photographic image of, 160; plan and guide route to, 155–160; validation of, 160–161
Success magazine, 71

T

Table manners, 131
Talents: cultivation of, 44–45; development of, 48; identification of, 208–209; listing of, 37, 38–39; parenting practices for nurturing of, 47–48
Talking candle, 78
Teasing, techniques for responding to, 134–136. *See also* Bullying
Television, 78
Terman, L., 147
Thompson, J., 130
Two Praise Rule, 127

U

U.S. News & World Report, 129
Unconditional love, 12, 24
Uniqueness, 51–52
University of California at Los Angeles (UCLA), Social Skills Training Program, 124–126
University of Chicago, 47
University of Michigan, 170, 219
University of Minnesota, 126
University of San Francisco, 67

V

Van Beethoven, L., 179
Victory dinner, 161
Victory log, 160

W

What to Do . . . When Kids Are Mean to Your Child (McCoy), 127
Wickwire, M., 179, 180–181
William F. Davidson School (Surrey, British Columbia), 3, 171, 227, 228
Wilson, W., 179
Wizard of Oz, The (Baum), 95
Wright University, 3

Writing, rebuilding conversation through, 66

Y

"You" messages, "I" messages versus, 15. *See also* Discipline, constructive

Z

Zagoria, L., 212
Zimbardo, P., 125

About the Author

Michele Borba, Ed.D., has worked with more than half a million parents and teachers over the course of more than two decades. A dynamic and highly sought-after speaker, she has presented hundreds of keynote addresses and workshops throughout North America, Europe, Asia, and the South Pacific on enhancing children's self-esteem, achievement, and behavior. Her down-to-earth speaking style, inspirational stories, and practical strategies appeal to audiences worldwide.

Dr. Borba is the author of more than thirty-six books, including *Self-Esteem: A Classroom Affair, Esteem Builders,* and *Character Builders,* and several audiocassette programs, including *The Five Building Blocks of Self-Esteem and Strengthening At-Risk Students' Achievement and Behavior.* Her latest video is *Working with Underachievers.* As a recognized expert on parenting and self-esteem, Dr. Borba has been a frequent guest on radio and television talk shows throughout North America. Her numerous awards include the National Educator Award, presented by the National Council of Self-Esteem; Santa Clara University's Outstanding Alumna Award; and the award for Outstanding Contribution to the Educational Profession, presented by the Bureau of Education and Research. She is on the board of directors of the National Association of Self-Esteem.

Dr. Borba was formerly a classroom and college teacher and has had a wide range of teaching experience, including work in regular education as well as work with children with learning disabilities; children with physical, behavioral, and emotional disabilities; and gifted children. She and her husband were partners in a private practice for troubled children and adolescents in Campbell, California. She received her doctorate in educational psychology and counseling from the University of San Francisco, her M.A. in learning disabilities, and her B.A. from the University of Santa Clara; she earned a life teaching credential from San Jose State University. She currently lives in Palm Springs, California, with her husband and three teenage sons.

Dr. Borba welcomes communication and inquiries from her readers and is available to conduct a wide variety of parent and teacher workshops. She can be reached at:

Michele Borba, Ed.D.

1205 Camino Mirasol Drive

Palm Springs, CA 92262

Office fax: (760) 323-5387

E-mail: BorbaM@aol.com